Prehistoric Indians of the Southeast

to
David L. DeJarnette

Prehistoric Indians of the Southeast

Archaeology of Alabama and the Middle South

· ·

John A. Walthall

The University of Alabama Press
University, Alabama

976
W17p
126927
Nov.1983

SECOND PRINTING 1982

Copyright © 1980 by
The University of Alabama Press
All rights reserved
Manufactured in the United States of America

Library of Congress Cataloging in Publication Data

Walthall, John A
  Prehistoric Indians of the Southeast.

  Bibliography: p.
  Includes index.
  1. Indians of North America—Southern States—
Antiquities. 2. Southern States—Antiquities.
3. Indians of North America—Alabama—Antiquities.
4. Alabama—Antiquities. I. Title.
E78.S65W34   976   79-13722
ISBN 0-8173-0020-1

Contents

Illustrations and Tables

TABLES

Preface

The project that culminated in this volume was originally suggested by Christopher Peebles and James B. Griffin in August 1974. At that time I was visiting Ann Arbor and, over lunch, the subject was casually discussed. As a newly appointed faculty member in the Department of Anthropology at The University of Alabama, I was in the process of planning courses on Alabama and Southeastern archaeology and had become aware of the massive amounts of published and unpublished data produced by over fifty years of archaeological investigation in the region.

Other than the now classic 1952 summary of Alabama archaeology by David DeJarnette, there were no other area syntheses available to aid in my compilation of lecture notes. Griffin and Peebles suggested that a new summary of Alabama archaeology would be useful and furthermore, that I was now in a position to write one. Being both young and naive I heartily agreed to meet the challenge. Two years later I found myself older, somewhat less naive, and in possession of a manuscript, which I hoped represented the type and quality of synthesis discussed in Ann Arbor.

It is appropriate for this volume to be dedicated to David L. DeJarnette, who, for almost half a century, has been the guiding force behind Alabama archaeology. While it was a coincidence that the initial draft of the study was completed at the time of DeJarnette's retirement from The University of Alabama in May 1976, it is nonetheless significant since this book essentially reports the contributions of the "DeJarnette Phase" of archaeological investigations within the state. If the reader is uninitiated and therefore excusably unaware of DeJarnette's impact on the archaeology of the state, one need only to refer to any chapter in the succeeding pages. DeJarnette is cited, quoted, or referred to numerous times in each of these sections. His efforts have been fruitful both in the quantity and quality of data they produced and in the generation of students to whom he taught an appreciation of prehistory.

Many people provided aid and encouragement during the time I was preparing the manuscript. I have attempted to justify their confidence, and if I have failed the fault is entirely my own. James B. Griffin, Charles Faulkner, Roy Dickens, Christopher Peebles, Jefferson Chapman, Bennie Keel, Ned Jenkins, Ben Coblentz, and Eugene Futato read draft versions and offered their valuable comments. Dr. Griffin was especially helpful and I benefited greatly from his detailed comments and expertise. Timely encouragement was frequently provided by Paul Nesbitt and Margaret Searcy. Ann Clark typed the original draft and contributed much of her own time to the production of the manuscript.

Many members of the Alabama Archaeological Society shared their data and knowledge of local sites and prehistory. The members of this organization should be extremely proud of their efforts. The Alabama Archaeological Society is proof of the valuable contribution that avocational archaeologists may provide in preserving our national heritage.

I also owe a great deal of gratitude to my wife, Nina. I began to write this volume during our first year of marriage and her understanding and patience were magnificent. She not only had to adjust to a new husband and a some-time writer, but, perhaps most difficult of all, to life with an archaeologist. Her success in this endeavor is a tribute to human adaptation.

Prehistoric Indians of the Southeast

1: Discovering the Past

This book deals with the prehistory of the region encompassed by the present state of Alabama and spans a period of some eleven thousand years, from 9000 B.C. and the earliest documented appearance of human beings in the area to A.D. 1750, when the early European settlements were well established. Forty years ago such a study could not have been undertaken. Only within the past four decades have remains of these prehistoric peoples been scientifically investigated.

Based upon information gathered by archaeologists working in the field and in the laboratory, it is now possible to divide this prehistoric cultural sequence into five developmental stages: Paleo-Indian, Archaic, Gulf Formational, Woodland, and Mississippian. The Paleo-Indian stage began with the migration into the state of the first bands of late Pleistocene hunters and gatherers. They armed themselves with spears tipped with specialized stone points, and their economy was based on hunting and scavenging now extinct gregarious mammals.

The Archaic stage began with the onset of modern climatic conditions. Archaic peoples also hunted with stone-tipped spears, but they added to its effectiveness by employing an *atlatl*, or spear-thrower, to increase the force and range of the projectiles. Modern game, especially deer, appear to have constituted their major source of protein. Archaic populations readily adapted to the diverse environments of Alabama, and their cultural remains are found in every area of the state. In some areas where the environment was particularly favorable, Archaic peoples developed specialized economies based upon a few high-yield natural foods, especially hickory nuts, shellfish, and deer. This specialization led to a more sedentary life and opened the way for the Gulf Formational stage.

The Gulf Formational stage began with the appearance of fiber-tempered and, later, sand-tempered ceramic complexes, mainly found in river valleys and along the coast, where semisedentary Archaic populations were established. The genesis of the Gulf Formational cultures apparently is not the result of major population movements or replacement. Rather, they appear to have diffused into Alabama through trade and culture contact with ethnic groups in surrounding regions.

The succeeding Woodland stage was primarily northern in origin. Major characteristics include cord- or fabric-impressed pottery, burial mounds, and cultivation of certain native plants as well as the tropical domesticated plants maize and squash. The bow and arrow were introduced into eastern forests during this time.

The earliest Woodland pottery comes from the northeastern United States and may ultimately have come from Old World sources, as the custom of constructing burial mounds. The earliest mounds are found in the Midwest and date to around 1000 B.C. The diffusion of these practices into the Southeast, which may in certain instances have involved actual population migration, occurred around the beginning of the first millennium A.D. These traits were integrated into local cultural systems and developed into many distinctive regional variations.

The culmination of Woodland development, combined with new traits derived from Mesoamerica, produced the apex of prehistoric culture in the Southeast, the Mississippian stage. The Mississippian is characterized by effective food production combined with age-old hunting and gathering practices, the construction of earthen pyramids supporting structures of timber and thatch, the rise of complex religious systems, and the development of chiefdoms. The earliest of these cultures date to A.D. 700 in the central Mississippi Valley region and were at their height from A.D. 1200 to A.D. 1400. After 1400, prior to the first European explorations in the area, the Mississippian cultures of the Southeast underwent a rapid demise, the causes of which remain an archaeological mystery. After A.D. 1540, European exploration and settlement in the Southeast caused rapid acculturation among aboriginal tribal cultures until, by 1800, there was little left of traditional customs and lifeways.

Three generations of southeastern archaeologists have tried to illuminate this complex prehistory. This endeavor dates back to the 1930s to the Tennessee Valley, where the first stratified sites were discovered. With this discovery came the realization that human beings had arrived in the Southeast at some unknown time in the distant past prior to the introduction of pottery and agriculture. This realization led to the formulation of what is now called the Archaic stage.

The recognition of an Archaic stage of cultural development in Alabama and the eastern United States was one of the major contributions of archaeologists working four decades ago. The initial recognition of the Archaic as a major cultural unit is attributed to William Ritchie (1932), based upon his archaeological investigations of aboriginal sites in New York State. In Ritchie's preliminary definition of the Archaic, two major negative characteristics were stressed: The culture (Lamoka) he placed into this integrative unit was separated from previously established cultural units by a lack of both pottery and agriculture. Ritchie's concept of the Archaic was further substantiated by archaeological investigations that were beginning in Alabama during the same year that his volume on the New York sites was published.

In the summer of 1932, Walter B. Jones and David L. DeJarnette of the Alabama Museum of Natural History began an archaeological survey of the

Tennessee River Valley. Some 237 sites were located and mapped during this initial survey. The following year the Tennessee Valley Authority announced that it would begin construction of three major hydroelectric dams that would flood considerable areas of bottomland in the Alabama portion of the valley. Professor William S. Webb of the University of Kentucky was called upon to direct archaeological salvage operations in the Tennessee Valley in both Tennessee and Alabama. Thomas M. N. Lewis and DeJarnette were selected to direct the field operations in Tennessee and Alabama respectively. Utilizing depression-era Civil Works Administration and, later, Works Progress Administration labor, excavations were begun in December 1933 in the area of northern Alabama to be inundated by the construction of Wheeler Dam.

During this project nineteen sites were excavated. Among these was a large shell mound designated Lu⁰86, which produced the first documented evidence of prepottery Archaic cultures in the Middle South. Webb (1939) noted that this site was stratified and that only the upper levels contained pottery. The lower levels contained large numbers of broad-stemmed projectile points, stone tools, and bone implements. He reported, "From a careful investigation of the occurrence of these flint spear points and their associations, the author is convinced that a spear-throwing, hunting, and fishing people who made no pottery and used no bows and arrows laid down the great shell midden at the base of mound Site Lu⁰86" (1939:180).

The term "Archaic" was first applied to the preceramic levels in the Alabama shell mounds during the Pickwick Basin survey that followed. This project began in May 1936 and was halted due to flooding in February 1938. All of the nine shell mounds excavated during this time were found to contain shallow, upper, pottery-bearing zones, and deep, lower, prepottery strata. Lists of selected traits were compiled and generalized mound profiles were constructed to facilitate comparison between these sites. The trait lists compiled for the Pickwick Basin shell mounds were then compared to those constructed for the shell middens of the Green River in Kentucky and many similarities were noted. Based upon this study, a cultural classification of these shell-mound dwellers was constructed in keeping with the Midwestern Taxonomic System then in vogue (Webb and DeJarnette 1942:319):

Pattern: Archaic

    Aspect: Pickwick

        Focus: Lauderdale (Alabama)
            Components: Long Branch, site Lu⁰67
                         Bluff Creek, site Lu⁰59
                         Perry, site Lu⁰25
                         Mulberry Creek, site Ct⁰27

Focus: Indian Knoll (Kentucky)
        Components: Chiggerville, site Oh_1
                       Indian Knoll, site Oh_2
                       Ward, site McL_{11}

In reports of the excavations of these shell mounds, Webb and his colleagues noted that, although the cultural materials recovered from the prepottery levels in these sites were highly homogeneous, culture change was apparent. Studies of the stratigraphic distribution of these materials revealed that, through time, new traits were added to the cultural inventory of these peoples while other traits disappeared. Based upon these observations a relative chronology was devised for these shell-mound occupations (Webb and DeJarnette 1948a). The prepottery occupations of these sites were divided into three broad periods: Archaic 1, 2, and 3. These periods were segregated on the basis of presence or absence of single attributes. For example, Archaic 3 began with the appearance of stone vessels and ended with the appearance of ceramics, which began the first of three pottery periods.

The major flaw in this system was its general nature. Diagnostic cultural assemblages were not recognized during investigation of the shell mounds, and intrasite comparison was founded upon single traits, some of which had great time depth and were attributes of several distinct assemblages. Thus, the Archaic occupations of these sites have been relegated to a single homogenous cultural unit, Lauderdale, which has been called a focus, phase, or culture by different archaeologists writing at various times. Only in the last few years has the nature of culture change displayed in the shell-mound strata begun to emerge. Even now, the outline is incomplete and a second monumental effort is needed to clarify this development.

By the end of the 1930s the Archaic was synonymous with "Shell Mound Archaic." James Ford and Gordon Willey (1941:332) in their synthesis of the prehistory of the eastern United States remarked, "It appears to be justifiable to apply the name 'archaic' to the earliest known cultural horizon in the East. The cultures of this period were 'archaic' in the true sense, horticulture was lacking, pottery is either absent or makes its appearance late in the stage, and the abundance, variety, and quality of artifacts do not compare with the more complex later developments. . . . A common feature of nearly all these sites is the fact that they are located at points where an abundant supply of shellfish was available and the occupation areas are marked by large accumulations of discarded shells."

Development of radiocarbon dating was the major scientific contribution during the late 1940s to the ongoing elucidation of the evolution of preceramic cultures in the East. Although several previous attempts had been made to devise absolute dating techniques for archaeological materials in this area, none proved satisfactory. Some archaeologists attempted to guess their way out of this dilemma. Thus Ford and Willey in their 1941 synthesis attempted to estimate absolute dates for the relative chronological sequence that had been established for the prehistoric cultures of the East on the basis of stratigraphy and seriation. Their chronology was brief. All of the known prehistoric manifestations in the East were placed into a 2,000-year span. The oldest stage, the Archaic, ended around A.D. 800 with the introduction of fiber-tempered pottery. When radiocarbon dates for shell-mound materials began to be announced, the Ford and Willey chronology proved to be much too condensed.

Shell-mound occupations from several areas were dated to between 2000 and 3000 B.C., and radiocarbon dating soon indicated that the initial occupation of some of these sites dated as far back as 5000 B.C. A single radiocarbon date was obtained on materials gathered during the depression-era salvage operations conducted on the shell mounds of Alabama. Deer antler from the 3.5- and 4-foot levels of the Perry site at Lauderdale proved to be 4,764 years old (± 250). This would date them between 3064 and 2564 B.C.

By 1950, the oldest documented prehistoric manifestation in Alabama was the shell-mound Archaic culture, which had been dated to some four or five thousand years ago. However, hints of even earlier occupations had already been noted. DeJarnette, in is 1952 summary of Alabama archaeology, devoted a brief but revealing passage to these materials. He related that three fluted projectile-point fragments similar in form to the Clovis and Folsom points, then being dated to between ten and twelve thousand years ago in the Great Plains, were recovered during WPA-TVA salvage operations in the 1930s. DeJarnette's discussion of these finds signaled the beginning of an intensive search for more. Remarkable results were obtained in later years in the form of substantial Paleo-Indian habitation sites in the Tennessee Valley.

The early finds of fluted points did not produce an immediate announcement of the existence of early man in Alabama. First, the salvage operations of the 1930s were limited to bottomlands that would be inundated by flood waters confined by dam construction. Time was an essential factor and excavations at more than one site were abruptly halted by early flooding. Only the more substantial sites—shell mounds, temple mounds, and burial mounds—were thoroughly investigated. Small archaeological sites in the valley floor that might have produced fluted points were not excavated. It must be noted also that all major Paleo-Indian sites that were later discovered in the Tennessee Valley were above the basin areas on upper terraces; there are some climatic indications that suggest increased rainfall during the late Pleistocene and cast doubt on the existence of Paleo-Indian campsites in the bottomlands.

Second, the three fluted points found during these salvage operations were discovered in perplexing context. Two fluted projectile point fragments were encountered in two widely separated Copena burial mounds, Lu⁰54 and Lu⁰63 (Webb and DeJarnette 1942:Plate 132.2), while a third was found

WPA Work Crew in the Guntersville Basin, 1939, AMNH 4 Ja 101

WPA Shell Mound Excavation in the Pickwick Basin, 1936, AMNH 95 Lu 59

at a small village site, Lu^{v}65, which was also thought to be associated with the Copena manifestation (Webb and DeJarnette 1942:Plate 207.1). This provenance and the fact that Copena blades, while unfluted, were similar in form to these fluted points added to the confusion. For a while, it seemed possible that fluted points in the Tennessee Valley were late in time and were made by the builders of the Copena burial mounds. Fluted points were added to the Copena trait list and were even used by one archaeologist as a diagnostic trait in demonstrating the existence of Copena peoples in the Nashville Basin (Jennings 1946).

In sum, the small quantity of fluted points discovered during the salvage operations of the 1930s, their fragmentary nature, and the problems raised by their context produced understandable conservative and even skeptical attitudes about their significance. It was not until much later that it was demonstrated that these fluted projectile points were diagnostic of an early period in eastern North American prehistory and that extensive Paleo-Indian habitation sites existed in that area. We now recognize these fluted fragments found during the WPA-TVA investigations as a type of projectile point called Cumberland. Their presence at the Copena sites appears to have been only a chance occurrence. Even as such, they served as a base for DeJarnette's recognition of the possibility that prehistoric man was in Alabama much earlier than had previously been recognized.

A significant step in the discovery of more Paleo-Indian materials in northern Alabama was taken in 1944 with the organization of the Tennessee Archaeological Society under the guidance of T. M. N. Lewis and Madeline Kneberg. Lewis and Kneberg were very interested in the scattered discoveries of fluted points in Tennessee and Alabama, and at the December 1950 meeting of the Tennessee Archaeological Society they called for help from among the amateur ranks in documenting finds made in the Tennessee Valley. This study aroused considerable enthusiasm among local professional and amateur archaeologists and led directly to the discovery and reporting of the first Paleo-Indian habitation sites in Alabama and the Southeast. During the following seven years three major Paleo-Indian habitation sites in the Tennessee Valley of Alabama and many additional finds of fluted points were reported in the Tennessee Archaeological Society publication, the *Tennessee Archaeologist*. These reports convincingly demonstrated the existence of a Paleo-Indian stage in Alabama prehistory.

The three Paleo-Indian sites reported during this time were discovered within a three-mile area on the upper terraces of the Tennessee River north of Decatur. The first reported and best known was the Quad site discovered by Frank J. Soday in 1951 (Soday 1952, 1954). Over a thousand Paleo-Indian artifacts were recovered from this site alone. Comparable amounts of these materials were recovered from two other, nearby sites, the Stone Pipe and Pine Tree sites reported by James W. Cambron (1955, 1956).

Thus by 1955 two preceramic manifestations had been documented in

Alabama, an earlier Paleo-Indian culture and a later shell-mound Archaic culture. However, the enormous amount of time thought to separate these cultures, and the heterogeneous nature of their assemblages, indicated a hiatus between these occupations. The recognition of this temporal and cultural gap between these manifestations raised many problems. Did the Paleo-Indians occupy the area and then leave to be replaced much later by culturally distinct shell-mound dwellers, or was there some intervening culture or cultures yet to be discovered that bridged this gap?

Answers were forthcoming. In 1953 members of the Chattanooga chapter of the Tennessee Archaeological Society discovered a cave shelter—Russell Cave—in the uplands above the Tennessee River in Marshall County, Alabama. The cave deposit was tested in 1953 and 1954 and proved to be deeply stratified. The potential of these deposits convinced the National Geographic Society to sponsor excavations at this site. Carl Miller, a Smithsonian archaeologist, summarily began a second phase of excavations at Russell Cave in 1956. Miller's initial investigation produced significant results. The lower strata at Russell Cave did not produce fluted points but did yield projectile points and stone tools that appeared to be related to these earlier assemblages. Radiocarbon testing on charcoal samples from these levels dated to eight thousand years ago (Miller 1956).

The materials from the lower levels of Russell Cave were culturally and temporally intermediate between the known Paleo-Indian and shell-mound Archaic occupations of this region. Only a small amount of data resulting from Miller's investigation was published in the form of two popular articles, and, unfortunately, these brief accounts were not followed by a technical report.

By this time, however, interest in the archaeology of the state had reached a new high with the founding of the Alabama Archaeological Society in 1955. Society members had already contributed much new and significant knowledge to the Paleo-Indian–Archaic problem. During the first years of the founding of their organization, they began to plan, in cooperation with local professional archaeologists, a problem-oriented archaeological research project directed toward expanding and corroborating the discoveries made by Miller at Russell Cave.

One major hurdle—financial support—lay in the path of their plans. Leading members of the society, spurred on by the enthusiasm of Dan Josselyn, one of the society's founding fathers, formed the Archaeological Research Association of Alabama, Inc., to generate financial support for excavations through public subscription. This unprecedented effort was highly successful and led to over a decade of fruitful cooperation between the society and University of Alabama archaeologists directed by David L. DeJarnette.

The archaeological projects sponsored by the society included two seasons of excavation at the now famous Stanfield-Worley bluff shelter (1961–1962) and investigations at rock shelters on Sand Mountain in Marshall and De-

David L. DeJarnette at Stanfield-Worley, 1961 (Courtesy David L. DeJarnette)

Kalb counties (1962–1964), at open-air sites in the Mud Creek drainage area of Colbert and Franklin counties (1961–1962), in Lamar County (1966), and in rock shelters in Franklin county (1967–1968). Most recently the society has provided funding for a study of the late Pleistocene deposits of the Black Belt region of central Alabama, where C. B. Curren has reported possible Early Man finds.

Of all of these projects, the Stanfield-Worley excavation stands alone in importance of the data produced. The deposits at this site yielded early Archaic assemblages dating to over nine thousand years ago, clearly bridging the gap between the Paleo-Indian and later Archaic occupations of Alabama (DeJarnette, Kurjack, and Cambron 1962). This work, combined with the results of earlier investigations, has demonstrated that the Tennessee Valley area of northern Alabama is one of the few regions in the East where cultural continuity can be documented between the Paleo-Indian and Archaic stages. The middle Tennessee Valley of Alabama is thus an extremely important area for the study of Early Man in the New World. It is only in such regions, where cultural continuity can be established, that the nature of man's changing adaptation to his environment can be fully traced.

The next stage to be discussed in this study, the Gulf Formational, has only recently been recognized by archaeologists working in the area. Many alterations and changes in interpretation will certainly be made as new data become available. As stated earlier, this stage is marked by the diffusion of ceramics into the Southeast, possibly resulting from cultural contacts with ethnic groups to the south in the Circum-Caribbean region. The Gulf Formational stage developed out of the Archaic and actually represents a type of culture climax based upon earlier achievements. It ends with the appearance of Woodland ceramics and burial mounds, which diffused from northern cultures to the Southeast during the final centuries B.C.

A more complete documentation of the discovery and development of this stage is given in chapter 5. However, it should be noted that, as in the case of the earlier two stages, the major traits of the Gulf Formational stage were discovered during depression-era archaeological projects. Concomitant with the recognition of preceramic cultures in Alabama came the recognition of the earliest pottery, a crude fiber-tempered ware closely followed by a much more sophisticated sand-tempered ceramic complex. The initial study of these early ceramic complexes and the cultures of which they were a part was a major contribution of archaeologists working forty years ago. Based upon these and new discoveries in certain key areas of the state (Walthall and Jenkins 1976), a picture of man's first eight thousand years in Alabama is now emerging.

The last two stages of eastern prehistory, the Woodland and Mississippian, were the first to be recognized in Alabama. By 1930, Woodland burial mounds and Mississippian temple mounds had been reported in all of the major river valleys of the state. The major burial mound complex discovered in Alabama, the Copena manifestation, had been originally reported by C. B. Moore during his turn-of-the-century explorations of the Tennessee Valley. However, it was not until three decades later that William Webb and David DeJarnette formally defined this mound complex and gave it the name "Copena." After a decade of intensive study, resulting in the excavation of over thirty structures, investigations of the Copena complex were halted by the outbreak of World War II. With the resumption of archaeological work after the war, research was shifted from the Tennessee Valley to other areas of the state where new dams and reservoirs were to be built. While other burial mound complexes were discovered in these areas, none was as elaborate or as widespread as Copena, which still remained somewhat of a mystery due to the lack of knowledge concerning its temporal position or cultural affiliations. In 1971 John Walthall began an investigation of Copena aimed at solving these two problems. The result of this study, which constituted Walthall's doctoral dissertation at the University of North Carolina, was the association of the Copena mounds with an indigenous Tennessee Valley Woodland culture stimulated by trade contacts with Hopewellian cultures in the Midwest. Radiocarbon dates submitted as part of this study indicate a temporal range extending from A.D. 100 to A.D. 500 for Copena (Walthall 1972, 1973a).

Since the early nineteenth century, temple mounds, later to be considered a hallmark of the Mississippian stage, have been recognized in several areas in Alabama. The largest group of such mounds was discovered near the town of Carthage, later renamed Moundville, on the banks of the Black Warrior River. The site at Moundville was thoroughly explored for the first time in 1905 by C. B. Moore, who dug pits into each of the twenty major structures. He discovered that Moundville had once been a major ceremonial center for a complex culture with a sophisticated art and technology. Scientific examination of the Moundville site was begun in 1929 by Walter B. Jones, David DeJarnette, and other personnel from the Alabama Museum of Natural History. Later, with the aid of a Civilian Conservation Corps work force, large areas of the site were excavated, revealing the remains of a sizable prehistoric town surrounding the mounds. Beginning in 1938, roads were built to the site and a museum was established in order to make Moundville accessible to the public. In recent years, Moundville has been the subject of two doctoral dissertations: Douglas McKenzie (1964) of Harvard University summarized much of the existing data recovered from Moundville; Christopher Peebles (1974), now of the University of Michigan, studied the social organization of the people who had once lived there. Peebles has continued his interest in Moundville, and his ongoing research should shed additional light on the origin and development of this great prehistoric settlement.

A major post–Moundville Mississippian development, the so-called Burial Urn culture of central Alabama, was first discovered by Moore and was the subject of intensive study by amateur members of the Alabama Anthropological Society during the 1920s and 1930s. This protohistoric complex derives its name from the unusual practice of placing the dead, especially infants, into large pottery vessels capped with often ornate bowls. The Burial Urn manifestation and related phases in other areas of the state represent the last totally aboriginal cultures of Alabama. Rare finds of Spanish and French trade objects in association with urn burials denote the beginnings of European contact that would so alter aboriginal life. Major recent studies of Burial Urn archaeology have been made by two former students of David DeJarnette, John Cottier (1970b) and Craig Sheldon, who wrote a doctoral dissertation on the subject (1974).

The following chapters, detailing current knowledge of the five prehistoric stages, are the product of intensive archaeological investigations in Alabama by scores of amateur and professional researchers. They represent no end product but are rather an initial step in our ongoing study of Alabama's prehistoric past. The extent of current industrial development and highway construction within Alabama and the damming of more and more rivers and streams underscore the necessity that an unprecedented effort be made to preserve the traces of prehistoric human beings that are destroyed every day by our own progress. The results of such efforts may disprove many of the interpretations made in this volume while allowing us to gain new insight into many now unanswerable questions. New problems will be created also, keeping many future generations of archaeologists busy, bothered, and happy.

2: The Environment

The region encompassed by present-day Alabama includes a wide variety of environments. This diversity is the product of a long process of geological upheavals, erosion, concomitant variations in elevation, and climate. The surface of this region rises gradually from Alabama's Gulf coast in the south to the Appalachian ridges and plateaus in the north. The climate of Alabama is humid subtropical, reflecting its proximity to the Gulf of Mexico and its latitude of approximately thirty to thirty-five degrees north.

Alabama's geographic position, topography, and air-mass activity all contribute to the temperate climate. Summers are hot and humid, with average daytime high temperatures in the ninety-degree range and nighttime lows in the high sixties. Harsh winter weather seldom occurs. Below-freezing temperatures normally last less than forty-eight hours. Average winter temperatures range from forty-two degrees in the Tennessee Valley highlands to fifty-two degrees near the Gulf. The growing season averages two hundred days in the north and three hundred near the coast. Precipitation reaches a peak from December to March, and flooding normally occurs during this season (Hays 1973).

Based on geological and geomorphic features, Alabama can be divided into four major physiographic regions or provinces: the Coastal Plain, the Piedmont, the Valley and Ridge, and the Cumberland Plateau. The physical and ecological characteristics of each province had significant effects on prehistoric aboriginal settlement in the Alabama region.

The Coastal Plain. The Coastal Plain province is characterized by low, rolling hills and shallow valleys. Elevations vary from sea level at the coast to some two to three hundred feet in the northwestern margin of the plain. This region is drained by four major rivers: the Tombigbee and Black Warrior in the west; the Alabama, which flows across the central section; and the Chattahoochee in the east. One of the most important subdivisions of the Coastal Plain is the Black Belt, a low valley stretching across central Alabama. The Black Belt, often referred to as the "canebrake" or "prairie" region, averages some twenty miles in width and contains extremely productive soils. Its unusual nature is due to its underlying bedrock formation, an outcrop of soft limestone known as the "Selma chalk." As this limestone weathers, it creates a dark, heavy soil. In areas where the soil is thin, the flora has many elements in common with the true prairie of the Midwest. In other areas where weathering has created deep soil deposits, a rich forest is present, similar to that of surrounding regions but including a number of cedar and oak species not found in contiguous woodlands (J. Thomas 1973).

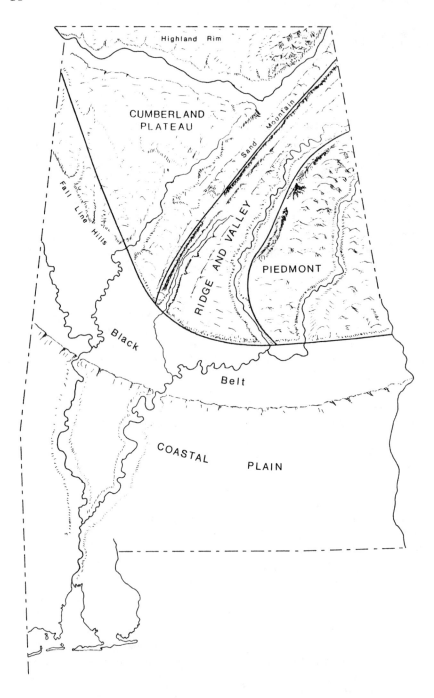

Major Physiographic Provinces of Alabama

Other areas of the Coastal Plain support three major vegetation communities. In the extreme southern portion of this region is the southern mixed forest, composed of tall trees with a mixture of broadleaf deciduous and evergreen species and several species of pine. Dominant species include southern white pine, shortleaf pine, longleaf pine, loblolly pine, white hickory, swamp chestnut oak, laurel oak, and white oak. In sandy areas, particularly near the coast, the forest becomes more open, consisting largely of pine. Food resources available to aboriginal gatherers were relatively sparse, and no major settlements were established in the forest interior during prehistoric times. Stone suitable for tool production is rare in this area; the only major source available were the Tallahatta quartzite formations in what are today Washington and Clarke counties in the extreme southwest of the state. Extensive aboriginal quarries are known in this area, and Tallahatta quartzite was widely traded in prehistoric times.

The northern areas of the Coastal Plain contain the southern extension of the oak-hickory-pine forest that covers most of the state. This diverse forest contains several species of oak, hickory, and walnut, which were extremely important to aboriginal gatherers. The southern floodplain forest, the most productive plant community in the Coastal Plain in terms of aboriginal subsistence, forms narrow north-south belts along the middle and lower reaches of the Black Warrior, Tombigbee, Alabama, and Mobile rivers. This forest is dominated by cypress and several species of oak. The abundance of oak trees, the occurrence of broad floodplains, and the proximity of other major forest regions creating diverse ecotones all contributed to the high population density found in this area during prehistoric and early historic times.

The Piedmont. The Piedmont province of east-central Alabama is a region of rolling hills and deep stream valleys underlain by igneous and metamorphic rocks that represent the roots of the ancient Appalachian Mountains. Within the Piedmont are several mountains, including Mount Cheaha, the highest elevation in Alabama at 2,407 feet above sea level. The Piedmont is drained by scores of small streams flowing into the Coosa and Tallapoosa river systems. The southern margin of the province, forming the fall line boundary, marks the contact between the crystalline rocks of the Piedmont and the sedimentary rocks of the Coastal Plain. In prehistoric times the Piedmont was important as hunting and collecting grounds for the inhabitants of settlements in the Coosa, Tallapoosa, and Chattahoochee valleys, and as a source of raw materials for the production of tools and ornaments. The Hillabee schist deposit was a major source of greenstone, steatite, mica, and graphite. Prehistoric steatite quarries have been discovered and reported at several locations along this formation, and objects made from Piedmont raw materials were widely traded. Steatite was manufactured into vessels, pipes, and ornaments, while celts, axes, and hoes were made from greenstone. Stone tips for spears and, later, arrows, as well as other chipped tools, were made from quartz cobbles found in Piedmont stream beds.

The Valley and Ridge Province. The Valley and Ridge province consists of a series of parallel ridges and valleys with a conspicuous northeast-southwest trend. These formations extend from northeastern Alabama to just south of Birmingham, where they meet the Black Belt to form an extension of the fall line. Some of the major ridges of this province are Red Mountain (which contains tremendous deposits of iron ore), Red Ridge, Shades Mountain, and Lookout Mountain. The oak-hickory-pine forest of this region is drained by the Coosa and Cahaba rivers. Archaeological exploration has only recently begun along the Cahaba, and little is known about the prehistoric settlement of this region. However, extensive aboriginal settlements are known in the Coosa Valley. The Valley and Ridge province and the corresponding Coosa River form a natural north-south corridor from highland Georgia. There is extensive evidence of contact between inhabitants of this area of Alabama and ethnic groups living in northern Georgia, stimulated, no doubt, by the fact that the Coosa Valley constituted a major route to the Piedmont quarries.

The Cumberland Plateau. The Cumberland Plateau, which encompasses most of northern Alabama, constitutes a wedge-shaped highland region bounded on the east by the Valley and Ridge province and on the west and south by the Coastal Plain. This province ranges in elevation from seven hundred feet in the south to over one thousand feet in the north, where the Tennessee River forms a sharp break in the plateau surface (Hooks 1973). Beyond the Tennessee River Valley, the plateau continues into Tennessee as the Highland Rim. The topography of the plateau is broken in the east by a long, narrow anticline extending into Alabama from east-central Tennessee. This anticline, the Sequatchie Valley, is followed by the Tennessee River from Chattanooga to Guntersville, where the river leaves the anticline and turns northwestward across northern Alabama. The Cumberland Plateau is drained by the Tennessee River to the north and by the Black Warrior River to the south.

The vegetation of this region is complex. Four major forest types are found within the plateau highlands: an oak-hickory-pine forest, an oak-hickory forest, cedar glades, and a mixed mesophytic forest.

The oak-history forest dominates much of the north-central portion of the state. This forest represents a southern extension of a plant community covering large portions of the Midwest as far north as Michigan and as far west as Nebraska. Major species in this forest include white oak, red oak, southern red oak, black oak, shagbark hickory, mockernut, pignut, elm, and black walnut.

The cedar glades are found in scattered patches throughout the Tennessee Valley and cluster in a large zone north of Guntersville where there are areas of very shallow soil over limestone bedrock. Red cedar is often the dominant, and at times only, species of tree. These cedar glades support a diverse herbaceous flora, many species of which belong to the mustard family. Cedar

Alabama Counties

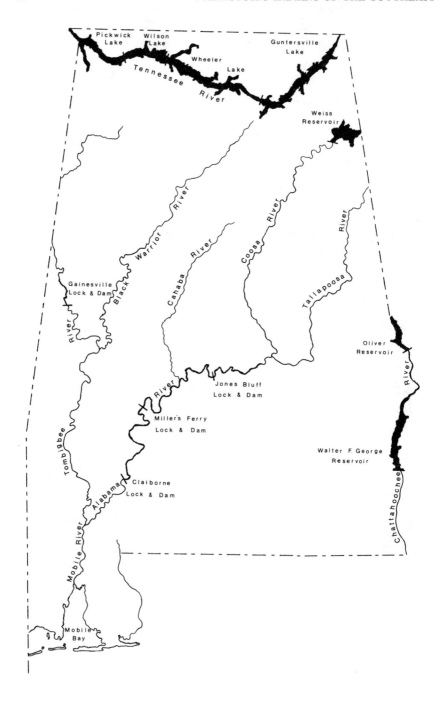

Major River Systems and River Basins Discussed in Text

was a favored wood for carving utensils and other objects during aboriginal times and many of the herbs found in the cedar glades are known to have been used by Indians in historic times for medicinal purposes. Game concentrates in these glades during the spring, and it is likely that these areas were extensively utilized on a seasonal basis by hunting and gathering parties.

The mixed mesophytic forest is confined to the Guntersville Basin region of extreme northeastern Alabama. Dominant trees in this plant community include several species of oak, basswood, hickory, maple, beech, poplar, chestnut, ash, sweet gum, and hemlock. This forest type appears best developed in moist ravines, particularly those with calcareous soils. Plant geographers have noted that this forest represents a remnant of a once vast forest that extended over large portions of the northern hemisphere. Similar remnants are found today in southeastern Asia (J. Thomas 1973).

The ecotones formed in the Cumberland Plateau province by river valleys, highland ridges, and diverse flora offered aboriginal populations an incredibly rich subsistence base. The highest population density in prehistoric Alabama was found in the river valleys of this region. The remains of the largest prehistoric town known in the Southeast—Moundville—is found in the Black Warrior Valley, and other extensive settlements were occupied in the Tennessee Valley. The earliest evidence of man in Alabama is also in the Cumberland Plateau region. One can imagine bands of hunters stalking herds of elephant and other extinct species that once roamed the valley corridors. The floodplains of these valleys provided a variety of wild plant foods and rich soils for cultivation. Extensive mussel beds in the rivers also provided a ready source of protein, as did the several species of mammals and birds that fed along the banks. As early as 8000 B.C., the uplands were extensively used during the fall and winter months when forest seeds drop and animals congregate in the highland forests. As Joseph Caldwell noted, the fall season in the southern highlands was once a time when "the hunting must have been good, the meat fat, and the pelts glossy."

3: Pioneer Hunters and Gatherers

The origin of man is not to be found in the New World. Abundant archaeological and paleontological evidence indicates that man first appeared in the tropics of the Old World. After a long period of cultural and physical development, he eventually began to migrate into temperate and even subarctic environments. The geological epoch that gave birth to man was the Pleistocene, dating back to more than three million years ago. During this time, the earth's surface underwent a series of drastic climatic and environmental changes, from glacial periods when much of the earth was covered by vast ice sheets to long, warm, interglacial periods that witnessed expansion of tropical and temperate zones.

The last major glacial advance, known as the "Wisconsin" in North America, began about seventy thousand years ago and ended about ten thousand years ago. It is this final Pleistocene development that is of particular interest to American archaeologists, for during this time man first reached the New World. The extensive glaciers that covered much of the northern hemisphere during the Wisconsin advance trapped large quantities of water, causing sea levels to drop over three hundred feet and in some areas exposing now-submerged continental shelves.

During these periods of low sea levels, the Bering Strait between Siberia and Alaska was a broad plain some thirteen thousand miles wide (Haag 1962). Across this expanse, herds of large mammals migrated from one continent to another. Paleolithic hunters, long adapted to the harsh environments of northeastern Asia, also moved through this area. Following ice-free corridors, they pushed southward into more favorable environments. Archaeologists are divided, however, as to when the first migrants crossed over the Bering Strait. Some argue that man reached the New World forty thousand years ago or even earlier, while others postulate a late migration some fourteen to sixteen thousand years ago, followed by relatively rapid population growth and colonization.

Early New World Cultures

The earliest definite evidence of man in the New World dates to about 10,000 B.C., based upon a number of radiocarbon determinations from archaeological sites where stone implements have been recovered near extinct animals. The lithic assemblages found at these localities have been assigned to an early cultural stage called the Paleo-Indian by many archaeologists.

These assemblages include a type of projectile point, with long channel flakes or flutes removed from one or both faces, that has no counterpart in the Old World. It is the product of a specialized technology and represents a culture already well adapted to the New World environment. This suggests that an earlier developmental stage existed in the New World that ultimately produced these later fluted-point complexes. The search for evidence of this early lithic stage has been long and tumultuous.

The history of this problem in American archaeology begins not in the New World but in Europe. In 1849 Boucher de Perthes reported the results of a ten-year study of the terrace deposits along the Somme River in north-western France. In these ancient gravel beds he had found worked flints of a distinctive, recurring type near extinct faunal remains. It was not until the summer of 1859, however—when a group of distinguished British scientists visited the Somme terraces and themselves found worked flints—that de Perthes's findings were authenticated. The reverberations of this discovery had a worldwide impact on the search for prehistoric man. Suddenly, scores of earlier finds of stone tools were announced throughout Europe and the exploration of prehistoric sites began in earnest.

These events in Europe did not go unnoticed in the United States. Stone implements were discovered by the thousands along the Eastern Seaboard; when these were compared to drawings of the Paleolithic artifacts of Europe, many were found to be similar in form and workmanship. Assertions of great antiquity were made for these New World finds on the basis of these typolog-ical comparisons.

However, the age of these artifacts and the claims of their numerous champions were the subject of considerable debate. During the late nineteenth and early twentieth centuries, scientific investigations, based upon accumulating archaeological and osteological knowledge, disputed these earlier speculations. Ales Hrdlicka, the dominant figure in physical anthropology in the United States at that time, discredited or cast serious doubt on the validity of the many finds of human skeletal material recovered from supposed Pleistocene contexts. His studies indicated that man must have entered the New World late in time, since all human skeletal remains that had been recovered in reliable prehistoric context were fully modern in physical appearance.

The coup de grace was apparently dealt Paleolithic man in the New World when William Henry Holmes published the results of a scientific study of some of the supposed Early Man sites along the eastern coast. Crudely worked stone tools had been collected from a series of sites in the Potomac-Chesapeake region, and these had been put forward in support of the An-cient Man theory. Holmes's (1897) pioneering functional study of these sites and the artifacts recovered from them demonstrated that these locations were not campsites of Paleolithic man, but rather quarries utilized by a number of aboriginal peoples even during the initial period of European colonization of the region. The crude stone tools proved to be quarry debitage—rejects, cores, flakes, and unfinished tools and implements used in the quarrying and production of lithic artifacts.

Thus, during the first quarter of this century, all evidence pointed to a relatively brief aboriginal occupation of the New World. All prehistoric remains were summarily placed into a restricted post-Pleistocene archaeological sequence. However, the idea of a "short chronology" for New World prehistory was soon shattered. Beginning in 1926, a series of archaeological discoveries were made in the American Southwest that provided irrevocable proof of the existence of man in North America during the Pleistocene. At Folsom, New Mexico, fluted projectile points were found with the remains of extinct forms of bison. Later, in 1932, at a site near Dent, Colorado, a number of larger, more crudely made fluted points were found in association with mammoth bones. It was clear that these animals had been the prey of hunters armed with stone-tipped spears. These discoveries reopened the entire question concerning the existence of an early lithic stage.

A Pre-Projectile Point Stage?

Since these landmark archaeological investigations, the idea of such an early lithic stage has found a number of proponents among American archaeologists. One of the leading figures is Alex Krieger, who has documented hundreds of sites that have yielded assemblages of crude, percussion-flaked tools—pebble choppers, scrapers, cores, and flakes. Krieger (1964) assigns them to what he calls a pre-projectile point stage because of the conspicuous absence of projectile points at a number of these sites. His theory is controversial among most archaeologists because the majority of these finds occur on the surface and have been subjected to disturbance. Doubt also exists concerning the identification of some of these objects as actual artifacts (Haynes 1973). The most convincing evidence for such a stage is based upon data recovered from sites in South America, where such crude tools have been found in stratigraphically early contexts. Some of these artifact-bearing zones have been dated by the radiocarbon technique to more than twenty thousand years ago (MacNeish 1971: Lanning and Patterson 1967).

The Lively Complex

Claims of great antiquity have recently been made for a number of finds of such crudely worked artifacts from sites in northwestern Alabama. Dan Josselyn, Matthew Lively, and several other amateur archaeologists spent a number of years systematically collecting off the surface in the upper Coastal Plain region of Lamar and Marion counties along the Mississippi border. On the eroded surfaces of sites in this area, Josselyn and his companions found numerous worked chert (jasper) cobbles and flakes. Studies of these collections (Josselyn 1965; Lively 1965) indicate that many of these artifacts are typologically similar to percussion-flaked implements found in early Paleolithic cultures of the Old World. On this basis, the hypothesis was made that these Alabama artifacts predated the fluted-point complexes and were part of a southeastern extension of the pre–projectile point stage.

The artifacts in question were identified according to technological and geological criteria. All of these Lively complex tools were made by percussion flaking and virtually all were made from cobbles of yellow-tan chert that occur in river-deposited gravels in the area. According to Josselyn, "It is a circumstance of considerable interest that all of the other artifacts on the Lively Complex sites, in some cases very abundant, are notoriously made of red jasper (excepting the fluted points, which as usual are exotic material)—while the Lively Complex utilized only the yellow jasper, which makes it conveniently separable from the enormous litter of red jasper on some of the eleven sites involved" (1965:5). Referring to the yellow jasper cobbles, Josselyn also notes that "Much of the material used is hardly adaptable to thin biface manufacture, but suffices surprisingly well for large, crude tools" (1965:4).

The major problem concerning the Lively complex is one of interpretation. Josselyn and his associates believe that these artifacts represent a single early lithic assemblage. This interpretation is certainly open to debate. If William Henry Holmes had studied these sites he would most probably have concluded that these materials represent quarry workshop debris. In his study of the quarry sites between Baltimore and Wilmington, Holmes recovered specimens that were, on the basis of form and technology, identical to the Lively complex artifacts. He further noted that all along the fall line of the inner edge of the eastern Coastal Plain large quantities of river-deposited cobbles were extensively quarried. The Lively complex sites are also located on the inner edge of the Coastal Plain, and extensive deposits of riverine gravels are found in the area. The presence of abundant broken cobbles and flakes on these sites indicates that the procurement and processing of local lithic materials were major activities conducted at these locations. These data strongly support the contention that many of the Lively complex artifacts represent by-products of lithic tool production.

The different choice of materials used in Lively complex artifacts and bifacially thinned implements noted by Josselyn is significant in interpreting the meaning of these finds. The yellow chert cobbles were found to be difficult to thin during flint-knapping experiments conducted by Josselyn. More recent experimentation conducted at The University of Alabama under the direction of C. B. Oakley indicates that heat treatment of the yellow cobbles substantially increases the amount of control the flint knapper is able to maintain during the removal of primary and secondary flakes. When the yellow cobbles were subjected to heat, they took on a pink-to-red hue iden-

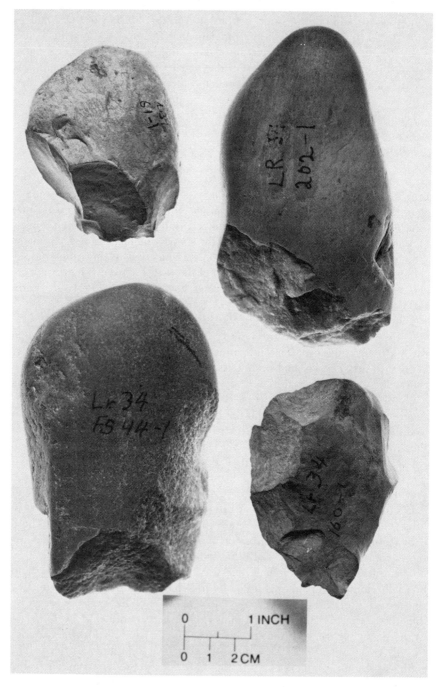

Pebble Tools from the Crump Site, Lamar County

tical to that of flakes and cores recovered from Lively complex sites. It appears that during certain occupations of these sites lithic materials were processed in two separate and functionally significant manners. Tools that required only slight modification were not subjected to heat, while materials to be made into thinned, bifacial implements were heat treated to facilitate reduction.

The question remains: Are all of the Lively complex artifacts quarry tools and workshop debris? It does not appear so. Many of these artifacts were utilized as choppers for a variety of tasks, while others appear to be specialized implements such as denticulate (serrated) tools for plant processing. The major problem that remains is to associate these tools with particular lithic assemblages. This was not possible at the multicomponent surface occurrences investigated by Josselyn. Toward this end, excavations by The University of Alabama were conducted at two stratified sites in the Lively complex area. Cultural zones dating from the Woodland and Archaic stages were found at these two locations: the Crump site and Stucks Bluff rock shelter (DeJarnette, Walthall, and Wimberly 1975a,b). Yellow jasper cobble tools and debitage, as well as red jasper bifaces and flakes, were found throughout both sites but were clustered in the Woodland levels. It appears that these percussion-flaked cobbles were utilized during several temporally isolated occupations of these sites. Paleo-Indian projectile points have also been noted in surface collections from some of Josselyn's sites, and some of the percussion-flaked cobbles may date to that cultural stage. Similar crude tools and heat-treated artifacts have been reported from isolated Paleo-Indian sites in other areas, most recently at the Wells Creek crater in Stewart County, Tennessee (Dragoo 1973).

The initial question concerning these artifacts still remains: Is it possible that some of the Lively complex materials predate the fluted-point stage? Until sites are located and investigated where crude tools are found stratigraphically beneath fluted-point zones, this question will remain unanswered and the theory of the pre–projectile point stage in the Southeast will continue to be a matter of conjecture.

The Paleo-Indian Stage

No such controversy exists concerning the Paleo-Indian stage. There is abundant evidence of this early hunting and gathering way of life, both in the western plains and in the eastern woodlands. In the West, these cultures have been divided into two sequential complexes, Clovis and Folsom. Four of the six sites where Clovis assemblages were found in association with mammoth remains have been dated by the radiocarbon technique to between 9500 and 9000 B.C. Hundreds of finds of these diagnostic projectile points in the East imply an occupation of this area by Clovis hunters during this time. The later Folsom complex has been dated to between 9000 and 8000 B.C., but projectile points of the specific Folsom type are restricted in range to the Great Plains. During this terminal Pleistocene period, groups of men in the East made a variety of fluted and nonfluted lanceolate-shaped projectile points, including the Cumberland, Beaver Lake, and Quad types of the Alabama area.

While fluted points have been recovered frequently from deeply stratified sites in the West, this has not been the case in the East. With few exceptions, all eastern fluted points have been recovered from eroded surface sites. Likewise, extinct animal remains have not been reported from Paleo-Indian sites in the East. However, hunting is implied in the tool forms found at these sites. Besides the fluted points used to tip throwing and thrusting spears, many biface knives and blades have been recovered; and uniface scrapers, knives, drills, groovers, and graving tools are common. As has also been noted:

> Some inferences as to other tools can be made, even though perishable artifacts are not normally found in the East. Slender cylindrical bone points with beveled bases have been found at the Clovis site in New Mexico, and bone needles, awls, and beads at the Lindenmeier site in Colorado. Wood would have been used for spears or darts, for handles, for shelter, for clubs, and for fire. Animal hides were probably used for clothing, cordage, and containers, and perhaps for shelter. [J. B. Griffin 1967: 176]

The Clovis Period

Distributional studies of Clovis points in the Southeast indicate that these artifacts are most commonly found in the plateau areas (Williams and Stoltman 1965). In fact, more fluted points have been reported from the Interior Low Plateau province of the Kentucky and Tennessee highlands than in any other area of North America. The occurrence of these numerous fluted points in this region has led some archaeologists to argue that the Clovis complex has an eastern origin (Mason 1962). While this theory is open to debate, the high frequency of Paleo-Indian artifacts in this area is significant. This concentration of fluted points most probably reflects the intensive hunting of late Pleistocene mammals attracted to the numerous salt springs found in this region. Large quantities of Pleistocene animal bones have been reported from a number of these salt springs. The only reported case in which a fluted point may have been found in association with mammoth bones in the East was at one of these springs, Big Bone Lick in Kentucky (Haynes 1966:109), where in 1898 a Clovis point was recovered. Unfortunately, the exact context in which it was found was not recorded. However, the recovery of this spearpoint does indicate the presence of Clovis hunters and raises the possibility that further investigation of these springs may lead to the discovery of mammoth kill sites in the East.

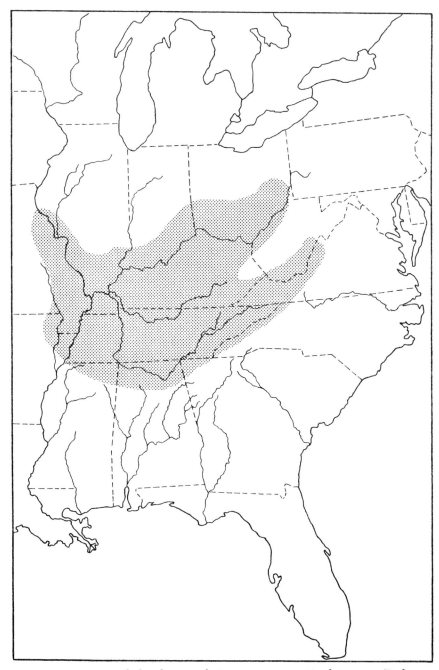

Major Concentration of Fluted Projectile Points in Eastern North America (Redrawn after Mason 1962)

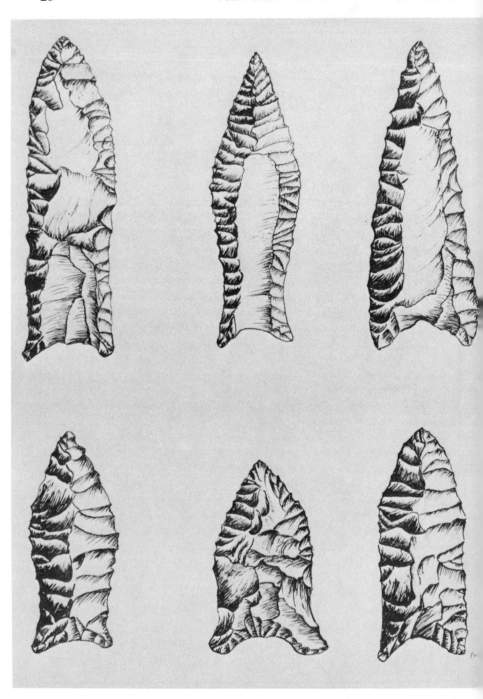

Some Paleo-Indian Projectile Point Forms from Alabama Sites

Paleo-Indian Projectile Points from the Middle Tennessee Valley (After Cambron and Hulse 1960)

The southern extension of the Interior Low Plateau province terminates in northern Alabama. In turn, more fluted points are found in this portion of the state than in any other area. The occurrence of fluted-point finds drops off drastically in Alabama as one moves from the northern highlands southward; only a few points of this type have been reported from the Coastal Plain. In northern Alabama, Clovis points most commonly occur in the Tennessee Valley.

Clovis sites are usually found on the upper terraces of the Tennessee River. Only a few isolated Clovis points have been reported from the bordering upland environments, which suggests that this region may have been wetter during the late Pleistocene than it is at present and that the Clovis economy was based upon the exploitation of valley resources. All of these early fluted-point sites were apparently temporary, open-air campsites. Excavations of numerous rock shelters in the Tennessee Valley region have been conducted, but Clovis points have not been found in this context.

The isolation of a distinct Clovis component has proved difficult because the sites on which they occur are heavily eroded and are usually multicomponent in nature. However, on the basis of typology it is possible to distinguish at least three periods of Paleo-Indian occupation. The Clovis occupation, which probably dates from 10,000 to 9000 B.C., is characterized by small campsites or isolated finds. The projectile points are made from a variety of local and nonlocal lithic material and are fairly consistent in form and manufacture. During the subsequent periods of the Paleo-Indian stage in this region, several interrelated trends emerge. Wider varieties of projectile-point forms appear; sites are more numerous and occur often in previously unpopulated areas. These trends suggest that there was an increase in population density and in territoriality and that a number of new resource areas were beginning to be exploited.

Later Developments—Cumberland and Quad

Based upon typological considerations and a limited amount of stratigraphic data, it is possible to distinguish two later Paleo-Indian periods in northern Alabama. The earlier, Cumberland period is characterized by narrow, lanceolate-shaped projectile points with constricted hafting zones. These points are normally fully fluted, although an unfluted and perhaps later variant, known as the Beaver Lake type, has been recognized. Cumberland points are thought to be contemporary with the fully fluted Folsom points of the Great Plains, for both are characterized by this apparently late technological development.

Cumberland and related projectile points do not occur over the wide geographical area that characterizes the Clovis forms. Most of these fully fluted eastern points are restricted to the Interior Low Plateau and surrounding regions. Cumberland points have been recovered, however, from a wider range of environmental zones than the earlier forms. While Cumberland points are frequently found in the Tennessee Valley, they also occur in the uplands. Four fluted point fragments identified as belonging to the Cumberland type have been recently recovered from a small rock shelter on Sand Mountain in northeastern Alabama (Clayton 1965). The recovery of these specimens represents the first discovery of Cumberland points in such a context. This site, called the Rock House by local residents of the nearby Asbury community in Marshall County, is in a steep bluff at the junction of two small streams. The living area within the shelter was approximately twenty feet in width and depth and from four to six feet in height at the time of investigation. Three cultural zones were exposed during the excavation of the shelter deposit. The bottom zone, overlying bedrock, proved to be a stratum containing early Archaic lithic material. The four Cumberland fragments and a Quad point were also recovered in this zone. Because of the uneven nature of the shelter floor, stratigraphic separation of the Paleo-Indian and early Archaic occupations was not possible. Another fragment of a fluted point was later reported by Margaret Clayton (1967) from the nearby Boydston Creek rock shelter in a similar context. The presence of these points in the lower cultural zones at these sites provides stratigraphic evidence of the early context of the Cumberland point and may signify initial economic exploitation of the upland microenvironments by regional Paleo-Indian groups.

The final period of the Paleo-Indian stage in Alabama is represented by the Quad and Beaver Lake point types. Quad projectile points have been described as medium-sized, broad, fluted or unfluted, with a constricted hafting area (Cambron and Hulse 1964). The Beaver Lake is a medium-sized lanceolate point with a recurvate blade edge. The shape of the point is similar to that of the fluted Cumberland type (DeJarnette, Kurjack, and Cambron 1962), and distribution is similar to that of the Cumberland form. However, Quad and Quad-like projectile points are more frequently found in highland and piedmont areas than the earlier types (Coe 1964). Evidence that Quad peoples used upland areas has been reported from several small rock shelters in the Tennessee Valley region. Quad and Beaver Lake points and a small associated lithic assemblage were found in the lower cultural zone at the Flint Creek rock shelter, and Beaver Lake points were recovered in the bottom cultural layers at Stanfield-Worley in Colbert County (DeJarnette et al. 1962) and at the Walls I rock shelter on Sand Mountain in Marshall County (Clayton 1965).

The Flint Creek rock shelter is on a tributary of Flint Creek in the Morgan County highlands south of the Tennessee River. Excavations revealed that this shelter was a multicomponent site with major Archaic and Woodland components (Cambron and Mitchell 1958; Cambron and Waters 1959, 1961). The bottom culture-bearing layer produced the two late Paleo-Indian points. This stratum was physically distinct from the overlying intermediate zone containing early Archaic Dalton material. Associated with the projectile points were a biface knife and a small number of uniface tools. Although the artifact inventory from this bottom zone was small, the recovery of this Quad assemblage stratigraphically below the early Archaic zone is of importance in determining the chronological position of the late Paleo-Indian stage in Alabama. Similar early Archaic materials have been dated by the radio-carbon technique to between 8000 and 7000 B.C. at other sites in the Tennessee Valley. This indicates that the final Paleo-Indian period of this region, represented by the Quad occupation, dates to the latter half of the ninth millennium B.C.

The Quad Site

In 1951 Frank J. Soday discovered a number of Paleo-Indian projectile points on the eroded surfaces of two parallel ridges across the Tennessee River from the city of Decatur. Subsequent visits to this location, which Soday (1954) named the Quad site, yielded over a thousand artifacts dating from the Paleo-Indian to Archaic times. This multicomponent site was near the valley edge on the upper terraces above the valley floor. Much of this area, including the southern portion of the Quad site itself, was inundated by the construction of Wheeler Dam. Before the completion of this reservoir, several oxbow lakes and swamps were present in the valley between the Quad site and the river.

Scattered on the surface of the Quad site Soday found numerous early Archaic projectile points and tools mixed with the Paleo-Indian materials. He was able to distinguish the Paleo-Indian assemblages from later occupational debris on the basis of raw material, degree of weathering (patination), and technology. Most of the Paleo-Indian artifacts were moderately to heavily patinated and had been made with a type of mottled, blue-gray chert. The Paleo-Indian artifacts recovered by Soday included Clovis, Cumberland, Beaver Lake, and Quad projectile points, as well as a variety of tools—scrapers, knives, gravers, drills, and choppers. Several channel flakes, removed during the fluting of projectile points, were also found. Bone tools were not present, probably due to the unfavorable soil conditions.

Limited excavations were conducted in 1959 on a portion of the Quad site that is submerged most of the year by Wheeler Lake (Cambron and Hulse 1964). Test pits revealed four thin strata of sand and clay, ranging from less than one foot to only two feet in total depth. One feature was encountered—a small pit containing reddish, sandy soil and a few partially charred raccoon bones. The cultural provenance of this feature could not be determined because there had been considerable mixing throughout the strata due to erosion and a slow rate of deposition. It was noted, however, that fire-cracked rock was present throughout the cultural zones.

A recent study of a sample of the lithic material from the Quad site has been conducted by Edwin Wilmsen (1968). Distributional analysis of the artifacts recovered during Soday's visits indicates that the cultural material was found in small, concentrated areas, generally widely separated. Wilmsen suggests that this pattern of concentration indicates that the site was periodically occupied by small groups of people rather than by a large group at one time. The very low ratio (2:1) between debitage and finished tools recovered at Quad implies that tools were imported in an essentially completed state and that little stoneworking other than tool repairing was done on the site. The presence of numerous projectile points and tools made from nonlocal stone and the low proportion of unfinished tools recovered tend to support this conclusion.

The wide variety of tools from the Quad site indicates that this locality was used as a base camp by hunting and gathering groups. Functional analysis of these tools suggests that they were used in hunting, butchering, hide-working, and plant-processing tasks. Sites of this nature have been called "multiple activity locations" (Wilmsen 1968). In contrast, some of the other Paleo-Indian sites studied by Wilmsen have been called "limited activity sites." These are sites, like quarries or the kill sites of the Great Plains, that

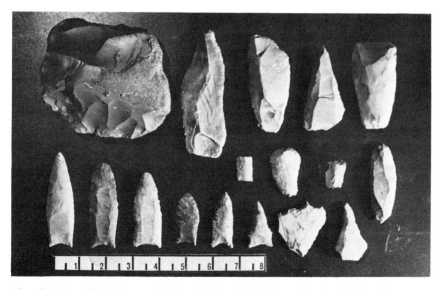

Fluted Projectile Points and Paleo-Indian Tools from the Quad Site (Courtesy Frank J. Soday)

are near certain kinds of natural resources and yield evidence of the exploitation of these resources as the primary activity practiced at the site.

Multiple activity locations are most often found in favorable camping areas. The area surrounding the Quad site must certainly have been such a favored locality. Along two miles of the valley edge, on either side of the Quad site, abundant Paleo-Indian finds have occurred. Besides numerous isolated fluted points, two other major Paleo-Indian habitation sites have been located in this area. The Pine Tree site (Cambron 1956, 1958) and the Stone Pipe site (Cambron 1955) have both yielded artifacts similar to those found at the Quad site, indicating that these localities also served as Paleo-Indian campsites.

It would appear that small groups of Paleo-Indian peoples often visited this area of the valley. Possible explanations for the intensity of the prehistoric occupation of this particular area can be offered. First, distributional study of Paleo-Indian sites in Colbert and Lauderdale counties has revealed that fluted points are often found near ancient ponds or lakes in the valley floor (Hubbert n.d.). These small bodies of water, like those below the Quad site, attract a variety of animal life and would have been favored locations for ambush hunting. Second, the reason for the founding of the modern city of Decatur across the river from the area of the Quad site may be of significance. Decatur was founded in 1821 at this particular place because it was the site of a well-known aboriginal crossing. Both men and animals forded the river at this point because of the treacherous shoal waters downstream and the high bluffs upstream. It may be, then, that a similar set of circumstances resulted in the establishment of temporary Paleo-Indian camps along this area of the river more than ten thousand years ago.

Paleo-Indian Culture

One of the primary aims of archaeology is the reconstruction of prehistoric cultures. This task is difficult because the nonperishable remains left by prehistoric peoples are usually few and reflect only a small portion of the total culture—especially in the case of the Paleo-Indian inhabitants of the New World. In most situations the archaeologist has only stone tools with which to work. Functional studies of these tools, such as that conducted by Wilmsen, can tell us a great deal about how certain tools were used and allow certain inferences to be made concerning the culture of which they were once a part. The interpretations of the functions of these stone implements are largely based upon recorded observations of tool use among contemporary primitive peoples. Such ethnographic analogy is one of the major techniques used by the archaeologist in attempting to understand prehistoric human beings and their ways.

The Band Level of Society

The late Pleistocene Paleo-Indian peoples were most probably on the band level of society, the least complex of all known social systems. Bands are groups of loosely related kinsmen who function as an economic and social unit. One of the major characteristics of this type of culture is the nomadism required by a hunting and foraging economy (Service 1966). This nomadic way of life limits the amount of material goods a people can accumulate, and it restricts community size. Known Paleo-Indian sites in Alabama are typically small and scattered in comparison to the more substantial camps and villages of later peoples. This observation suggests that population density was very low at this time, even in the Tennessee Valley region where most of the fluted points were found. This type of sparse settlement pattern is characteristic of contemporary hunting and gathering band societies like the Australian aborigines or the Kalahari bushmen. According to Elman Service:

> The band is usually a vague entity without very definite boundaries. The domestic family is often the only consistent face to face group, although brothers and their families may meet from time to time and sometimes hunt and forage together. The next largest group, the band itself, may take its definition merely from the fact that its members feel closely enough related that they do not intermarry. In some instances they also define themselves territorially, as inhabitants and "owners" of a foraging range. [1966:7]

Based upon further ethnographic analogy, the following predictions can be made concerning Paleo-Indian society. The economic division of labor was by age and sex differentiation. Adult males hunted, worked stone, and made and repaired weapons, while adult females took care of the children, gathered plant foods and firewood, constructed shelters, worked animal hides, prepared food, and did the cooking. These groups were male dominated, with leaders chosen on the basis of skill or age. The bands themselves probably averaged twenty-five individuals, and marriages were exogamous, that is, outside the group (Birdsell 1968).

Marriage between bands served to promote unity and cooperation among families sharing a geographical range. In times when abundant food resources were available, several bands would join together to procure food. At these times, probably on a seasonal basis, ceremonies were conducted, marriages made, and goods were redistributed among the people through gift giving and barter. It is likely that information concerning the availability of certain resources in various areas of the overlapping foraging territories was also exchanged. The presence of the exotic cherts on some of the Tennessee Valley campsites can be accounted for as representing exchange items from kinsmen in surrounding regions.

Were Elephants Hunted in Alabama?

The answer may be yes. There is a growing body of data that suggest that mammoth and mastodon were hunted in eastern North America as well as on the Great Plains. This question is an integral part of a broader problem that American archaeologists are attempting to solve: What was the nature of Paleo-Indian economy? Because the diet of these early peoples consisted solely of wild plants and animals, knowledge of the environment in which they lived is essential.

The land inhabited by the Paleo-Indian peoples of the East was subject to the influences of continental glaciation. During the maximum advance of the Wisconsin period, when the ice sheets moved southward into Ohio, much of what is now the Interior Low Plateau was probably spruce park land. To the south were boreal forests, like those found in Canada today, followed by zones of deciduous forest. As the ice sheets retreated northward, these environments began to shift. By the terminal Pleistocene, the mixed coniferous forest covering much of northern Alabama was replaced by a deciduous forest climax. To the south, the Black Belt region was a rolling prairie, while the Coastal Plain environment was much the same as it is today, a mixed broadleaf and pine forest. Fossil remains recovered from Alabama and surrounding states indicate that mammoth and mastodon were present in the Tennessee Valley during the late Pleistocene, while the Black Belt region supported a large variety of animal life that included, besides elephants, giant ground sloth, elk, bison, and horse (Hay 1923; Kaye 1974).

In some areas of the northeastern United States, archaeologists are able to see clear distinctions between Paleo-Indian occupations and later Archaic cultures. However, in the Southeast there appears to have been an early adaptation by Paleo-Indian bands to the developing oak-hickory forest environment. Cultural development, as reconstructed on the basis of the excavated sites already discussed, indicates real cultural continuity between the Paleo-Indian and Archaic stages in northern Alabama. While there is abundant evidence of hunting found at these sites, the gathering of plant foods in this rich environment must have also been of considerable economic importance. Service (1966) has noted that where the environment permits, band groups universally depend heavily upon vegetable foods as a major portion of their diet.

Because of the lack of animal remains at late Pleistocene sites in the East, Paleo-Indian hunting patterns are difficult to define. It may be assumed that these strategies varied according to environmental potential. Small game probably played a significant role in the hunting activities of most groups, while larger animals were a primary prey in others. However, the idea of the Paleo-Indian hunter as the eternal nomad following migratory herd animals wherever they roamed cannot be supported by current anthropological research. These groups, especially in the more densely occupied regions, were territorial. The term territorial "implies that the members of a given social group moved within an area which was more or less delineated by social factors, by the proximity of other such groups, by considerations of distance, by familiarity with the environment, and by natural obstacles" (Wobst 1974:151).

It appears to be fairly clear that the Paleo-Indian habitation of northern Alabama was much more substantial than in areas to the south. Paleo-Indian sites in this region are located either in the main valley or in the uplands near mountain passes and corridors, probably because of the proximity to migratory routes of large herd animals. Although this statement is speculatory, there is a certain amount of data available to support such a contention. The distribution of Paleo-Indian projectile points in the Southeast has been compared with the distribution of mammoth and mastodon remains from this region. While the results of such a correlation are tenuous at best, there was a substantial overlap between these two variables (Williams and Stoltman 1965). The Paleo-Indian groups inhabiting territories in the Tennessee Valley region possibly relied much of the year on small game and plant foods, but, when herds moved through seasonally, hunters could have taken these animals in two ways. First, groups of men could have taken part in collective hunts or drives. Second, scavenging of migratory animals that died as a result of disease, drowning, or old age either could have supplemented hunting activities or constituted a major source of protein during certain seasons. The position of the Quad locality and other Paleo-Indian sites near a ford of the Tennessee River may have some correlation with this type of activity.

Whatever role these large herbivorous mammals played in the economy of the Paleo-Indian peoples of north Alabama, it seems certain that toward the end of the Pleistocene the range of these animals no longer extended into this region. During this time there was a gradual shift to a more intensive hunting of modern fauna and the development of a general foraging pattern that signals the beginning of the next stage of cultural development in Alabama, the Archaic.

4: The Archaic Stage

The recognition of an Archaic stage in North American archaeology has a long history. The term was first used in 1932 by William Ritchie when he applied this concept to a series of preceramic assemblages from sites in New York State. Since that time numerous excavations have been conducted at preceramic sites throughout North America. The vast amount of temporal and cultural diversity displayed by many of these geographically distant components has led to many revisions of Ritchie's original definition. The problems in terminology encountered by archaeologists attempting to integrate their preceramic data have been summarized by Gordon Willey and Philip Phillips (1958:104–11) and by Douglas Byers (1959:229–32), among others.

Most of the definitions of the Archaic currently in use place emphasis on three factors: adaptation, time, and technology. A standard interpretation of this sort was offered by Willey and Phillips in their volume on archaeological method and theory:

> We may briefly define the Archaic as the stage of migratory hunting and gathering cultures continuing into environmental conditions approximating those of the present... there is now a dependence on smaller and perhaps more varied fauna. There is also an apparent increase in gathering; it is in this stage that sites begin to yield large numbers of stone implements and tools that are assumed to be connected with the preparation of wild vegetable foods....
> Of primary interest as stage criteria are the heavy ground-stone woodworking tools generally regarded as prerequisite to the successful occupation of forest environments—axes, adzes, wedges, gouges, etc. [1958:107–08]

Recent investigations of stratified rock shelters and open-air sites in eastern North America have indicated that the Archaic stage began nearly ten thousand years ago and ended some seven thousand years later. This long cultural sequence has been traditionally divided into three sequential periods. The first of these temporal segments, the early Archaic period, is characterized by notched and stemmed projectile points, uniface flake tools, and, in northern Alabama, by a more intensive utilization of rock shelters as habitation sites. This initial Archaic period dates from approximately 8000 to 6000 B.C. The following period, the middle Archaic, dating from 6000 to 4000 B.C., is characterized by the appearance of ground and polished stone implements; a wide variety of bone tools; flexed burials, often accompanied by mortuary goods; and the first major occupation of riverine shell middens. In late Archaic times there were many innovations, including the develop-

Major Pre-ceramic Sites in Northern Alabama

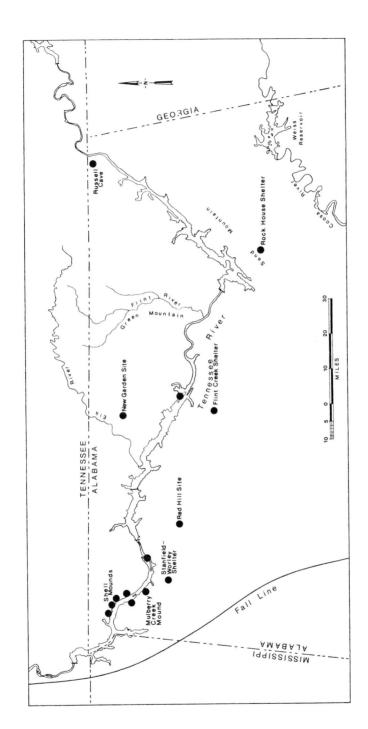

ment of limited spectrum economies based upon a few high-yield natural foods, and the earliest cultivation of native annuals. This final period in the Archaic sequence dates from 4000 B.C. to the diffusion of Gulf Formational pottery into the Alabama region. Ceramics of this sort were introduced around 1000 B.C., thus establishing a terminal date for the Archaic stage in this area.

Much of our knowledge of the latter two periods in the Archaic sequence in Alabama is derived from the monumental depression-era excavations of the great shell middens on the Tennessee River (Webb and DeJarnette 1942, 1948a, b, c, d). However, a considerable amount of important information concerning both these later periods and the initial Archaic occupation of Alabama was obtained during investigations of two deeply stratified rock shelters in the Tennessee Valley region. Before beginning an inquiry into the nature of culture change during the Archaic in Alabama, it would perhaps be important first to describe these two extremely significant sites—Russell Cave and the Stanfield-Worley bluff shelter.

Russell Cave

In 1953 Russell Cave was discovered by members of the Chattanooga chapter of the Tennessee Archaeological Society (P. H. Brown 1954). The site is in Jackson County, Alabama, some four miles west of Bridgeport. The cave consists of two chambers situated fifty feet above the present valley floor in Doran Cove, one of many small valleys and hollows in the limestone escarpment along the edge of the Tennessee Valley.

The lower or south chamber of the cave contains a stream that flows out of the mountain through this passageway. This stream is a permanent water supply, ranging from a depth of a few inches to more than a foot in wet seasons. In the back portion of the lower chamber is an opening leading upward to the second room. Only this upper chamber appears to have had human occupation.

The upper room has an entrance 110 feet wide and 25 feet high. The floor of this chamber extends some 150 feet into the mountain, providing a large, relatively dry living area. The habitation area is restricted to the interior of this room because the front terrace extends for only a few feet before dropping off some 30 feet to the stream bed below. A test trench was begun in this room in the fall of 1953 by the original discoverers. This initial excavation consisted of a trench 40 feet long, from 3 to 8 feet in width, carried down some 6 feet below the floor surface. Work on this trench continued through the following two years. During this time the excavators were joined by Bettye Broyles, a professional archaeologist, who soon recognized the scientific importance of their discovery. Broyles (1958) published the results of these early investigations and interested the Smithsonian Institution in making a full-scale investigation of the site.

Russell Cave (Courtesy David L. DeJarnette)

In 1956, in conjunction with the National Geographic Society, Carl Miller, a Smithsonian archaeologist, began a three-year excavation of Russell Cave (Miller 1956, 1958). Although a final report of these investigations is yet to be published, Miller's excavations revealed that the upper chamber contained cultural deposits over fourteen feet in depth. The presence of cultural zones well below middle Archaic materials, coupled with a radiocarbon date of 6210 ± 300 B.C., clearly indicated that man had been in Alabama well before the first occupation of the riverine shell middens. Miller's investigations were also important because they demonstrated that deeply stratified rock shelters existed in the highland Southeast, which might shed further light on the development of the Archaic stage.

On 11 May 1961 the National Geographic Society generously purchased Russell Cave and 310 surrounding acres for the people of the United States (see the September 1967 issue of the *National Geographic* magazine). With the establishment of Russell Cave National Monument, the administration and the responsibility for protection of the site was given to the National Park Service. This federal agency has since established an impressive visitor center near the site location that is open to the public all year round.

In 1962 John W. Griffin, archaeologist for the National Park Service, began a third and final excavation of a portion of the upper chamber. The results of this investigation have been compiled in a summary report (Griffin 1974) and artifacts recovered are on display in the center museum. They reveal a long sequence of cultural adjustment to the surrounding oak-hickory forest environment and represent a lasting tribute to human ingenuity and adaptability. Seven stratigraphic zones containing cultural material were found in the excavation unit dug during Griffin's investigation. The upper four levels, Zones A–D, contained Mississippian and Woodland ceramic and lithic assemblages. The lower depths of these pottery-bearing zones contained an early Middle Woodland component that was dated to 150±200 B.C. Ceramics from this level were characterized by a fabric-marked surface treatment.

The bottom three strata contained prepottery Archaic stage materials. Zone E related to a late Archaic occupation culturally similar to middle levels in the well-known Tennessee River shell middens. Below this stratum, Zone F was encountered. The major occupation represented in this middle Archaic level was associated with the Morrow Mountain complex. Dates of 4300 ± 190 B.C., 4030 ± 200 B.C., and 4360 ± 140 B.C. were obtained on charcoal samples from this zone. Five flexed burials were recovered from this stratigraphic unit. None of these interments was accompanied by grave goods. The bottom stratum, Zone G, contained a variety of early Archaic projectile points and cultural debris, indicating widely separated occupations of short duration. One burial, representing the oldest known human remains in Alabama, was found in this level. This interment, an infant burial, was dated at 6550 ± 320 B.C.

The data recovered from these strata suggested to Griffin that this location was sporadically occupied by small bands or work parties during the late fall and winter months. The lower levels contained cultural materials reflecting a wide range of economic activities, indicating that this site was used as a temporary campsite by family groups. A larger proportion of projectile points in the cultural inventory of the upper strata was recognized as implying that the function of this site had changed through time, until, in the final period of prehistoric occupation, Russell Cave served as an overnight refuge for small hunting parties.

Stanfield-Worley Bluff Shelter

The Stanfield-Worley site is a large rock shelter in a small valley in the upland forests near Tuscumbia, some seven miles south of the Tennessee River in Colbert County. The sandstone overhang forming the shelter extends some fifty feet out from the rear wall, creating a protected living area containing some 8,000 square feet of floor space. A shallow stream and a number of small springs are present near the shelter, providing a permanent source of water. Excavations conducted within the living area and on the

talus slope outside the shelter indicate that this site was intermittently occupied by man for more than eight thousand years.

The discovery and investigation of this important archaeological site
created considerable public interest and resulted in a fruitful cooperative
effort combining the skills of both amateur and professional archaeologists.
The archaeological potential of the shelter was first discovered by members
of the Alabama Archaeological Society, and the resulting excavations were
funded with public donations raised and administered by the Archaeological
Research Association of Alabama, Inc. Professional supervision, tools, and
equipment were provided by The University of Alabama, and labor was
volunteered by students, Boy Scouts, members of the archaeological society,
and other interested citizens. An unprecedented total of more than three
hundred donors and participants took part in this endeavor.

Test excavations, conducted under the direction of David L. DeJarnette,
were begun at Stanfield-Worley in the late summer of 1960. More extensive
investigations were carried out in the summers of 1961 and 1962. The 1961
excavations consisted of two 5-foot-wide trenches parallel to the back wall of
the shelter. These trenches were later connected to the test units dug in
1960. This resulted in the isolation of two blocks, each 10 feet wide and 40

Stanfield-Worley Bluff Shelter (Courtesy David L. DeJarnette)

feet long. The exposed profiles of these control blocks contained four strati-graphic zones above the sterile sand and gravel underlying the site. Each zone was given a letter designation, with the zone nearest the surface and thus the "youngest" termed Zone A and the bottom cultural stratum labeled Zone D. The results of the 1961 excavations have been published (DeJarnette, Kur-jack, and Cambron 1962), and from this report the following cultural se-quence can be summarized.

Zone A was a light gray-brown fill varying in thickness from 2 to 4.5 feet. This zone contained large amounts of Woodland pottery and lithic material. Mississippian pottery was less abundant (163 sherds), but over 240 Missis-sippian triangular points were recovered from the site, suggesting that the shelter served as a male-oriented hunting camp during this final prehistoric occupation.

Zone B averaged only .5 foot in thickness and contained middle and late Archaic lithic material. Three burial pits, which originated in this zone, contained flexed interments accompanied by middle Archaic Morrow Mountain lithic and bone assemblages.

Zone C was a sterile layer of yellow sand and clay and varied in thickness from .3 to .8 foot. Under this stratum was the bottom cultural layer, Zone D.

Zone D was a dark brown midden stratum containing early Archaic lithic materials and a small amount of animal bone. Charcoal from this level was submitted for radiocarbon testing. These tests produced two dates, 9640 ± 450 and 8920 ± 400 years ago. These dates indicate that the shelter was first occupied during the early portion of the seventh millennium B.C.

The Stanfield-Worley bluff shelter is one of the most important prehistoric sites excavated in Alabama. The cultural material from the stratigraphic zones illuminate the evolution of prehistoric societies in northern Alabama over a period of almost nine millennia. Perhaps the most significant informa-tion obtained is that from the lower cultural zone, which contained remains of prehistoric cultures in transition from an earlier Paleo-Indian lifeway to the Archaic stage. These early Archaic assemblages compare favorably with western post-Folsom, Plano-tradition materials, indicating an early de-velopment of the Archaic stage in this region of the Southeast.

Early Archaic Horizons

Excavation and analysis of cultural material from stratified sites such as Russell Cave and Stanfield-Worley have revealed a detailed picture of the initial development of the Archaic stage in eastern North America. It is apparent that in some areas—the Great Lakes region for example—there was a cultural hiatus between the Paleo-Indian and Archaic stages. This void in the archaeological record is thought to represent a depopulation of these areas followed by repopulation by culturally distinct peoples. In these northerly regions such population movements appear to have been precipitated by large-scale environmental change directly attributable to glacial fluctuations (Fitting 1970).

In the nonglaciated areas of the southeastern United States, climatic and environmental changes at the end of the Wisconsin period were neither drastic nor sudden. Rather, there was a gradual climatic alteration. Similarly, culture adaptation in response to these factors was gradual, almost imperceptible in some areas. Culture change during this transition was marked by transformation in projectile-point styles.

Projectile points have served as temporal indicators since the realization by some prehistorians "that when an occupation zone can be found that represents a relatively short period of time the usual hodgepodge of projectile points types are not found—only variations of one specific theme" (Coe 1964:8). Based upon this axiom, it is possible to subdivide the early Archaic period into a number of horizons characterized by certain projectile-point styles or themes (Tuck 1974). Four such pan-eastern horizon themes can be recognized during this time, and each appears to have been represented in the Alabama region. In turn, in the middle Tennessee Valley region where intensive archaeological investigations have been conducted, it is possible to define local phases corresponding to the earliest of these horizons. As work continues in other portions of the state, it may be possible in the future to define such phases in these areas as well.

The Dalton Horizon

Dalton projectile points are small-to-medium blades, lanceolate to pentagonal in form. Serration of the blade edge and grinding in the hafting area are common characteristics. Points of this type were frequently resharpened, and many specimens exhibit concave bases and a pronounced steeple shape. Resharpening was apparently done while the point was still hafted. This process was accomplished by pressure flaking on opposite faces of each blade edge, producing a bevel or parallelogram cross section (Tuck 1974:73). Toward the latter portion of the Dalton horizon, there was an apparent alteration of hafting techniques marked by the appearance of a variety of side-notched forms (Coe 1964:120).

In general, Dalton horizon points are restricted in eastern North America to areas south of the Ohio Valley. Within the Southeast, points of this type are most common in riverine environments of the highlands. Stephen Williams and James Stoltman have compared the Dalton distribution to that of fluted points and have offered a hypothesis to account for the contrasts revealed during their study.

Of 253 Dalton points on record in Alabama, all were found in counties bordering on the Tennessee River. The same pattern carries northward into western

Tennessee where 89 of the 95 Dalton points in the sample come from Tennessee River counties. The interesting aspect of the Tennessee pattern is that *not one* Dalton point has been reported from the Interior Low Plateau, except where it is adjacent to the Tennessee River. Besides a general contraction in areal distribution of the Dalton tradition compared to the earlier fluted point traditions, available evidence suggests an increasing Dalton concentration into the Tennessee Valley of northeastern Alabama and western Tennessee and into the Green River basin of western Kentucky. Since it is in exactly these three areas that we later find the classic expression of the Shell Mound Archaic culture, we offer the working hypothesis that the Dalton distribution pattern reflects the onset of a new economic adjustment. With the depletion of the herds of big game animals, new sources of food were sought, or more likely, old supplementary subsistence patterns were intensified in favorable localities. As a result, the Dalton peoples laid the foundation for the subsistence pattern which we are to recognize later as "Archaic" in northern Alabama and western Tennessee and Kentucky. [1965:678]

Since the publication of the Williams and Stoltman study, Dalton points have been reported from other areas within Alabama. These recent finds, while not in any way contradicting their conclusions, do indicate that the Dalton peoples also began to inhabit new resource areas in the Coastal Plain region. David Chase (1966) has reported the recovery of four Dalton horizon points from the lower levels of a stratified multicomponent site on an old terrace of the Alabama River in Lowndes County in the central portion of the state. Points of this type also occur as scattered surface finds in the coastal uplands to the south in Baldwin and Clarke counties (Trickey and Holmes 1971).

Table 1:   Middle Tennessee Valley Archaic Development

Period (B.C.)		Horizon	Culture or Phase
Late Archaic	1000		Lauderdale
Middle Archaic	4000	Morrow Mountain	Sanderson Cove
Early Archaic	6000	Bifurcate Kirk Big Sandy Dalton	Doran Cove New Garden Red Hill
	8000		

The most significant of these recent Dalton finds were discovered during salvage operations on the Tombigbee River near Gainesville in western Alabama. Dalton materials have been recovered from two stratified sites in this area: At site 1 GR 1 two points were found in the basal culture-bearing zone, while two more were recovered at site 1 GR 2 stratigraphically beneath later Archaic zones (Nielsen and Moorehead 1972; Jenkins: personal communication). Both of these sites are within a mile of each other on the eastern banks of the Tombigbee. Associated with the Dalton horizon points at 1 GR 2 were numerous chert cobbles and flakes. Most of these flakes and one of the points were made from Tallahatta quartzite, a material quarried and widely traded during later periods. The nearest source of this material is some one hundred miles south of this section of the Tombigbee. The lithic debitage recovered from this zone indicates that weapons and tools were made and repaired during the Dalton occupation; plant foods were also collected and prepared, as grindstones, a muller, and carbonized hickory nut and acorn fragments also found in this level attest. The lack of storage facilities suggests that this site was occupied during the fall when such nut foods were available.

In the Tennessee Valley region a local Dalton phase may be defined—the Red Hill phase. Red Hill components occur on both open-air sites and in rock shelters. Major components have been reported from such open-air sites as the Klein site in the Mud Creek–Town Creek drainage area south of the Tennessee River in Franklin County (Brock and Clayton 1966) and at the Red Hill site in Lawrence County (Waters 1959). Although the artifacts from the latter site were found on the surface, they appear to represent an almost pure Dalton horizon component. The Red Hill site, situated on an elevated ridge in the upland forests overlooking a stream on one side and a marsh on the other, was apparently used as a temporary camp. Other artifacts recovered from this locality include end and side scrapers, uniface and biface knives, gravers, spokeshaves, flint debitage, a large flint chopper, pitted nutting stones, a quartzite pebble hammerstone, and a piece of ground hematite (an iron ore) (Waters 1959:77). Most of these tools are related to maintenance activities, suggesting occupation by a family or band unit.

In the Tennessee Valley proper, Red Hill phase open-air sites most often occur on upper terraces. These sites are usually multicomponent in nature, yielding a wide range of Paleo-Indian and early Archaic materials. Artifacts dating to later periods are generally rare. In contrast, Paleo-Indian and early Archaic artifacts are uncommon in the bottomlands and along the present riverbanks where numerous sites dating to later prehistoric periods yield evidence of intensive occupation. This pattern may be due to the effects of two climatic events—the Valders and the Cochrane glacial advances, both of which were minor. Ice sheets moved only as far as the Great Lakes during the Valders (centering around 8500 B.C.) and only two hundred miles south of Hudson Bay during the Cochrane (centering around 7200 B.C.) (Barlow

1971; Olafson 1971). These glacial advances had little effect on southern environments, probably only resulting in climates somewhat wetter than at the present. This humid climate possibly made the valley floor unsuitable for habitation during Paleo-Indian and early Archaic times. However, with the onset of a more arid climatic episode in eastern North America at about 6000 B.C., rainfall diminished. This reduction in humidity opened up the valley floor for settlement while also making certain riverine resources available, apparently for the first time.

Red Hill phase assemblages have also been recovered from stratigraphically deep levels in several rock shelters in the uplands surrounding the Tennessee Valley. In the northeastern portion of the state, one Dalton point was recovered from the bottom culture-bearing zone at Russell Cave, while nine Daltons were recovered from the Rock House shelter, and four were found in basal levels at the Boydston Creek shelter (Clayton 1965, 1967). Both these latter sites are small rock shelters on Sand Mountain in DeKalb County.

In the northwestern area of the state, a major Dalton component was discovered in the basal level of Stanfield-Worley. This level, Zone D, was a sealed cultural layer containing at least two early Archaic components, a Dalton occupation and a later Big Sandy occupation. Radiocarbon dates from this zone average at approximately 7300 B.C.; however, the Dalton assemblage probably dates nearer to 7700 B.C. and possibly even two or three centuries earlier.

Chipped-stone tools from this level included long, flat flakes with pressure flaking around the edges for use as knives or scrapers, and small gravers and thick uniface scrapers made from rectangular-, oval-, or triangular-shaped flakes. Animal food-scrap bone was also recovered. Analysis of this sample of five thousand bone fragments indicate that the whitetail deer was the most common mammal hunted. Also present were the remains of raccoon, rabbit, squirrel, gray fox, chipmunk, wood rat, porcupine, skunk, turkey, bobwhite, and turtle (Parmalee 1962).

The chipped-stone assemblage recovered from Zone D reflects activities associated with hunting and the manufacturing of stone tools and wooden implements such as spear or dart shafts. Specialized plant-processing tools were not reported from this zone. This may be the result of sampling error or may indicate that this rock shelter served as a limited activity location, perhaps a winter hunting camp.

In summary, it appears that the Dalton horizon materials represent the cultural remains of descendants of Paleo-Indian peoples in the Southeast. Similarities in the lithic assemblages of both peoples strongly suggest such a relationship. Although it cannot yet be demonstrated, it is likely that the Tennessee Valley open-air and rock-shelter campsites were components of a seasonal economic cycle. Social structure was still at the band level, but population increases apparently occurred. As noted by Williams and

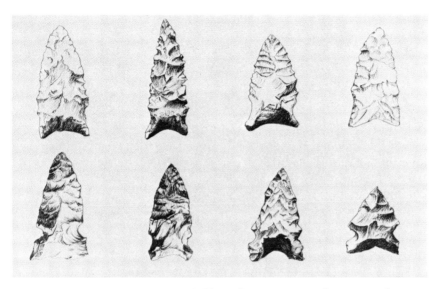

Projectile Points from Zone D, Stanfield-Worley. *Top row*, Dalton Projectile Points; *Bottom row*, Big Sandy Projectile Points (Redrawn after DeJarnette, Cambron, and Kurjack 1962)

Stoltman, there appears to have been a definite trend toward a riverine-oriented economy during this time.

Hunting activities are well documented at the Alabama Dalton sites, and evidence of plant collecting and processing is emerging at a number of different localities. However, the lack of storage facilities at these sites suggests that during the lean winter months Dalton bands had to rely on hunting as a major food source. The Stanfield-Worley site and other rock shelters occupied during this time may represent such upland winter hunting camps.

Big Sandy Horizon

Big Sandy projectile points are characterized by sidenotching, steep triangular blades, and frequent serration of blade edges. Grinding in the hafting area is common on most specimens and beveling through resharpening is a typical structural trait. There is a considerable overlap in the late Dalton and Big Sandy side-notched forms, strongly suggesting culture continuity (see, for example, the Dalton points illustrated by Lewis and Kneberg [1958:66–70] from the Nuckolls site).

Big Sandy points are found over a greater area of the East than the earlier Dalton forms. Big Sandy sites are reported from Arkansas to Florida, and scattered surface finds have been reported as far north as the Great Lakes region (Fitting 1970:70). However, in Alabama the distribution of Big Sandy points is similar to that of the Dalton forms. Only a few have been reported from the Coastal Plain, while most are found in the Tennessee Valley region.

Like the Dalton points, Big Sandy forms have been recovered from both open-air and rock-shelter sites in northern Alabama. In fact, most sites producing Dalton points have also yielded Big Sandy points. Again, strong cultural continuity is implied, as suggested by the chipped-stone tool assemblages associated with these horizons. Dalton and Big Sandy tool kits are almost identical. On the basis of current data, the Big Sandy horizon components in the middle Tennessee Valley can be placed into a regional phase, the New Garden phase.

Two major trends can be distinguished during the transition from the Dalton Red Hill phase to the Big Sandy New Garden phase. First, there appears to have been a definite increase in population density in the Tennessee Valley during this time and, second, there is a marked increase in evidence of intensive hunting. The suggestion of population increase from Dalton to later early Archaic times is based upon the occurrence of Big Sandy points on many more sites than the Dalton forms and a higher percentage of Big Sandy points on sites where both types are found. This was illustrated in a recent study of a large sample of Archaic projectile points collected from surface sites in Madison County. From a sample of 3,315 points that could be easily placed into some thirty established Archaic types, Oscar Brock (1969) of The University of Alabama noted that there was an increase in the quantity of points through time. This sample contained 91 Dalton horizon points, 510 Big Sandy points, and over 1,000 corner-notched Kirk horizon points. A brief survey of published site reports in the Tennessee Valley indicates that this trend is not isolated in Madison County alone but exists throughout the valley region.

Big Sandy points have also been found in a number of rock shelters in this region. A New Garden phase component was present in the upper portion of Zone D above the major Dalton component at Stanfield-Worley. At Cave Springs (Moebes 1974) to the east in Morgan County, Big Sandy points were found in large numbers. In the cultural zones of this stratified cave shelter, 131 Big Sandy points were recovered while only 6 Dalton forms were found. Further to the east, 3 Big Sandy points were reported from the lower half of Zone G, the bottom culture-bearing level at Russell Cave (J. W. Griffin 1974). Similarly, at the small Walls I rock shelter on Sand Mountain, Clayton (1965) reported the recovery of 17 Big Sandy points. Dalton forms were not present at this latter site.

As with the Dalton Red Hill phase, it is difficult to establish a settlement pattern model for the New Garden phase occupation of the middle Tennessee Valley region. Three, or possibly four, types of sites that may represent components of a single-settlement pattern are known. Rock-shelter sites apparently represent either hunting camps or multiple activity base camps, perhaps occupied during the winter months.

Two functional types of open-air sites can be distinguished. First, a number of such sites that have been reported appear to represent limited activity work camps. The New Garden site is an example. This site is on a small hill overlooking Sulfur Creek in Limestone County (Lenser 1959). The occupied area had a maximum extent of 250 feet by 100 feet along the knoll summit. This high ground was intensely cultivated for a number of years, and all cultural material was found on the surface or in the disturbed plow zone. A sample of 140 pieces of worked, dark gray chert was collected from this area over a span of several years. This lithic collection contained 42 Big Sandy points in various stages of manufacture, flake knives and scrapers, biface knives, several expanded base drills, large cutting tools, and a high percentage of workshop debris. This assemblage suggests that the site was a temporary Big Sandy horizon work camp located near a source of high-quality raw material. The dark gray chert used in the production of the stone tools recovered from this site occurs in nodular form in the nearby creek bed. Besides the stone tool associated with flint knapping, a number of tools recovered from New Garden apparently constituted a tool kit for plant processing. The steep-edge end scrapers, knives, and large cutting tools could have been used in the production of wooden spear shafts and other similar implements.

Second, several sites have been reported that have major New Garden occupations appearing to have been multiple activity locations. The Quad site, the Stone Pipe site, and the Pine Tree site have already been noted in the preceding Paleo-Indian discussion. These sites are linearly distributed along a three-mile strip on old upper terraces paralleling the right bank of the Tennessee River. Paleo-Indian materials were recovered from all of these sites. However, all appear to have been more intensely utilized during the early Archaic period. Cambron and Hulse (1960) report that, from a sample of 41 projectile points recovered during their test excavations at the Quad site, 22 (54 percent) of the points were side-notched Big Sandy types. Similarly, 118 of 283 points collected from the surface were of this type. A comparable situation has been reported from the two nearby sites. At the Pine Tree site, 25 Dalton, 110 Big Sandy, and 141 corner-notched Kirk horizon points were collected on the surface. At the Stone Pipe site, only about 6 Dalton points were recovered, only 36 corner-notched points, and 103 Big Sandy points.

Wilmsen, in his study of the lithic materials from the Quad site, noted that the Paleo-Indian materials did not constitute the major occupation. His

observations concerning the later (early Archaic) occupations appear to apply
to the Stone Pipe and Pine Tree sites as well as to the Quad site.

> The Quad site . . . appears to have been occupied periodically by no more than
> a single band at a time, perhaps over a span of several thousand years. The
> earliest inhabitants made fluted and basically thinned projectile points and
> probably followed a hunting way of life similar to that described for Linden-
> meier. The first occupation does not constitute the major component of the
> site. Later inhabitants hunted intensively, as is seen in the large numbers of
> projectile points they left behind, but also depended on plant product collect-
> ing. The generally steep distal retouch and the high proportion of heavy doubly
> retouched tools suggest wood working or fiber shredding. Whether this kind of
> activity increased in importance with succeeding occupations cannot be de-
> termined from the data at hand. But a selection for heavier, thicker tools made
> from flakes with steeper striking angles and greater lateral inclination is a major
> characteristic of the site. We may assume that this selection reflects the in-
> creased desirability of such characteristics, resulting from increasing exploita-
> tion of a forest-riverine ecology. [Wilmsen 1968:32]

Kirk Horizon

The typical artifact for this horizon is a medium-sized, corner-notched
projectile point. In Alabama several variants of this theme have been noted,
including the Lost Lake, Decatur, and Plevna types. The type designated
Pine Tree Corner Notched by Cambron and Hulse (1964) appears to represent an early variety of the Kirk Corner Notched form. This relationship is
supported by the recovery of points (Charleston Corner Notched) stylistically similar to the Pine Tree, from cultural zones below the Kirk occupation
at the Saint Albans site in West Virginia (Broyles 1971:56–57). In the latter
part of the Kirk continuum some points were manufactured with a modified
hafting area, resulting in a variety called the Kirk Stemmed (Coe 1964:70).

All of the Kirk varieties commonly exhibit deep serrations on the blade
edges. Many of these specimens also exhibit beveling of the blade as a result
of resharpening. These two technological characteristics suggest that many of
these artifacts served functions other than as projectile tips. Microscopic
examination of similar points recovered from the Rodgers Shelter in Missouri has revealed wear patterns on blade edges indicating use as knives for
cutting animal and plant materials (Ahler 1971). The range of the Kirk horizon points appears to be concentrated in the forested portions of eastern
North America, suggesting that these multipurpose artifacts were
specialized tools adapted to a woodland environment. These Kirk points
appear to have diffused over much of the East during a period extending
from 7400 B.C. to 6500 B.C. (Chapman 1976). Supporting dates have been
obtained from Kirk zones at Russell Cave, Saint Albans, and three sites in
the Little Tennessee Valley of eastern Tennessee. (J. W. Griffin 1974;

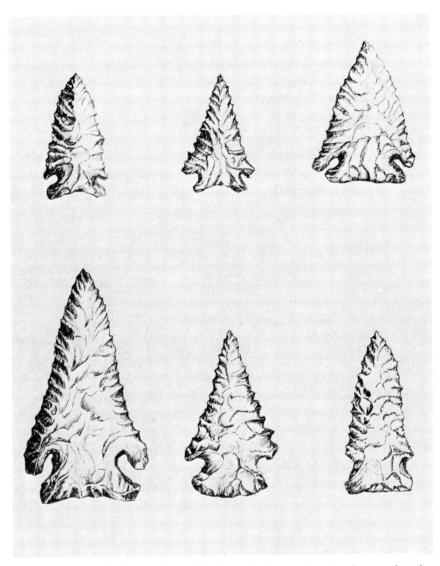

Early Archaic Kirk Horizon Projectile Points (Redrawn after Cambron and Hulse 1964)

Broyles 1971; Chapman 1976). In the middle Tennessee Valley region Kirk horizon materials can be placed into a single classificatory unit, the Doran Cove phase.

The Kirk points from Russell Cave were recovered in the upper portion of the bottom stratum, Zone G. A large cultural inventory was recovered from this level. The chipped-stone assemblage was very similar to that reported for the Dalton and Big Sandy horizons. However, a wide range of bone and antler tools was also recovered, including bone and antler ornaments and awls and needles for processing animal hides into garments and containers. The presence of antler flakers and drifts and numerous chert cores and flakes indicates that tools were produced and repaired during this occupation. Cane-matting impressions were also found in this zone, implying that weaving was known and that mats for flooring and shelters were used and, perhaps that baskets were made.

It is possible that the Doran Cove people were Alabama's first anglers. A bone fishhook, the earliest known in the Southeast, was recovered from this level. The presence of drumfish, gar, and buffalofish remains indicates that these early fishermen had some luck with their primitive tackle. The oldest human burial yet found in Alabama was discovered in this zone—the interment of an infant buried in a shallow pit in the cave floor (J. W. Griffin 1974).

No plant-food storage pits were found in this Kirk zone, but the presence of mortars and mullers suggests that such foods were processed at this site. Jefferson Chapman (personal communication) has also recovered grinding stones from Kirk zones at the Rose Island and Icehouse Bottom sites on the Little Tennessee River, though charred acorn and hickory nut fragments were also present.

It appears that the Doran Cove people excelled in hunting and trapping. Zone G contained the remains of 18 species of mammals, 10 species of birds, and 6 species of reptiles and amphibians. At least 20 turkeys, 155 squirrels, 8 deer, 5 raccoons, 3 skunks, 4 porcupines, 1 bobcat, and a now extinct form of peccary were taken during the early occupations of this shelter (Weigel et al. 1974). Though data is limited, Russell Cave seems to have been utilized as a camp by small bands of hunters and gatherers during the late fall and winter. The wide variety of cultural material associated with the Doran Cove phase occupation suggests a vigorously expanding population well adapted to a riverine-forest environment.

Bifurcate Horizon

This final horizon of the early Archaic period is marked by the appearance of small projectile points with indented, bifurcate stems. The blade edges of these points are usually serrated. These St. Albans and, later, LeCroy points appear to have developed out of Kirk forms, since many of these later points exhibit indented bases and serrated blade edges. Several variants of the bifurcate theme have been recognized, including an apparently earlier side-notched form named the Saint Albans Side Notched (Broyles 1971). These points were recovered at the Saint Albans site in strata above the Kirk horizon and below LeCroy zones, suggesting an intermediate temporal and stylistic position.

At Saint Albans, the earlier side-notched, bifurcate-stem points were dated to approximately 6700 B.C., while the LeCroy forms were dated to 6300 B.C. Three radiocarbon determinations, ranging from 6110 B.C. to 6850 B.C., were obtained from LeCroy zones at the Rose Island site in east Tennessee. However, based upon current information, the later date of 6110 ± 350 B.C. seems to be more reasonable for this final early Archaic occupation (Chapman 1975).

James Fitting (1964) has noted a wide spatial distribution and temporal range for bifurcate projectile points in North America. The LeCroy and related types can be distinguished from much later bifurcate-stem projectile points and appear to have a geographical range in the East similar to that of the earlier Kirk horizon points. It should be pointed out, however, that there are many fewer bifurcate points reported from the Alabama region than either the earlier Kirk or Big Sandy forms. This should not be construed as evidence of a population decline or as an indication of a decrease in hunting

Bifurcate-stem Projectile Points from Madison County (Brock 1969)

activities. Rather, this pattern of LeCroy points sparsely distributed over a large area appears to imply a relatively brief temporal span for this particular theme or style.

Bifurcate points have been reported in stratified context from three rock shelters in northern Alabama. Four examples were recovered from the lower levels of Stratum II at the Flint Creek rock shelter (Cambron and Waters 1961) and three were found in Zone G at Russell Cave (J. W. Griffin 1974). At Stanfield-Worley, one point of this cluster was reported from Zone C, Block 2 (DeJarnette, Kurjack, and Cambron 1962). These finds clearly demonstrate the early Archaic context of the Bifurcate horizon in Alabama.

Bifurcate points have also been recovered from a number of open-air sites in the Tennessee Valley region of Alabama. One site has been reported near the Tennessee River in Lauderdale County (Hubbert 1961:47). This small site is on the top of a ridge in the old river floodplain. The ridge originally ran at a thirty-degree angle toward the river, paralleling a small stream that once emptied into the river a short distance away. Pickwick Lake now inundates this area and the surface of the ridge summit is exposed only in the late fall and winter when the waters of the reservoir are at their lowest level.

The assemblage collected from the eroded surface of this site consisted of several bifurcate points, a point identified as a Greenbrier, a biface knife, and uniface flake tools including end and side scrapers and knives. No ground-stone implements were present. Based upon the evidence available, this site appears to have functioned as a small hunting camp during late early Archaic times. Inasmuch as this Alabama bifurcate assemblage was a surface find, only a small amount of information concerning this occupation can be inferred. However, bifurcate assemblages in a stratified context have been recovered from sites excavated in other areas of the Southeast. A much more complete picture of early Archaic culture is now emerging from these excavations.

The first major bifurcate occupations to have been discovered in a stratified context were found at the Saint Albans site in West Virginia. Nearer to Alabama, two open-air localities—the Rose Island and Icehouse Bottom sites—have recently been investigated and found to contain sealed bifurcate zones. These sites are in the Little Tennessee River Valley and were excavated by Jefferson Chapman in cooperation with the University of Tennessee Tellico Archaeological Project (Chapman 1975, 1976).

The upper zones of the Rose Island site contained an early Woodland component at approximately 5.5 feet below the surface. Some 2 to 3 feet below the early Woodland stratum, Chapman discovered sealed early Archaic occupation zones. Twenty-seven bifurcate points were recovered from these strata during the 1973 field season. Additionally, some 107 pieces of worked chert were recovered. This chipped-stone assemblage included chisels or gouges, utilized flakes, knives, and a number of scraper forms. Chapman also reported that some 5,600 unworked flakes and 90 core fragments were found in the LeCroy zone. The cherts used in the manufacturing of these tools were local varieties. A large amount of hematite and geothite was also found in this zone. These related minerals produce red ocher when ground. Some eight sources of these minerals are located within a 24-mile radius of Rose Island.

Plant foods were also processed at this site during the bifurcate occupations. Pitted cobbles, or anvil stones, and hammerstones were also recovered from these zones. Direct evidence of plant-food preparation was recovered in the form of large masses of charred acorn and hickory nut fragments. A total of 47 features were recorded during the 1973 excavation, including fired areas on hearths; small globular pits; and a number of large, irregular, shallow pits or basins containing concentrations of nutshell fragments. All of these data combine to form a picture of an economic procurement system of nut-food collection, storage, preparation, and cooking.

The excavation of the Rose Island site produced important data concerning early Archaic economy and adaptation. Much more information was recovered from this site than at locations previously mentioned due to a number of circumstances. First, the deposition rate at this site was heavy and effectively sealed the LeCroy zone from contamination by later prehistoric peoples, a problem frequently encountered in heavily used rock shelters. Second, paleobotanical preservation was good, allowing recovery of a considerable amount of food debris. Third, and not least in importance, the excavation was carefully conducted and a large amount of midden and pit fill was processed through a flotation system (water screening), allowing near maximum recovery of preserved plant materials.

The Rose Island site appears to have been a base camp occupied during the fall months, with more substantial occupation than in previously recorded early Archaic settlements. There are a large number and variety of features, including storage facilities in which nut foods, rich in protein and carbohydrates, could have been stored, allowing the site to be occupied for as long as several weeks before the population was forced to move to winter hunting camps. The economic activities, preparation and storage of nut foods, increased sedentism, and a shift in economic scheduling, recorded by Chapman at the Rose Island site, point to a new perception of the environment and signal the beginning of the next period in the Archaic sequence, the middle Archaic.

Middle Archaic Adaptation

The middle Archaic period, extending from approximately 6000 to 4000 B.C., is marked by three interrelated events, one natural and two cultural. First, around 6000 B.C., the Altithermal interval began, bringing warmer and drier climates than at present. This climatic episode was followed by the

establishment of modern, stable climates, probably between 4000 and 3000
B.C. Second, there was a change in the economic scheduling activities of
certain populations resulting in increased territorialism and regional diversity. And third, there was the appearance by diffusion or innovation of a
series of new technological developments, especially involving ground-
stone, bone, and antler implements.

In Alabama, and over all of eastern North America, little is known concerning this important Archaic period. Many of the cultural traits of the
better-known late Archaic period, with its emphasis on shellfish collecting,
were introduced during this time. The middle Archaic period marks a turn-
ing point in Archaic economy and adaptation, and it deserves much more
intensive study than it has so far received.

At the present time, only a single pan-eastern middle Archaic archaeological horizon can be recognized in the Alabama region, apparently due to two
major factors. First, little comparative research has been done on archaeological manifestations dating to this period. Although there is an abundance of excavated material from several regions—including much of the
Tennessee Valley shell-mound material—pertaining to this period, it has not
been reported in full or in a manner that permits comparison. These materials are a rich, documented source of raw data for a score of new doctoral
candidates to study.

Second, a major trend that clearly accelerated during the middle Archaic
was increased territoriality and population growth resulting in much regional
stylistic diversity. This, in turn, produced a proliferation of projectile-point
styles, including the abundant undifferentiated straight- and expanded-stem
Archaic types. In many cases, thousands of these diagnostic projectile points
have been lumped into provisional categories, again impeding comparative
study. This is the result, in large part, of the failure of many archaeologists
working in various places at various times to isolate distinct Archaic assemblages.

Morrow Mountain Horizon

The one middle Archaic projectile-point theme that has been isolated at
several sites in the East is the Morrow Mountain complex. Points of this type
are characterized by small-to-medium-sized triangular blades with short,
tapered stems. The Morrow Mountain point and some of its several variants
were first stratigraphically isolated in eastern North America by Joffre Coe at
the Doerschuk site in the Morrow Mountain area of the North Carolina
Piedmont (Coe 1964). These points appeared in the cultural sequence at this
site without any apparent stylistic antecedents. Below the Morrow Mountain
zones at Doerschuk was an occupational layer characterized by straight-stem
points with notched bases. These Stanley projectile points with their indented bases and often serrated blade edges apparently represent a carry-

Ground Stone Implements, AMNH 90 Ms 65

Morrow Mountain Projectile Points from Madison County (Brock 1969)

over from early Archaic bifurcate types. This cluster has not been widely recognized in the Alabama region.

Coe noted that points stylistically related to the Morrow Mountain form extend from as far west as Gypsum Cave in Nevada to New England. Points of this type have since been found in stratigraphic context at a number of southeastern sites. Caldwell (1954) has reported that such points are characteristic of what he refers to as the "old quartz" industry of the Georgia Piedmont. Artifacts associated with this complex, including Morrow Mountain points, were recovered three feet below a late Archaic shell midden along the Savannah River during his excavations at the Lake Springs site. Caldwell (1958:8–9) has suggested that this old quartz complex represents pre–shell mound Archaic hunters and gatherers who followed a nomadic way of life in the Piedmont forests.

Similar projectile points have been reported by Lewis and Lewis (1961) in the Three Mile component at the Eva site on the lower Tennessee River. At this shell mound, Morrow Mountain points were recovered stratigraphically above a deeper middle Archaic shell midden containing large, basally notched Eva projectile points and below a late Archaic zone typified by a variety of stemmed types. The bottom Eva component was dated by the radiocarbon method to 5200 ± 500 B.C. The Eva projectile-point type is an apparent local form concentrated in the lower Tennessee Valley. These points become less frequent in sites up river, and while Eva points have been found in northwestern Alabama they have not been reported as far east as the Guntersville Basin area. Some authors recognize a development of the Morrow Mountain projectile point out of ancestral Eva forms (Long and Josselyn 1965). While there is a certain amount of stylistic blending of later Eva forms (Eva II) and Morrow Mountain varieties, this relationship is yet to be convincingly demonstrated, although it remains a distinct possibility.

Morrow Mountain points and several related types have been recovered from a number of sites in Alabama. In the Coastal Plain region they have been found at the Tensaw Creek site in Lowndes County and on several surface sites in Lamar County on tributaries of the Tombigbee River (Chase 1966; Long and Josselyn 1965). Recently, DeJarnette, Walthall, and Wimberly (1975b) have reported the discovery of Morrow Mountain points in the lower levels of a sealed Archaic stratum at Stucks Bluff rock shelter on the Buttahatchee River in Lamar County. A date of 4500 ± 120 B.C. was obtained from a hearth associated with a Morrow Mountain point. Some of the most important data concerning this middle Archaic horizon come from the Tennessee Valley region, where Morrow Mountain occupation can be placed into a local phase, the Sanderson Cove phase. In the highlands surrounding the Guntersville Basin area of northwestern Alabama, some rock shelters have been found to contain Sanderson Cove assemblages. Clayton (1965, 1967) has reported the investigation of nine small shelters inhabited during the middle Archaic. The Morrow Mountain occupations were difficult or impossible to isolate in the shallow floor deposits in these sites. However, at the Boydston shelter, a cultural layer, Zone B, was found to contain a heavy Morrow Mountain occupation associated with biface and uniface tools and numbers of pitted nutting stones, manos, and mortars.

Morrow Mountain points were also recovered from the middle Archaic Layer F at Russell Cave (J. W. Griffin 1974). In comparing the chipped-stone assemblages from this zone and the early Archaic zone, Layer G, Griffin noted, "Although most of the other artifact types occur in both layers, there is a distinct drop in the proportion of uniface stone tools to bifacially worked ones (excluding projectile points). Some 73 percent of the Early Archaic tools are uniface while this drops to 23 percent in the Middle Archaic" (1974:112).

Five of the six burials found in Russell Cave during Griffin's excavations are associated with the middle Archaic occupations. All of these burials were interred in a flexed position. Burials included two infants (one associated with a Morrow Mountain point), one adolescent, and two adults (male and female). Both adults exhibited heavily worn teeth, suggesting a coarse, gritty diet. Carbon samples taken from the pits containing the two adults produced test dates of 4300 ± 190 B.C. and 4310 ± 190 B.C. These dates correspond very well with Coe's estimate of 4500 B.C. for the initial Morrow Mountain occupation at the Doerschuk site.

Some of the most significant data concerning the Sanderson Cove occupation of the middle Tennessee Valley area were recovered during the excavations at the Stanfield-Worley site in northwestern Alabama, where eleven burials were found. Three of these burials (Numbers 6, 8, and 11) were associated with Morrow Mountain stone- and bone-tool assemblages (DeJarnette, Kurjack, and Cambron 1962:80–82). Burial 6 was that of an adult of undetermined sex in a fully flexed position; burial goods included four Morrow Mountain points, two triangular Morrow Mountain variants, three biface blades, and an antler atlatl hook. Similar atlatl hooks consisting of a short, thick piece of antler with a small spur were found in association with middle Archaic Three Mile component burials at the Eva site, representing the earliest known form of this artifact in the Southeast.

Burial 8, a mature male, was found in a common pit directly above Burial 11, also an adult male in a flexed position. Associated with Burial 8 were seven Morrow Mountain points, one triangular variant, one Crawford Creek point, one White Springs point, two cores, one flake knife, three end scrapers, a pebble hammer, ten bone awls, an antler flaker, and a turtle shell. Most of these implements appear to be components of a weapon-processing tool kit that probably belonged to the male with whom they were buried. Found in association with Burial 11 were four Morrow Mountain points and an expanded base drill.

Burials 7 and 9 were also possibly associated with the Morrow Mountain occupation of Stanfield-Worley. These two burials, an adult and an adolescent, were found near the back wall in two adjoining circular pits. A turtle shell had been placed into the grave of Burial 9. This turtle shell and the one associated with Burial 8 may have functioned as rattles. Turtle-shell rattles have been reported from burials at a number of shell mounds in the East. At the Eva site, such objects were recovered from Three Mile component burials (Lewis and Lewis 1961:87–89). Some of these turtle shells contained small pebbles or drumfish teeth as rattle stones.

The importance of these Sanderson Cove phase burials found at Stanfield-Worley lies in their associations of contemporaneity. That is, they contained a number of artifacts used at the same time and once part of a single culture. From the data recovered from these burials we know that these peoples made projectile points that archaeologists have assigned to the Morrow Mountain, White Springs, and Crawford Creek types, and that these points functioned as tips for spears propelled by atlatls with antler hooks. These projectile-point forms and the chipped-stone tools found with them constitute a single archaeological assemblage. Along with the bone-tool assemblages, these associated artifacts make up an isolated material culture that can be used as a comparative unit. Thus, it is evident that there are a large number of similarities between the Stanfield-Worley burials and those associated with the Three Mile component at the Eva site, which suggests that they were roughly contemporaneous and raises the possibility that these peoples shared a common culture. This comparison also indicates that the Morrow Mountain peoples were some of the earliest inhabitants of the great shell mounds of the Tennessee River.

One case in point is the Mulberry Creek shell mound on the left bank of Mulberry Creek at its junction with the Tennessee River in Colbert County. This extensive site was excavated during the WPA-TVA archaeological survey of the 1930s (Webb and DeJarnette 1942:235–66). The deposits of shell at this site were about 20 feet deep and covered an area of some 60,000 square feet. The strata in this mound consisted of multiple zones of shell and cultural debris interspersed with layers of sterile river-deposited sand. One unusual feature, a level consisting entirely of flint-chipping debitage, was encountered 9 feet below the surface. Under this stratum were three more layers of shell, the lowest of which had been laid down on a sloping sandbar near the river edge. These lower zones contained bone and antler points, bone awls, fishhooks, and an antler shaft straightener similar to those found in the lower (Eva) component at the Eva site. This suggests that the initial occupation of the Mulberry Creek site dates to the early portion of the middle Archaic during the sixth millennium B.C.

Excavations carried down to the water line on the eastern side of the mound along the bank of Mulberry Creek revealed a number of burials, including ten apparently made during the early stages of occupation. Found at a depth of between 10 and 14 feet below the mound surface, these burials originated from an upper occupation zone, most likely the area encompass-

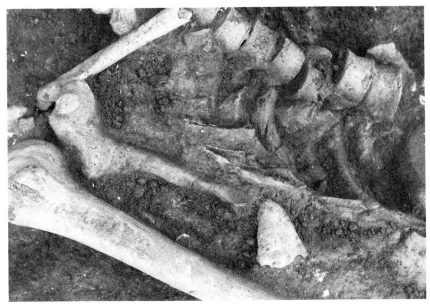

Burial 84 with Morrow Mountain Projectile Points In Situ, Mulberry Creek Shell Mound, AMNH 117 Ct 27

Morrow Mountain Burial at Stanfield-Worley (Courtesy David L. DeJarnette)

ing the flint workshop layer at the 9-foot level. These interments (Burials 82, 83, 84, 85, 86, 88, 89, 92, 93, and 94) are similar to the Three Mile component burials at the Eva site and to the Morrow Mountain burials uncovered at Stanfield-Worley. Six deserve detailed consideration.

Burials 83, 84, and 85 had been placed into a common, circular grave dug into a sand layer 13.8 feet below the surface. They rested on the bottom shell midden, which indicates that these individuals were buried after the initial occupation of the site and after a subsequent flood. Webb and DeJarnette (1942:245) in their description observed, "Multiple burials are not usual in shell mounds and the form of flexure was not common. None was fully flexed. In each case the arms were extended and the legs flexed back on the body." The burial position of these individuals was not the only thing unusual about them—all three had met violent deaths. The rib cage of Burial 83, an adult male, had been penetrated by three projectile points. One of these points was a Morrow Mountain type, while the other two were fragmented on impact and cannot be identified. Burial 84, also an adult male, was associated with seven Morrow Mountain projectile points. Four were found in the thoracic cavity, two were firmly embedded in the spinal column, and one was found in the mouth cavity. One of the two points found in the spinal column "had entered the body from the front and had lodged in the centrum [center part of the vertebra]; the other had penetrated from the rear, and was embedded between two neural processes" (Webb and DeJarnette 1942:245).

Burial 85, a male adolescent, had been placed into the burial pit first, then a cache of artifacts was placed between the left arm and the body. These objects included two bone awls made from deer ulnas, one biface knife, and two Morrow Mountain projectile points. This individual also had a projectile point firmly embedded in the spinal column (Webb and DeJarnette 1942:Plates 274,275,289.2, and 290.1).

Burial 86, a partially flexed adult male, was found near the other burials at a common depth. Near the left elbow a perforated ground-stone cylinder (an atlatl weight) had been placed (Webb and DeJarnette 1942:Plate 290.2). (Three cylindrical atlatl weights were recovered in association with antler atlatl hooks in Three Mile component burials at Eva [Lewis and Lewis 1961:66].)

Burial 88, also a partially flexed adult male was found several feet away from Burial 86 at a depth of 11.2 feet. A number of objects had been placed carefully into the grave (Webb and DeJarnette 1942:Plates 291.2, 300.1, and 302.1). Among these were four Morrow Mountain points and six White Springs points (called "Sykes points" by Lewis and Lewis). A large spear-point with diagonal notches, producing an expanded stem and barbed shoulders, was found among these grave offerings. Artifacts of this type were called "Cypress Creek points" at the Eva site, where they occurred in the Eva and Three Mile components. An antler chisel, a bone flaker, and a large rodent incisor were also recovered. Two dog burials (sacrifices?) had been placed near the grave, one at the knees and one at the head of Burial 88. Fifteen dog burials, some in association with Morrow Mountain burials, were found in the Three Mile component at Eva. Burial 93, a partially flexed adult male, was found in close proximity, with a Morrow Mountain projectile point in the thoracic cavity.

These burials from the lower levels at the Mulberry Creek shell mound reveal much significant information concerning the Morrow Mountain horizon and middle Archaic culture. However, they also pose several problems. First, what was the nature of the Sanderson Cove phase occupation of this locality? It seems certain that shellfish were collected by these peoples, as demonstrated by several shell middens above the Morrow Mountain burials and an initial shell lense below the interments. Also, the site was possibly used as a limited activity location—a flint-knapping station—during the middle Archaic. The volumes published on the numerous shell mounds along this portion of the river indicate that zones of chipped and fire-cracked rock were fairly common in these sites. A number of sites found back from the river in the valley floor did not contain shell but appeared to be covered by a solid layer of chipped stone.

Robert Work (1961:1–75) reported a cursory examination of one of these, the Swan Creek site, in the north mud flats of the Tennessee River a few miles downstream from Decatur, an area now flooded for a good deal of the year by Wheeler Dam. The eroded surface of this site is paved with a four-to-eight-inch-thick layer of fire-cracked stone, flint chips, and other cultural debris; only a few Woodland or Mississippian artifacts were found on the surface. The site appears to have been occupied during the middle-late Archaic continuum. From a sample of 85 typed points recovered from the surface, 27 (32 percent) were Morrow Mountain points, while 6 (7 percent) Eva points were found. If this sample is representative, as it appears to be, this high proportion of Morrow Mountain points suggests a major middle Archaic occupation of this site. It should also be noted that the often mentioned, and prolific, Pine Tree site (Cambron 1956) is located along the edge of the valley nearby. The projectile-point sample from the Pine Tree site also contained a large number of middle Archaic specimens (101 Morrow Mountain points, 4 Eva points), indicating a major occupation during this time.

A second question concerning the Sanderson Cove Phase is: What is the meaning of the violent deaths at Mulberry Creek? It is possible, of course, that these may have been ritual killings. A more probable explanation, however, can be found in the nature of the middle Archaic economy. Competition for favored localities may have produced conflict among populations living in the region.

With the coming of a drier climate during the Altithermal interval, the valley floor of the Tennessee River became more inhabitable and certain resources, including freshwater shellfish found in large numbers in the shallow shoal waters, became available for exploitation. During the middle Archaic there was a shift in the scheduling of economic activities to include this resource. This new seasonal round constituted the beginning of the late Archaic narrow spectrum economy (Winters 1974:x–xi), based upon deer, mussels, and nut foods. Because large beds of mussels are found only at certain places along the river, camps had to be established nearby. According to Webb and DeJarnette:

> The most obvious fact about the shell mounds is that they are on the immediate bank of the river, so near that they are at times subject to erosion by the river and to silting by floods. They are always adjacent to a shoal . . . , on which great quantities of *Mollusca* of many species were to be found. . . . Not only was there a great variety in the food of this kind, but its never-failing supply encouraged men to live near a certain source. Seemingly, they did not carry the mussels very far from the shoals before using them for food. It may be . . . that the huge amount of shell in any midden has all come from the river in the immediate vicinity. . . . Wherever shoals appeared in the river, there on the bank, often on both sides of the river, and sometimes on islands nearby, shell mounds are to be found. [1942:307–08]

In a discussion of narrow spectrum harvesting economics, Winters (1974:xi) noted that one characteristic of cultures of this sort was evidence of increased internal and external conflict, suggesting that this conflict was the product of competition for limited food resources. Individuals who died violently also have been found in burials at Archaic shell mounds of the Indian Knoll culture of the Green River area in Kentucky, at the Riverton site on the Wabash River in Illinois (Winters 1969), at the Eva site in Tennessee, and at other Tennessee Valley sites in northern Alabama. Later, as the population density of the Tennessee Valley shell mounds increased, and as food resources fluctuated, further conflict possibly erupted at various times as groups attempted to take over more productive shell-gathering stations.

In summary, the data now emerging concerning the middle Archaic people in northern Alabama suggest that these groups added an important item, shellfish, to the Archaic diet and introduced a number of new cultural traits into the area. Among these are the atlatl with antler hooks and ground-stone weights; flexed, round-grave burials often accompanied by utilitarian grave goods; a variety of bone tools; antler-tip projectile points; turtle cups or rattles; and perhaps specialized grinding stones such as the bell pestle. The earliest recorded remains of the Indian dog also are of this period. Some were buried "as though they were someone's best friend" (J. B. Griffin 1967:178). Some data also suggest competition and conflict among groups inhabiting the Tennessee Valley area of northwestern Alabama. This conflict appears to have occurred in several regions in the East where narrow spectrum economies were being established and where key resources were restricted. In establishing themselves in favored localities, these middle Archaic peoples laid the foundation of one of the most efficient gathering economies ever developed in a temperate riverine-forest environment.

The Late Archaic

The late Archaic period witnessed the arrival of modern climates and environments in Alabama. During this time there was a marked increase in population growth, and many uninhabited or sparsely populated areas were settled. New technological innovations were introduced into Alabama, among the most important of which were stone vessels and fiber-tempered pottery. The latter serves as a marker for the beginning of the succeeding Gulf Formational stage. Many of these technological developments diffused into the Alabama area as part of a pan-eastern interaction sphere that emphasized burial ceremonialism and exchange with other groups of scarce raw materials and finished products.

Sites dating to the late Archaic period have been reported from all over Alabama. In the Mobile Bay region, Trickey and Holmes (1971) investigated several shell-gathering stations containing late Archaic components. These sites are linearly distributed along a mile of the shoreline of Tensaw Lake in the delta of the Alabama and Tombigbee rivers. Five middens were tested, all containing large amounts of *Rangia cuneata* shells, a brackish-water clam.

Archaic cultural materials were sparse at these sites. However, at Bryant's Landing No. 4, the bottom zone of the shell midden apparently had been laid down during the late Archaic, even though diagnostic materials such as stone tools were not found. This conclusion is based upon a radiocarbon determination obtained from materials found in this lense. The date 2139 ± 250 B.C. falls clearly into the late Archaic continuum. Above the Archaic components at these sites were layers containing fiber-tempered pottery and Bayou La Batre ceramics (Wimberly 1953a, 1960). One of these Bayou La Batre shell middens was dated to 1129 ± 200 B.C., possibly indicating an early occupation by Gulf Formational peoples. Data indicate that the first major prehistoric occupation of the Mobile Bay area dates to the late Archaic period. These shell middens along Tensaw Lake apparently were occupied intermittently, perhaps on a seasonal basis, by small bands of hunters and gatherers. Recent study suggests that both the availability of shellfish and the habitability of these locations were subject to long-term tidal fluctuations in Mobile Bay (Trickey and Holmes 1974).

Further north, in the Coastal Plain region of central Alabama, another group of late Archaic peoples settled along the Alabama River, a manifestation that has been named the Milbrook phase. Two components have recently been reported. David Chase, who first recognized this phase, excavated one of these sites in Lowndes County. This multicomponent locality, the Tensaw Creek site, contained five levels, Level 1 representing the plow zone. Levels 2 and 3 contained a high concentration of late Archaic materials, including three major late Archaic projectile-point types, Savannah River (35 percent), Elora (34 percent), and Gary (11 percent) (Chase 1966). Numbers of chipped-stone bifaces and other tools, mainly constructed from local quartzite materials, were found in these zones. Steatite bowl fragments were also recovered.

Eighty-seven fiber-tempered sherds (Stallings Island Plain) were present in these two levels, with the majority (80 percent) concentrated in Level 2. Feature 15, a deep storage pit containing a large amount of carbonized hickory nutshell and hackberry seeds, could be assigned to this terminal Archaic occupation. A radiocarbon date of 1350 ± 100 B.C., obtained from a sample of these ethnobotanical materials, appears to be a reasonable date for the end of the Archaic in this area (Chase: personal communication).

Eugene Futato (1973) has reported recent University of Alabama excavations at a second Milbrook phase site. This locality, the Honeymoon site (1 Ee 101), is on an old river terrace between Cobbs Swamp and Crescent Lake above the Alabama River near Montgomery. The site originally covered some ten acres, but much of it was destroyed by removal of soil for highway fill. Excavations in the remaining portion revealed six natural and cultural zones, labeled A–F, with Zone F representing the red clay subsoil. Zones C and D contained large amounts of Milbrook phase materials.

Within these two zones, two late Archaic living floors were found, which Futato suggests may represent the partial remains of a single camping activity on the site. A stone-lined hearth was associated with one of these areas. Artifacts found on these living floors include large numbers of projectile points, blades, and scrapers. The absence of storage pits and plant-processing tools, coupled with the predominance of hunting and butchering implements, suggests that the Honeymoon site was used frequently during the Milbrook phase as a hunting camp.

Futato recognized the close similarity between the Milbrook phase material culture and that of the Stallings Island culture of Georgia. The two sites reported indicate that the Milbrook phase economy was based upon intensive riverine-oriented hunting and gathering. Unlike some contemporary ethnic groups in other areas, shellfish do not appear to have been among their major resources. The large number of cultural traits held in common between this central Alabama late Archaic phase and the Stallings Island culture probably reflect similar adaptations to the riverine habitats of the southeastern Coastal Plain.

Tennessee River Shell-Mound Dwellers

Along the banks of the middle Tennessee River in northern Alabama a number of large shell mounds have been found. Many of these sites have been subjected to excavations of varying degree and quality (Moore 1915; Fowke 1928: W. S. Webb 1939; Webb and DeJarnette 1942, 1948), which have shown that they are not "mounds" in the proper sense. That is, they are not intentional structures like the burial or temple mounds of later peoples. Rather, these "mounds" consist of massive accumulations of cultural debris, mainly great middens of mollusk shell and other refuse interspersed with river-deposited sand and gravel. Cultural materials found in these structures represent the remains of many generations of peoples sharing a common tradition. These middens are concentrated in the western portion of the middle Tennessee Valley (Lauderdale, Colbert, and Limestone counties) where shallow shoal waters provided ideal environments for over sixty species of freshwater shellfish.

Although the first settlement of these shell mounds appears to have begun during the middle Archaic period, the major occupation dates to late Archaic times, approximately 4000 to 1000 B.C. These components can for the present be placed into a single, broad classificatory unit, the Lauderdale culture. These Lauderdale occupations were first recognized during the WPA-TVA archaeological surveys of the 1930s, though they were termed a "focus" in keeping with the Midwestern Taxonomic System then in vogue. Later, the "focus" was called a "phase" by Lewis and Kneberg (1959). In reclassifying these preceramic occupations as a "culture," it is here recognized that the long temporal span and internal diversity represented within these shell mounds indicate that future researchers may subdivide these occupations into a number of discrete classificatory units probably based upon changes in projectile-point themes. Certainly much more intensive research and re-study is needed in order to understand this local late Archaic sequence. Until such work is conducted, we can only continue to lump these pre-ceramic occupations into a single unit.

For much of the late Archaic period these shell mounds served as base camps where a variety of maintenance activities were conducted. The living floors within these middens lay upon the accumulated garbage of bygone days. Many times, clay was brought to the site and simply spread over the shells and other debris. Scattered post holes in and around these prepared floors attest to only crude shelters (DeJarnette 1952:274). Fired areas and fire basins floored with stone have been found on or near these areas. The lack of substantial dwellings seems to have been due to occupation in the warm late spring and summer months when only minimal shelter was neces-sary. Each small, clay lined area may represent the living quarters of a nuclear family, members of which may have been born, have lived and died, and have been buried on these shell heaps. Several families probably oc-cupied each shell mound at the same time. These groups were tied together by kinship bonds forming a band society that may have included peoples living on nearby shell mounds.

The material culture is impressive when compared to that of earlier peoples, due in part to a more sedentary way of life allowing greater accumulation of material wealth. Large steatite and sandstone bowls, not easily transported, were quarried, often at distant sources, and used as cooking receptacles and, at times, as mortuary offerings. These vessels, like their later ceramic counterparts, represented a major development in the culinary arts. Assemblages of chipped-stone, ground-stone, bone, and antler implements are indicative of a diverse technology. Leather garments were probably fashioned by using bone awls, needles sharpened with grooved shale abraders, and shell and bone pins. The art of weaving was evidently known; remains of a fabric breechclout were found with one burial. The shell-mound Archaic Indian adorned himself with necklaces and bracelets. He had beads of marine and freshwater shell and of stone and bone. His charms were made of animal and human teeth; he had pendants of shell and bar gorgets of stone (DeJarnette 1952:274).

The environment of this part of the western middle Tennessee Valley was diverse, providing an abundant supply of nutritious foods. This area can be divided into five subregions—the Chert Belt, Upland Coastal Plain, Little Mountain, Valley Lands, and Plateau (Harper 1942:16), each of which is characterized by a distinct biota. The late Archaic peoples were probably not adapted to any specific microenvironment within this ecosystem, but rather to a series of plants and animals that often ranged across several habitats. However, certain plants and animals may have been more plentiful in certain of these microenvironments. For example, shellfish were found in much greater number in the river shoal waters of the valley proper than in tributary streams, and the different species of nuts were more abundant in the uplands surrounding the river valley (Jenkins 1974:185).

Howard Winters (1974) has described the late Archaic economy of certain eastern North American peoples as a limited spectrum economy, based upon a few essential resources—in this case deer, mussels, and nut foods. The late Archaic subsistence and settlement patterns in the western portion of the middle Tennessee Valley have been the subject of recent research by Ned Jenkins of The University of Alabama. His study sheds light on one of these limited spectrum economic systems and provides comparative data concerning the evolution of this type of economy in eastern North America.

There were three major procurement systems: (1) shellfish collecting and fishing, (2) hunting, and (3) harvesting of plant foods. According to Jenkins, each was based on a technology involving implements (projectiles, mortars, atlatls, conical holes, etc.) and facilities (baskets, storage pits, stone-lined fireplaces, etc.).

> In turn, these procurement systems were regulated by seasonality and scheduling. Seasonality was imposed on man by the nature of the wild resources themselves (Flannery 1968), such as the period of the availability of nuts, or the river level during the different seasons, which controlled the availability of shellfish. Scheduling was a cultural activity which resolved con-

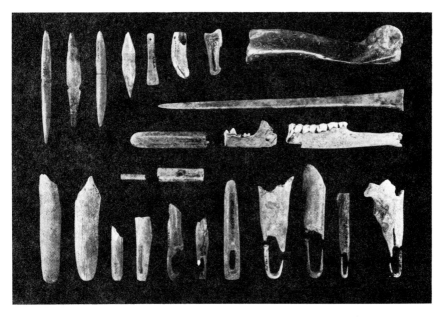

Late Archaic Bone Tools. *Bottom row, right,* Fishhooks, AMNH 156 Ma 48

Late Archaic Carved and Polished Bone Pins, AMNH 175 Ct 27

Burial with Cache of Five Steatite Vessels at Flint River Site, AMNH 102 Ma 48

Steatite Bowl (Courtesy Frank J. Soday)

flict between procurement systems. An example of scheduling in the western Middle Tennessee Valley would be the simultaneous availability of shellfish in the valley proper, and acorns in the uplands for a brief period in September and October. During such a period these people would have to schedule their activities; i.e., make a decision over one or the other food product. [1974:183–85]

Based upon biophysical studies of the present western middle Tennessee Valley area and upon current archaeological data, Jenkins has offered the following hypothetical settlement and subsistence model (1974:186–87). From May through October these peoples lived on shell mounds by the river in macroband groups composed of several related families. Subsistence was based upon collecting shellfish, fishing, hunting riverine fauna, and gathering plant foods that were available. Because plant-processing implements such as mortars and mullers are fairly rare at these sites, it seems that plants such as greens (*Chenopodium, Iva*) and fruits (*cherries, mulberries*) that do not require specialized preparation were gathered. Toward the end of October these late Archaic groups split into smaller family units (microbands) and moved to the upland microenvironments surrounding the valley. This move was the product of two factors: (1) cultural scheduling to take advantage of seasonally available upland resources, and (2) increased seasonal precipitation and high water impeding the procurement of riverine resources. The upland settlements were occupied from November through April. During this time they subsisted on harvested and stored nut foods and animal protein supplied by hunting and trapping. During the late fall and winter period, precipitation increases to a yearly high of 4.8 to 5.6 inches. Beginning in May and continuing through to October, rainfall diminishes to an average of 3 inches per month. In May the people returned to the shell mounds, renewing the yearly cycle. This settlement pattern fits the criterion of the central-based, wandering type (Beardsley 1955:138) and allowed greater sedentism over much of the year than had previously been possible.

The economic procurement systems utilized by these late Archaic peoples during their seasonal cycle can be summarized as follows:

Shellfish collecting and fishing. The shallow shoal waters of the western middle Tennessee Valley provided an abundant food supply for a large part of each year. Morrison (1942) has studied the shellfish remains from a number of the large midden deposits in this area. His research indicates that the vast majority of the species collected by these peoples were found in very shallow waters, a meter or less in depth. For example, of the 100 species of mussels found in this region, 40 occur only in small tributary streams or in deep water. Of the remaining 60 species, 56 were collected by these late Archaic peoples. In a one-cubic-yard sample of material from the Bluff Creek shell mound, Morrison found 52 species of mussels, 29 species of freshwater snails, and 38 species of land snails—a total of over 57,000 individual shells. The immense volume of shellfish remains from these midden deposits can be appreciated if one takes into consideration that the Bluff Creek site alone contained an estimated 25,000 cubic yards of material.

These middens were occupied for several thousand years in some cases, yet shellfish remained an important supplement in the diet on a seasonal basis and were a major reason for the return of the people to the river each year. Although low in nutrient value when compared to mammalian species (Parmalee and Klippel 1974) shellfish nevertheless served as an abundant, reliable, and easily procured source of food. Shellfish also did not require elaborate preparation; they were often steamed over beds of hot rocks or at times eaten raw. With the introduction of stone and pottery vessels, they may have been boiled separately or added to stews.

In a recent ethnozoological analysis of the vertebrate fauna from the Little Bear Creek shell mound, C. B. Curren (1974) noted that of some 1,200 bone fragments only four belonged to a fish species (drumfish). Curren attributes this low percentage of fish remains to two factors—differentiated preservation of these small bones and sample error. Inasmuch as the excavated materials from this site were not screened, only those fragments of bone large enough to catch the eye were recovered and only a representative sample was saved. Fish must have played a more important role in the diet than is indicated in this sample. The presence of fishhooks and net sinkers in the cultural inventory of these late Archaic cultures imply that fish were taken by both line fishing and netting. Weirs of stone and wood were known in other areas during this time and were perhaps also constructed in the shallow shoal waters by these people. Other forms of traps were probably also utilized.

Hunting. Intensive hunting was practiced both during shellmound and upland occupations. Larger animals were taken by ambush hunting, while some species of smaller mammals were probably taken in traps. Hunting equipment included stone, antler, and bone-tipped projectiles propelled by atlatls, which were at times fitted with antler hooks and ground-stone weights. Biface stone choppers and knives were used in the butchering process. At shell-mound camps, deer was the most common vertebrate taken, while raccoon, beaver, turkey, opossum, gray fox, gray squirrel, rabbit, and turtle served as secondary protein sources (Curren 1974). Migratory bird remains have not been reported from these late Archaic sites and, again, this may be due to differential preservation, sampling error, or both. This region of the Tennessee Valley is situated on a major flyway, and it would be unusual if these Indians did not take advantage of an abundant and easily taken food source. Deer was the major animal hunted in the uplands, and squirrel and raccoon were also favored prey (Parmalee 1962).

Venison was a favored meat. As with the buffalo of the Plains Indians, the deer was intensively exploited both as a food source and as a source of raw materials. The whitetail deer has an average live weight of two hundred pounds, about half of which is usuable for food. Rather than discard the

Late Archaic Stemmed Projectile Points, AMNH 182 Lu 25

remainder, the Indians made the antlers into projectile points, fishhooks, and a variety of awls, needles, pins, flakers, spatulas, saws (mandibles), scrapers, scoops, hammers, and ornaments. The hide, often tanned with a solution made of deer brain, was made into containers, foot gear, and garments. Sinews and entrails provided cordage, thread, and thongs. Heads, skins, and antlers were dried and used as decoys, stalking devices, and ceremonial costumes.

Harvesting. Analysis of floral remains from late Archaic sites in the western Middle Tennessee Valley indicates that nut foods were a primary source of food. Greens, berries, and tubers were probably also gathered in season, and squash and some native annuals, such as the sunflower, may have been cultivated. Grindstones and perhaps wooden implements were used to prepare some of these foods. Storage pits were often dug to cache part of the gathered produce, especially nuts. Nut crops such as acorn, hickory nut, and walnut begin to drop in late September and continue to fall throughout the autumn and part of the early winter seasons. Fierce competition probably erupted over these crops, more between man and beast than man and man.

Many species of nuts are found in all of the microenvironments surrounding the river valley. This diversity was important to the Indian, for most

Tightly Flexed Late Archaic "Sitting" Burial at the Perry Site, AMNH 14 Lu 25

species of nut-producing trees do not yield a crop every year. If trees in one habitat failed to yield, trees in other, nearby microenvironments might produce an abundant crop, allowing gathering activities to continue uninterrupted.

Nut foods, especially hickory nuts, are a rich source of carbohydrates, fats, and protein. They were apparently gathered in large quantities and, in some cases, stored for use during the lean late winter and early spring months. One small winter upland camp (Fr 524) was recently excavated by University of Alabama personnel in the Bear Creek area of Franklin County (Oakley and Futato 1975). Large storage pits were present and were found to contain abundant amounts of hickory nutshells. A sample of carbonized material from one of these features yielded a date of 1650 ± 180 B.C. Late Archaic stemmed points of the Little Bear Creek type were found in the pit. Because this type was the dominant projectile-point cluster at this site, it may in the future serve as a marker for a terminal Archaic phase.

5: The Gulf Formational Stage

During the 1930s archaeologists working in eastern North America became increasingly aware of the need to integrate and synthesize the voluminous amounts of information on prehistoric Indian life accumulated from a century of research and field investigation. Several attempts at synthesis were made, most notably by James B. Griffin (1946) and James A. Ford and Gordon R. Willey (1941). Technological developments in the archaeological sequence served as major definitive criteria in all three of these integrative models. Ultimately, there emerged a sequence of four developmental stages in the prehistory of the East: Paleo-Indian, Archaic, Woodland, and Mississippian. We are here concerned with the intermediate stages, the Archaic and Woodland. The Archaic, as defined in the Northeast, was characterized by such traits as ground-stone tools, large-stemmed projectile points, stone vessels, and tubular pipes. On the other hand, the emergence of the Woodland was marked in the Northeast and Midwest by the appearance of such traits as cord- or fabric-impressed pottery and burial mounds. Southeastern archaeologists imported this Archaic-Woodland dichotomy and applied it to their sequences as well, with considerable success for a time.

However, as more data and more precise chronologies emerged in the southern Coastal Plain region it became apparent that such a simplified model did not always accurately reflect internal developments being recognized in local and regional sequences. Fiber-tempered pottery and other early ceramic complexes were a major classificatory problem, as was the placement of the Poverty Point culture (see Willey 1966 and Jennings 1974 for examples of attempts to deal with this dilemma). Were these developments late Archaic or early Woodland? Some archaeologists, at times with success (Bullen 1974), opted for a transitional placement for some of the early ceramic-producing cultures. But over extensive areas of the southern Coastal Plain other cultures, appearing as a culmination of indigenous Archaic life, were abruptly replaced by new technological and cultural complexes radiating out of the Midwest and southern Appalachia. Because the term "transitional" implies continuity from one development to the next, these manifestations cannot properly be considered transitional.

While not believing that abandonment of the established developmental model is necessary or even desirable, many southeastern archaeologists feel that some sort of modification is in order. Ned Jenkins and John Walthall presented a research paper at the 1975 Southeastern Archaeological Conference in which these related Coastal Plain cultures were drawn into an intermediate cultural stage—called the Gulf Formational stage—between the

Archaic and Woodland (Walthall and Jenkins 1976). In order to illuminate better the origins and growth of the cultures assigned to this stage, the southern Coastal Plain was divided into two subregions: (1) an eastern region extending from eastern Alabama to the Atlantic coast and (2) a western region encompassing the area between the Tombigbee drainage of western Alabama and the lower Mississippi Valley. The Gulf Formational stage began in the eastern region with the appearance of fiber-tempered pottery and ended with the spread of southern Appalachian and northern ceramics into the Southeast. In the interim several major developments occurred. In order to trace these, the Gulf Formational stage is divided into three sequential periods, early (2500–1200 B.C.), middle (1200–500 B.C.), and late (500–100 B.C.). A discussion of each of these periods and Gulf Formational culture in Alabama follows.

The Early Gulf Formational Period: 2500–1200 B.C.

The beginning of the Gulf Formational stage is marked by the appearance of fiber-tempered pottery at littoral harvesting stations along the southern Atlantic Seaboard. Two ceramic-producing cultures from early Gulf Formational times are found in this area. Stallings Island of the Georgia-Carolina coast and the Orange culture of northeastern Florida. James Stoltman (1972a) and Ripley Bullen (1972) have recently produced syntheses of these manifestations, and their studies are the major sources used in the following summary.

Stallings Island sites are found along the Savannah River in the interior Coastal Plain and along the coast near its mouth. Most are shell middens. Mussels were gathered from the river inland and oysters were collected along the shoreline. In both areas, the Stallings Island occupation began around 3000 B.C. and continued for some two thousand years. Three major types of sites can be recognized according to their locations: (1) inland shell middens such as the type site at Stallings Island (Clafin 1931) and the Groton Plantation site recently excavated under Stoltman's direction; (2) floodplain sites, such as Clear Mount and Rabbit mound in the Savannah swamp; and (3) coastal shell rings (Williams, ed. 1968; Hemmings 1970). These latter sites are ring-shaped middens with embankments of oyster shell and cultural debris ranging from 2 to 9 feet in height and 20 to 50 feet in breadth at the base. Enclosed by the embankments are flat, central areas ranging from 100 to 150 feet in diameter. These enclosed areas are devoid of occupational debris. The function of these shell rings is not known, although it is interesting to note that they are not confined solely to the Savannah coastal region but are found, at roughly contemporaneous times, along the coasts of Florida, Mississippi, and Colombia. Antonio Waring (Williams, ed. 1968), who made a major study of the Stallings Island shell rings, believed that they

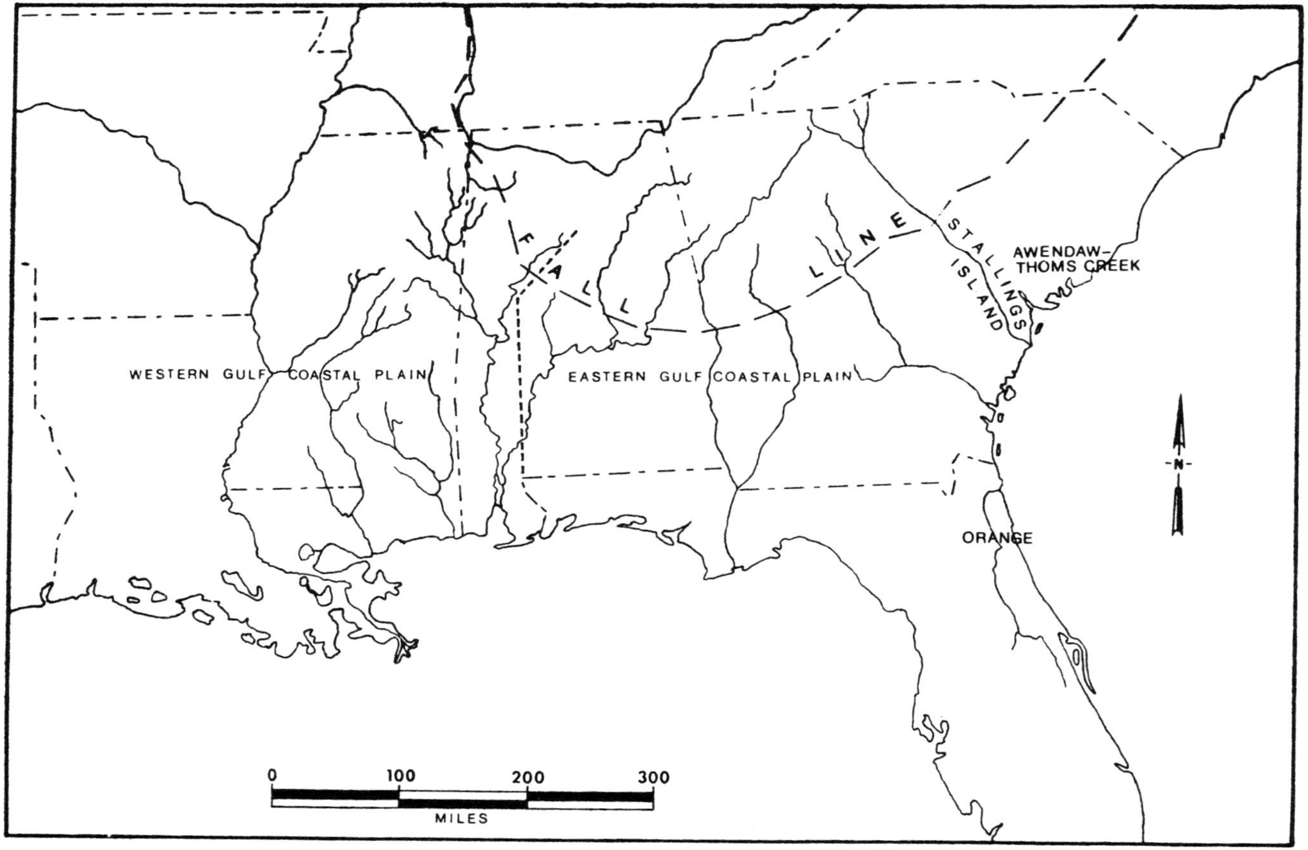

AWENDAW–
THOMS CREEK

STALLINGS
ISLAND

ORANGE

F A L L   L I N E

EASTERN GULF COASTAL PLAIN

WESTERN GULF COASTAL PLAIN

N

0   100   200   300

MILES

were intentionally constructed ceremonial enclosures of some sort. An alternative theory is that they represent habitation sites where refuse was carefully discarded around a centrally located residence area.

Stallings Island material culture is rich and varied. Stone was chipped into large-stemmed projectile points, knives, drills, stemmed scrapers, and other tools. Steatite, from upland Piedmont sources, was fashioned into vessels and grooved and perforated "net sinkers," which may have actually served as cooking stones. Baked-clay spheres, which have been dated to 1750 B.C. at a shell ring on Sapelo Island, may also have functioned as cooking stones for roasting or baking in pits. In the Sapelo Island midden they were found to decrease in frequency as fiber-tempered pottery increased. This trend is probably indicative of a major change in culinary techniques as direct-heat boiling in ceramic vessels became popular.

Polished ground-stone axes, atlatl weights, and gorgets have been noted at some Stallings Island sites. Bone and antler were also important raw materials in tool manufacturing. Bone awls, atlatl hooks, fishhooks, and projectile points are common. The most distinctive bone artifacts are ornamental pins, slender, carefully polished, and often decorated with finely engraved lines.

Stallings Island pottery, the oldest in North America, appeared around 2500 B.C., well over a thousand years before Woodland ceramics were known in the Northeast. Stallings Island vessels were tempered with vegetable fibers and were modeled from a single mass of clay. Only one vessel form is known, a simple wide-mouthed bowl. Most of the fiber-tempered sherds found in the Savannah shell middens are undecorated, but punctate, incised, and simple-stamped embellishments occur. Punctations, made with fingernails, hollow reeds, or blunt-end tools, are the most common form of decoration, while simple stamping is rare (found at only two sites and comprising only 1 percent of the total sherd count). Apparently, plain ware appeared first. At the Bilbo site, a circular shell midden 100 feet in diameter and 5 feet deep, Waring noted that plain sherds were found in the lower strata while decorated sherds increased in frequency in the upper zone.

One hundred and fifty miles to the south of the Savannah River, archaeologists have recognized a second major fiber-tempered ceramic complex, the Orange series. Orange pottery is found in large shell middens along the Saint Johns and Indian rivers on the Atlantic coast of Florida. In his most recent study of this complex, Bullen (1972) noted that the lower levels of a number of these sites are preceramic. Plain pottery appears in the local sequence around 2000 B.C., while decorated ware appears at approximately 1600 B.C. When Bullen salvaged a remnant of the once huge Bluffton midden on the Saint Johns River, he found that, though the deposit was 16 to 18 feet deep, pottery was confined to the upper 4 to 7 feet, and decorated sherds were found in only the upper two feet. Much of the midden, however, had been destroyed by commercial operators who used the shells for road construction.

The major Orange ceramic vessel form is a shallow, flat-based pan, circular to rectangular in shape. The most common decorative technique used by Orange culture craftsmen was incision, at times combined with punctations to form a wide variety of designs, varying from scrolls to herringbone motifs and crossed bands. Shell and bone were the major raw materials used in tool production. Large univalves were made into gouges, picks, celts, and hammers. Bone was worked into pins, awls, fishhooks, and projectile points. Chipped stone is relatively rare at Orange sites, but stemmed points and scrapers have been found. A few steatite vessels appear to have been imported from northern Coastal Plain areas.

A site located in the lowlands of Colombia on the northern coast of South America has played an important role in recent discussions concerning the origin of southeastern fiber-tempered pottery. Puerto Hormiga is one of a group of shell middens excavated by Gerardo Reichel-Dolmatoff (1972) near an old colonial canal, the Canal de Dique, which follows the course of a former river through the coastal marshes. The site is a large shell ring composed of cultural debris, oyster shells, and shells of the genus *Pitar*. The ring measures 255 feet from north to south and 280 feet from east to west. The surrounding embankment varies in width at the base from 53 to 82 feet and rises above the river bottoms to a height of about 4 feet. The flat area within the ring is about 132 feet in diameter (Willey 1971:268–70).

Table 2: Gulf Formational Cultures and Chronology

Date	Period	Eastern Area	Western Area
100 B.C.			
	Late	Early Woodland	
500			Tchefuncte Alexander
800	Middle		Bayou La Batre
		Saint Johns	Poverty Point
		Norwood	Wheeler
		Refuge	
1200			
		Thom's Creek	
1500	Early		Late Archaic
2000		Orange	
		Stallings Island	
2500 B.C.			

Reichel-Dolmatoff's excavations at Puerto Hormiga revealed that shell and other cultural debris were confined entirely to the ring embankment. Both the surrounding bottomland and the central area within the ring were devoid of such remains. Reichel-Dolmatoff believes that the shell ring represents the refuse from several dwelling structures, housing 50 to 100 people, once clustered in a circle in the marsh. The cultural material recovered from the Puerto Hormiga shell ring included potsherds, shell tools, and stone implements. Hammerstones and pitted anvil stones, perhaps used in the preparation of corozo palm nuts, were common, but no stone projectile points were found. Large shells were made into axes, hammers, gouges, and scrapers. Baskets and mats were woven of locally available plant fibers. The most striking aspect of the Puerto Hormiga assemblage is the remarkably varied and contemporary ceramic industry. Both crude, fiber-tempered pottery, modeled from a single lump of clay, and a more sophisticated, sand-tempered pottery have been found in the embankment deposits. The sand-tempered ware was made by the coil technique and was decorated by incision, punctation, modeling, rocker stamping, and dentate stamping. A typical design element used was incised zones filled with punctations or rocker stamping. Vessel forms include a semiglobular bowl and some shallow, elongated pans. While these ceramic types continued to be produced until 1000 B.C., both complexes have been consistently dated to between 3100 and 2500 B.C., making the Puerto Hormiga pottery one of the earliest ceramic complexes in the New World.

In his opening statements introducing a symposium of papers on southeastern fiber-tempered pottery, James Stoltman (1972b) reviewed the current evidence concerning the origin of this ceramic complex. The data at hand suggest two alternative hypotheses: (1) Fiber-tempered pottery in the Southeast is an independent invention, perhaps modeled after stone-vessel forms; or (2) Fiber-tempered pottery diffused into the Southeast from some other region. If the first hypothesis is valid, then the appearance of these ceramic forms at shell middens in both the Southeast and Colombia represents a classic case of parallel evolution. The second hypothesis raises the question: Could the fiber-tempered ceramics found at Puerto Hormiga represent the ultimate source of early southeastern pottery? James A. Ford (1969) spent the last years of his life compiling evidence to support his hypothesis that a number of historical ties existed between Latin American Formative cultures and the Southeast. There are three major factors supporting this view:

1. In both regions, fiber-tempered pottery and, it should be noted, decorated, sand-tempered ware are associated with coastal shell middens with a similar economic adaptation and level of cultural development.

2. Radiocarbon dates suggest a chronological overlap between these two complexes, with the Puerto Hormiga material being five to six hundred years earlier.

3. The two regions are connected by prevailing winds and ocean currents, with a general south-to-north movement.

Against the diffusionists' argument is the total absence of archaeological sites of the appropriate type or age anywhere along the Caribbean and Gulf coasts between Puerto Hormiga and the eastern Coastal Plain of the Georgia-Florida area. In spite of this, a number of archaeologists believe the many similarities between the southeastern Gulf Formational and the Latin American Formative cultures are too numerous and specific to represent independent innovations. If such contact did indeed exist, what form did it take? Ford championed colonization by seagoing migrants. On the other hand, both Stoltman and Bullen have emphasized that along the southern Atlantic coast fiber-tempered pottery appears as a nondisruptive addition to artifact assemblages whose development predates the appearance of ceramics by at least a thousand years. Stoltman also notes that, if actual population movements were involved between Latin America and the Southeast, one would expect to find an assemblage of demonstrably intrusive traits indicative of a site-unit intrusion. Inasmuch as no such sites are currently known, fiber-tempered pottery appears more likely to be a trait-unit intrusion into the Southeast, if, in fact, it is intrusive at all and not a local innovation.

The Middle Gulf Formational Period: 1200–500 B.C.

During the middle Gulf Formational period, mineral tempering (sand, grit, etc.) became popular in the ceramic industries of the eastern Coastal Plain settlements. Fiber-tempered pottery meanwhile was diffused westward along the Gulf coast, where by 1100 B.C. it had spread into the interior to form the Wheeler series. Stallings Island ceramics were succeeded by the sand-tempered pottery of the Thom's Creek (1300–1100 B.C.) and Refuge (1100–600 B.C.) phases. According to Drexel Peterson (1970, 1971), Refuge pottery is a coiled, sand-tempered ware decorated by simple stamping, dentate stamping, punctation, and incision. Open bowls and straight-sided cups with flat bases are major vessel forms. Both Thom's Creek and Refuge pottery appear to have evolved from the preceding Stallings Island ceramic complex, with certain traits, such as dentate stamping, appearing for the first time, perhaps as the result of diffusion from other Coastal Plain communities.

In Florida, two ceramic complexes replaced the earlier Orange series. In the northeast, Saint Johns pottery appeared, a chalky ware made in the same form as Orange vessels, decorated with simple techniques such as incision, punctation, and pinching (Bullen 1972). In northwestern Florida, David Phelps recognized a contemporary ceramic complex, the Norwood series, a semi-fiber-tempered pottery containing various amounts of sand, with one known decoration, simple stamping. At the Tucker site on the northern Gulf

Middle Gulf Formational Cultures

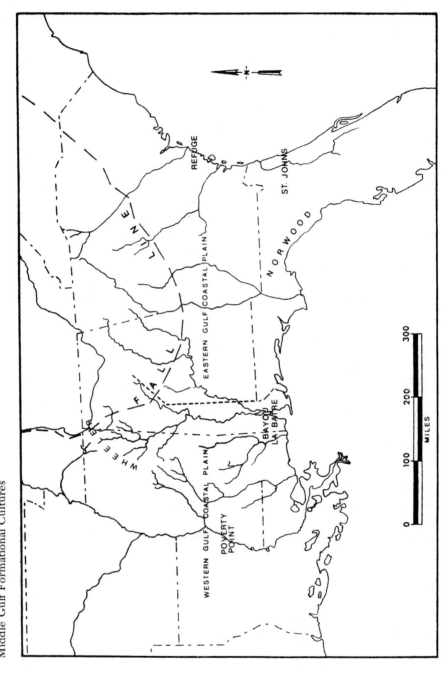

coast of Florida, Phelps obtained a radiocarbon date of 1012 ± 120 B.C. for Norwood pottery. Bullen (1972) noted that during this time there was an acceleration in trade as red jasper beads, Poverty Point-type clay balls, and steatite vessels diffused to Florida from the west and north and Saint Johns pottery spread westward among Gulf coast settlements to the lower Mississippi Valley.

Sometime after the diffusion of fiber-tempered pottery to the settlements of the western Coastal Plain, a totally new ceramic complex appeared, perhaps also ultimately derived from the Latin American Formative. This complex, which appears along Mobile Bay at Bayou La Batre sites, consists of sand-tempered pottery vessels with podal supports or annular (ring) bases, decorated with rocker or dentate stamping. There are no known precedents for these ceramic modes in the Southeast. While in the eastern area there is clear continuity in form and decoration between fiber- and, later, mineral-tempered wares, no such genetic relationships exist in the western area.

The middle Gulf Formational also witnessed the flowering of the Poverty Point culture in the lower Mississippi Valley, a development unparalleled in early North American prehistory. The Poverty Point site, on the edge of Macon Ridge overlooking the Mississippi floodplains, incorporates earthen mounds and embankments in a geometric design oriented according to the cardinal directions. Six concentric, semicircular earthworks with a maximum diameter of 1,200 meters are situated in the central area of the site, which at its height must have been the largest settlement in eastern North America. The earthworks are dissected by four aisles or interstices that radiate from an interior plaza at irregularly spaced intervals, forming five sets of concentric semicircles. On the outer edge of the western ridge is Mound A, a large earthen structure that is thought to represent a giant bird with spread wings. The major north-south axis of the site (7° to 8° west of true north) passes through this mound. A second structure, the Motley mound, lies 2,400 meters to the north of Mound A. Slightly smaller than Mound A, it may be an unfinished bird effigy mound. Along the major north-south axis are two more mounds; Mound B, 225 meters north of Mound A; and the Jackson mound, 2,800 meters to the south (Gibson 1974).

The Poverty Point site is strategically located near the confluence of six major rivers—a position that would have allowed its inhabitants control over the flow of trade goods between other communities. Jon Gibson (1974) believes that Poverty Point represents a chiefdom, and certainly the huge earthworks and enormous amount of labor required for their construction support such a contention. Gibson also has postulated that the subsistence base of the Poverty Point culture was centered around the intensive exploitation of forest-edge resources. No cultigens (cultivated plants) have yet been reported at Poverty Point sites. Although there are no known occurrences of chiefdoms developing in the absence of food production, Gibson considers it possible because of the unusually rich natural resources of this area. Poverty

Point villages were founded along ecological boundaries where at least two contrasting ecosystems merged. In the lower Mississippi Valley this would have assured the highest possible yield of game and plant-food resources (nuts in the forests and wild seed plants in the mud flats of the Mississippi bottoms).

The material culture of Poverty Point reflects both an Archaic heritage and widespread trade contacts with other, often distant regions. Three types of pottery have been recovered from the earthworks at Poverty Point: fiber-tempered Wheeler ceramics; later, sand-tempered Alexander pottery; and a clay-tempered ware. This latter Tchefuncte complex is a coiled pottery with deep cup or wide-mouthed pot forms sometimes having tetrapodal supports. Rim bosses were added below the vessel lip, and rocker stamping with a smooth or notched tool was frequently applied to the vessel surface.

Stone suitable for use in lithic tool production is almost nonexistent in this region, so such materials were a major import. Stone vessels from Piedmont sources to the east, sometimes with rims decorated with incised lines, are well represented in the cultural inventory. Tubular pipes of clay or stone; sandstone whetstones and saws; small celts; adzes; atlatl weights; large-stemmed projectile points; and hematite plummets, some with incised designs, are also known. Three unusual technological complexes set Poverty Point apart from previous developments (Webb 1968):

1. A microflint industry existed involving the striking of prismatic blades from egg-shaped flint cores. Perforators, end scrapers, side scrapers, and needles were manufactured from these blades. This flint-working technique allowed maximum efficiency in a land where stone is at a premium.

2. Poverty Point craftsmen also developed an interesting lapidary industry that produced several forms of perforated and nonperforated beads and pendants. A cache of lithic materials discovered among the embankments appears to represent a beadmaker's kit. Of the 56 objects found in the cache, most are sawed, partially shaped, or perforated bead blanks of red or green talc, though red jasper was also a favorite raw material used in bead production. With the cache were a drill and a large-stemmed blade; wear along the blade's edges suggests use as a lapidary saw (Webb 1968). Bead forms vary from short to long tubular types, to globular and disk shapes. Zoomorphic beads commonly include effigies of birds or locusts.

3. Clay was used to make objects other than pottery. Anthropomorphic figurines, always portraying females, were modeled out of solid clay. It was also used to produce the diagnostic "Poverty Point objects"—masses of various shapes, about fist size, apparently used in place of rock in hot-stone cooking in pits. These objects were not carefully made; a handful of wet clay was simply formed into a spherical cylindrical, or biconical shape in the hand or between cupped palms. Thousands of these clay balls have been recovered, some in association with hearths or roasting pits.

The Wheeler Culture

By 1300 B.C., fiber-tempered pottery had begun to diffuse westward as it was adopted by various semisedentary Coastal Plain ethnic groups. Punctation, one early decorative treatment that may have originated in the ancestral Stallings Island ware, was being applied to vessels at shell-midden sites along the Pearl River estuary on the Mississippi coast by 1200 B.C. Sherwood Gagliano and Clarence Webb (personal communication) believe that one of these, the Claiborne site—a horseshoe-shaped shell midden—was occupied for only a short time; radiocarbon dates suggest around 1100 B.C. The cultural material recovered includes almost 13,000 Poverty Point-type baked-clay objects, steatite vessels, and fiber-tempered pottery. A cache of 10 steatite vessels has been reported, and, as with the fiber-tempered pottery of this region, two vessel shapes were represented—a flat-based beaker and a simple open bowl. Several of these steatite containers were decorated with incised lines on the exterior below or on the vessel lip. The fiber-tempered ceramic sample included 98 plain sherds (90 percent) and 11 punctate sherds (10 percent). Six "untempered" sherds, two of which were decorated with incisions, were also found and are reminiscent of the Saint Johns series of Florida.

Plain and punctate fiber-tempered pottery spread from the coastal settlements to interior ethnic groups, reaching the lower Mississippi Valley Poverty Point sites and settlements in the upper Tombigbee River drainage area and western middle Tennessee Valley by 1000 B.C. This fiber-tempered ceramic complex was adopted, and for a brief period produced, by Poverty Point peoples in essentially unmodified form. Four sites (Poverty Point, Jaketown, Tchefuncte, and Teoc Creek) have yielded some two hundred fiber-tempered sherds. Plain ware is by far the most common type (84 percent), and punctation is the only major decorative treatment (15 percent).

The fiber-tempered ware that spread northeastward from the Pearl River estuary has a longer history of use than that of the lower Mississippi Valley. The sites where it is found in the upper Tombigbee Basin and Tennessee Valley comprise the Wheeler culture. Jenkins and Walthall have divided the Wheeler culture into two phases, the Bluff Creek phase of the western middle Tennessee Valley and the Broken Pumpkin Creek phase of the upper Tombigbee drainage area. Two additional decorative treatments were added to the original ceramic complex in these areas, probably sometime between 1000 and 800 B.C. Simple stamping, though proportionally rare, is found in ceramic samples from both areas. This treatment may have also ultimately diffused from the eastern Coastal Plain, but I suspect that it was an independent local innovation by Wheeler potters attempting to copy the exterior tool markings of their stone vessels. A third decorative technique—one found only in the fiber-tempered ceramics of this area—is dentate stamping, a late

Fiber-tempered Vessels. *Right to left,* Wheeler Plain, Dentate Stamped, Punctate

temporal marker in the local sequence. It occurs in higher frequency in the
upper levels of stratified sites and is carried over into the succeeding, sand-
tempered Alexander series (Mandeville Stamped). Jenkins (1975a) has offered a plausible hypothesis to account for its introduction. He believes that
dentate stamping was borrowed from Bayou La Batre peoples to the south,
who commonly decorated their pottery with impressions of the notched edge
of a scallop shell rolled across the wet vessel surface. That upper Tombigbee
peoples were in contact with Bayou La Batre groups in the lower Tombigbee
area is demonstrated by the presence of Bayou La Batre Scallop Impressed
sherds at the Broken Pumpkin Creek and Metzger sites and by spear points
of Tallahatta quartzite at several Broken Pumpkin Creek phase sites. This
lithic material has its source in Clarke County in the lower Tombigbee area
of the Bayou La Batre territory and was a favored raw material of both ethnic
groups.

Several sites that can be assigned to the northern Bluff Creek phase have
been excavated and reported. By and large, they are spatially distributed
around the Pickwick Basin area of Lauderdale and Colbert counties in extreme northwestern Alabama. Only scattered occurrences of fiber-tempered
pottery have been noted at sites up or down the river from this core area.

Within this territory, Bluff Creek phase sites are found in two major environmental zones—in the river bottoms near shellfish beds and in the upland fall line hills to the south, where both open-air sites and bluff shelters were occupied. These sites appear to be components of a central-based, wandering settlement pattern like that described for the late Archaic. The riverine middens were warm-weather collecting stations, and the upland sites have yielded evidence of fall-winter hunting and gathering activities.

Wheeler sherds have been recovered in small amounts at several shell middens within the Pickwick Basin (Haag 1942). However, over 72 percent of the fiber-tempered sherds recovered in the basin were found at only two shell middens, the Bluff Creek and Perry sites (Webb and DeJarnette 1942), where the proportion of decorated sherds is much higher than in any other area where Wheeler pottery is found. At Bluff Creek, one of the few stratified Wheeler sites known, plain and punctate appear in the lower levels, and simple- and dentate-stamped wares increase in frequency in the upper zones.

Lu⁰ 59	Plain	Punctate	Simple Stamped	Dentate Stamped
3–0 feet	30%	24%	4%	42%
6–3 feet	55%	32%	1%	12%

Both Bluff Creek and Perry were base camps. They are some seventeen miles apart and may have been occupied by two related macrobands occupying adjacent territories. The Perry site is on the upper end of Seven Mile Island, which suggests that some type of water craft was used during this time, perhaps dugout canoes. Among the cultural materials recovered from the Wheeler zones at these sites are stemmed projectile points, chipped bifacial tools, a variety of bone and antler implements, and sandstone and steatite vessels, some decorated with incised lines in the rim area. Sherds from stone vessels have not been recovered at sites in the uplands, suggesting that these containers were cached when the groups moved to their fall collecting grounds. Fiber-tempered pottery vessels, though crude in comparison to later ceramics, could easily be made while groups were in residence in the uplands, thus solving a transportation problem, for they did not have to be carried but could be manufactured on the spot.

Upland sites with Wheeler components have been reported in Colbert and Franklin counties (Jolly 1971, 1974; DeJarnette, Kurjack, and Cambron 1962; Stowe 1970). Joseph Benthall (1965) has noted that a major projectile-point type associated with Wheeler ceramics in the Tennessee Valley is the Cotaco Creek form. Cotaco Creek points are medium-to-large-stemmed blades with rounded shoulders. The blade edge is straight to excurvate, and the stem is straight or slightly expanded. This projectile-point cluster may represent a horizon marker in certain areas of eastern North America. In Pennsylvania and New York these points are called Perkiomen points and occurred between 1300 and 1000 B.C. in association with steatite vessels and

Cotaco Creek Projectile Points from Madison County (Brock 1969)

early pottery (Ritchie 1965:150–56). Benthall has also noted that Cotaco Creek points have been associated with preceramic terminal Archaic zones and subsequent early Alexander assemblages, an observation that has since been supported by excavations at the Buzzard Roost Creek rock shelter in Colbert County (Jolly 1974). There, Cotaco Creek points were clustered in the Wheeler zones and occurred in small numbers in lower and higher levels. Direct evidence for the association of Wheeler ceramics and Cotaco Creek points has been recovered from a burial discovered at a shell-midden site in Perry County, Tennessee, on the lower Tennessee River. Associated with this flexed burial were a Wheeler Plain flat-based bowl, two Cotaco Creek points, an expanded-base drill, a biface knife, an antler wrench, two perforated ground-stone gorgets, and two antler flaking tools (Benthall 1965:43–46).

In the upper Tombigbee Basin, several sites with Broken Pumpkin Creek phase components have been reported. Both open-air campsites and rock-shelter occupations have been reported along the Buttahatchee River, an eastern tributary of the Tombigbee (DeJarnette, Walthall, and Wimberly 1975a, b). To the south, Wheeler ceramics were found in the lower zones of two riverbank middens, 1 Pi 15 and 1 Gr 2, during the salvage excavation of sites to be inundated by the construction of the Gainesville Lock and Dam, one of several reservoirs being built as part of the Tennessee-Tombigbee Waterway System (Jenkins and Nielsen 1973; Jenkins 1972, 1975b). Only scattered remains of shellfish were found in these zones, indicating that this resource was not a major food of Broken Pumpkin Creek peoples. Studies of the floral and faunal remains from these sites do suggest, however, that other riverine resources were intensively exploited.

Two major Broken Pumpkin Creek base camps have been reported in the upper Tombigbee region. The Metzger site on Sun Creek in Clay County, Mississippi, some ten miles north of Starkville, has been excavated by Richard Marshall but is yet to be fully reported. However, all three Wheeler decorative treatments have been reported in the ceramic sample. Another base camp has been discovered on Broken Pumpkin Creek in Noxubee County, Mississippi, some twenty miles west of the Gainesville Reservoir. A surface sample from this site has been collected and studied by Jenkins and Walthall, who noted a large amount of Wheeler pottery. Perforated bar gorgets, steatite and sandstone vessel fragments, and stemmed points of Tallahatta quartzite were also present in the study sample. These materials suggest widespread trade connections with groups to the north, south, and west and reflect the strategic location of the Broken Pumpkin Creek site. William Myer (1928) in his study of Indian trails notes that major east-west and north-south trails converged in this area. One of these trails, connecting the lower Mississippi Valley and the Tombigbee, appears to have followed the course of Broken Pumpkin Creek to the Noxubee River, downstream to its confluence with the Tombigbee at the lower end of the Gainesville Basin.

The Pickwick Burial Complex

James B. Griffin (1967:178) has characterized the second millennium B.C. as a period of considerable population growth, clear regional adaptations, and interregional exchange. This last trait included trade of raw materials and finished products as well as diffusion of stylistic concepts and ideology. This interaction appears to have reached a peak, or climax, from about 1500 to 500 B.C. (Quimby 1960:49).

The most striking manifestations of interaction appear in certain burial "cults" or "cultures" in the Midwest and Northeast. The major burial complexes of this northern interaction sphere include Ritchie's Meadowood culture (1965:198–99) to the east and the Red Ocher burial complex of the western Great Lakes and upper Mississippi Valley. Fitting (1970:81–87) also associates the Glacial Kame and Old Copper culture of the Great Lakes region with these complexes.

Ritzenthaler and Quimby (1962) have defined the Red Ocher burial complex on the basis of seven nuclear and eleven peripheral traits. Nuclear traits include:

(1) the use of red ocher (hematite) to cover the grave, (2) burials in a flexed position in pits in sand (although cremations and bundle burials have been reported), (3) the presence of large white ceremonial blades, ellipsoidal in shape which taper toward a truncated base, (4) turkey-tail blades of blue-gray Indiana hornstone, (5) small, unnotched ovate-triangular cache blades which may occur in large numbers, (6) the presence of worked copper beads, celts, awls, or points, and (7) tubular marine shell beads.

Red Ocher complex peripheral traits include:

(1) interment in mounds, (2) use of cremation or bundle reburial as a method of interment, (3) the presence of galena cubes, (4) circular or ovate shell gorgets, (5) birdstones, (6) bar amulets, (7) three-hole rectangular gorgets, (8) tube pipes, (9) grooved axes, (10) celts, and (11) Early Woodland pottery.

Contemporaneous with these northern complexes was a southern interaction sphere centered in the Coastal Plain and contiguous areas of the Southeast. Cultures participating in this exchange included Stallings Island to the east, the terminal Lauderdale culture and the Wheeler culture of Alabama, Orange and Saint Johns in Florida, and Poverty Point to the west in the lower Mississippi Valley. The late Indian Knoll populations of Kentucky appear to have enjoyed a marginal geographical position in respect to the northern and southern spheres and to have exhibited characteristics of both. The major characteristic exchange items of the southern interaction sphere included steatite and sandstone products (vessels, tubular pipes), marine shell gorgets and beads, (usually red jasper), stone bead effigies (C. H. Webb 1968), and fiber-tempered pottery.

For comparative purposes it is possible to delineate a burial complex, derived from this terminal Archaic–Gulf Formational diffusion, represented by certain shell-mound burials in the western middle Tennessee Valley. These burials and their associations constitute a mortuary tradition that can be termed the "Pickwick Burial complex." In applying this term to these burials it is recognized that (1) the major traits of this complex are centered in the Pickwick Basin area of the Tennessee Valley, and (2) this mortuary tradition spans a period encompassing both late Lauderdale and Bluff Creek phases and perhaps extends into Alexander times as well.

Burials relating to the Pickwick complex are usually flexed on the side or in a sitting position and were placed into pits dug into the shell mounds or into nearby sand-beach deposits. Cremation was also practiced, and some individuals were decapitated (perhaps postmortem) before burial. Mortuary offerings generally accompanied only a small percentage of individuals. For example, at the Long Branch shell mound (Lu°67) only 17 of the 68 late Archaic burials contained grave goods (Webb and DeJarnette 1942).

Children and infants, however, were usually buried with mortuary offerings. This practice, combined with the limited number of adults of both sexes buried with mortuary goods, may reflect emerging concepts of status among these semisedentary groups. These concepts may be the product of interaction with contemporary populations on a higher cultural level. Jon Gibson (1974) believes he has evidence that the Poverty Point and related peoples of the lower Mississippi Valley were reaching a chiefdom level of sociopolitical organization. Certain distinctive traits in the material cultures of the Poverty Point ethnic group and the Pickwick peoples suggest exchange and interaction between these cultures. Examples include the presence of Wheeler and Alexander ceramics, steatite vessels, effigy beads, red jasper beads, Motley projectile points, and tubular stone pipes. Diagnostic Poverty Point effigy beads have been recovered both in the Pickwick Basin and in the upper Tombigbee drainage area of Lamar County (Jolly 1971: C. H. Webb 1971).

Burial goods found in Pickwick Burial complex association include all three of the functional categories defined by Howard Winters (1968) in his study of the Indian Knoll cultural burials. These include utilitarian items (projectile points, bone and antler tools, stone vessels, Wheeler ceramic vessels, etc.), ornamental items (shell beads and pendants, stone gorgets and beads, etc.), and items of a ceremonial nature (human skull bowls and awls, cut animal jaws, etc.).

The mortuary goods recovered in Pickwick burials can also be divided into two categories according to source area: (1) items made from locally available raw materials such as bone, antler, and indigenous lithic materials, and (2) materials that reflect trade with ethnic groups in other areas. It appears that objects of this type were most often exchanged as finished products. These artifacts include steatite containers and tubular pipes that may have been quarried from the Hillabee schist deposits of the Piedmont area of east-central Alabama. Extensive soapstone quarries have been reported in this area (Jones 1939; Wright 1974). Objects of steatite are more numerous in the Guntersville Basin area and may have been directly procured from the source areas by these people and then traded downstream to the Pickwick peoples.

Many Pickwick burials were accompanied only by strings of red jasper and shell beads. The jasper beads were carefully drilled and polished and vary in length from .6 to 2.25 inches, averaging .25 inches in diameter. Since jasper of this type is quite common in the upper Coastal Plain region, it is possible that these beads were locally produced. The shell beads are of several varieties, most generally disk or tubular in shape. Some of the disk beads were made from locally available mussels while others were manufactured from marine shell.

Other mortuary goods reflected long-distance trade, such as copper beads (Atkeson 1959), and perhaps flint blades, from the Great Lakes region. Caches of triangular flint blades similar to those reported in the northern burial complexes have been found in Pickwick burials. Some of these may have been made of exotic (nonlocal) materials. A stronger case for long-

Cache of Blades from Pickwick Burial Complex Grave (Courtesy Frank J. Soday)

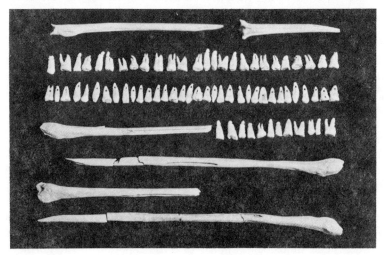

Perforated and Notched Human Teeth and Awls Associated with Burial 60 at the Bluff Creek Shell Mound, AMNH 120 Lu 59

distance trade of flint blades can be made for other blade forms. One such case is a cache of turkey-tail blades of blue-gray chert (Indiana hornstone?) recovered from a Pickwick complex burial at the Limestone Creek shell mound (Liᵛ35). This burial was found eroding out of a sand-beach between the shell mound and the river. The interment was that of a male dwarf, only 38 to 40 inches tall, who had been about seventeen years old at the time of death. This individual may have been accorded special status by his people. Beside the fully extended burial, near the right pelvis, a cache of five blades, ranging from 7 to 10.5 inches in length, was found. All but one of these long, bipointed blades had the characteristic turkey-tail notch at one end. A similar cache of turkey-tail blades made of blue-gray chert has been reported from a site to the south in Fayette County (Steve Skelton: personal communication). This particular cache consisted of three turkey-tail points ranging from 12.5 to 13.5 inches in length and 1.75 inches in maximum width. All of these points had been ceremonially killed. Although skeletal material was not found in the pit from which these mortuary offerings were taken, it is probable that they were once associated with a now-decomposed human burial. A third cache of large, bipointed blades has been reported from another Pickwick burial. Two large-stemmed points made of similar blue-gray chert were associated with this cache (Fundaburk and Foreman 1957: Plate 70).

Finally, mention must be made of a quite extraordinary Pickwick complex burial. This interment (Burial 60) at the Bluff Creek shell mound (Webb and DeJarnette 1942:115–16) was an adult male and apparently a dentist-shaman. He had been buried headless in a flexed position. Associated with this burial were a fox jaw, two animal-bone awls, five long awls made from fibulas, and 131 human teeth. Many of the teeth had been notched or perforated for suspension, perhaps to be worn as an advertisement or as ceremonial paraphernalia.

Bayou La Batre Culture

The inception of the Bayou La Batre culture is marked by the appearance of the earliest, coiled, grit-tempered ceramics in the Alabama region. This ceramic complex has been found at several shell-midden sites in the area of Mobile Bay northward some seventy miles up the floodplain forest belts of the Tombigbee and Alabama river systems. This pottery was first recognized as a distinct ceramic complex by Steve B. Wimberly (1953, 1960) during his analysis of materials recovered during 1940–1941 WPA excavations of archaeological sites in Mobile and Clarke counties.

Bayou La Batre ceramics are tempered with moderate amounts of coarse sand and fine gravel. There are two basic vessel types in this assemblage: a flaring-side cup or beaker and a globular pot. Both forms are known to have either annular (ring) bases or four small wedge- or mammiform-shaped feet.

The most common surface finish (used on some 20 to 30 percent of this ware) is rocker stamping applied randomly with the edge of a scallop-shell tool. The rocker stamping was apparently applied by holding a large scallop shell with the inner face almost parallel to the vessel surface and rocking it back and forth as it moved forward. The impressions were carelessly applied and run either parallel or vertically to the rim, covering the entire vessel surface from rim to base.

Three major Bayou La Batre sites have been reported. The first of these is the type site itself, which is a shell midden on the left (northeast) bank of Powell's Bayou, at its confluence with Bayou La Batre in southwestern Mobile County. The shell midden is a large one, running some 200 feet along the shoreline and extending some 100 feet into the forest interior. Three excavation units were dug into the midden during the WPA investigation of the site, producing some 2,500 pottery sherds. Of this number, 2,100 sherds (85 percent) are associated with the Bayou La Batre occupation; 11 are plain, fiber-tempered sherds; and the others are either the remains of trade vessels or ceramics produced by later peoples. One of the interesting aspects of the materials recovered from this site is the dearth of lithic material. The chipped-stone assemblage consisted of only 9 stemmed projectile points, 6 reamers, 4 drills, and 1 chipped fragment. The most common raw materials used in the manufacturing of these implements were jasper and Tallahatta quartzite found to the north in Clarke and Washington counties. The absence of chips or other knapping debitage suggests that these few lithic tools were transported to the site in a finished state. The only other lithic artifact recovered from the site was a fragment of a ground-stone, perforated, reel-shaped gorget made from red micaceous slate. The low number of stone tools in comparison to the ceramic assemblage (2,100 specimens) is striking. This contrast is due, at least in part, to the lack of suitable local lithic sources but may also be the result of a preferred use of weapons without stone tips in hunting activities (blow guns?) or subsistence activities that did not require such implements. Projectiles tipped with sharpened, fire-hardened wood or cane may have been the dominant type of weapon used during the occupation of these littoral sites, or gathering of shellfish and plant foods may have been the sole activities.

The second major site that has yielded important information concerning the Bayou La Batre culture is Bryant's Landing No. 4 along Tensaw Lake, discussed in chapter 4. At this site, one of a series of small shell middens, Trickey and Holmes (1971) found Bayou La Batre ceramics in stratigraphic context below middle Woodland pottery-bearing zones and above a late Archaic shell layer. Radiocarbon dates were obtained on materials from all three zones. The Bayou La Batre zone was dated to 1129 ± 200 B.C., while the late Archaic and middle Woodland zones were dated to 2139 ± 250 B.C. and 79 ± 150 B.C. respectively. These dates and the stratigraphic sequence at Bryant's Landing No. 4 confirm Wimberly's earlier relative chronology

Bayou La Batre Vessels

based upon ceramic seriation. At the Bayou La Batre site, he placed the Bayou La Batre ceramics in a chronological position between fiber-tempered pottery and middle Woodland Porter materials. The combined results of these investigations suggest a temporal placement in the second half of the first millennium B.C. for the Bayou La Batre culture.

The most recent Bayou La Batre site to have been reported is 1 Ck 45, a shell midden on the Tombigbee River north of Jackson in Clarke County. Limited testing at this site by David Chase (1972) revealed a deeply buried shell midden containing a single-component zone, the first such pure Bayou La Batre occupation yet discovered. Unlike the Mobile County site, 1 Ck 45 yielded a large amount of lithic materials. Chase reported that thousands of chips and spalls of Tallahatta quartzite were recovered, indicating that lithic tool production was a major activity at this site. Finished implements in the lithic sample recovered by Chase include biface blades, knives, scrapers, a graver, and projectile points. The projectile points were all stemmed, medium-to-large points similar in form to the late Archaic Pickwick and Little Bear Creek types of the Tennessee Valley. Bone tools were also recovered, including awls made from deer bone, an antler punch, a gouge, and a barbed fishhook.

A comparison of the Bayou La Batre site and 1 Ck 45 produces both similarities and contrasts. Shellfish were collected at both sites, brackish-water clam at the former and freshwater mussel at the latter. Both sites yielded a large number of potsherds, indicating that ceramic vessels were an important item in the culinary activities at both settlements. Here the basic similarities end, however. There is little evidence to suggest hunting at Bayou La Batre, while at 1 Ck 45 there is abundant evidence—numerous projectile points, butchering and processing tools, and faunal remains, mainly whitetail deer. This contrast in hunting activities may be the result of (1) different adaptations by separate groups of people, one on the coast and one in the interior forest; or (2) the fact that these two sites represent units of a seasonal settlement pattern of a single or related population (for example, a summer littoral gathering station and an interior winter hunting camp). Only further research will yield a solution. These two alternatives provide a good set of working hypotheses to be tested in the field at some future date.

The Late Gulf Formational Period: 500–100 B.C.

The late Gulf Formational is marked by three major events: (1) the final disappearance of fiber-tempered pottery, (2) the rise of the Tchefuncte and Alexander ceramic series in the western region, and (3) the appearance of early Woodland Deptford pottery in the east. Deptford ceramics have some characteristics (such as sand tempering and podal supports) in common with Gulf Formational pottery and may have at least partially developed out of Gulf Formational forms. However, Deptford vessel surfaces were finished with wooden paddles upon which parallel lines or grid patterns were carved, a trait that sets Deptford apart from previous ceramic complexes. During this period, Bayou La Batre peoples produced their traditional pottery forms in the Mobile Bay region. To the north, however, a major ceramic complex appeared for the first time, the Alexander series.

The Alexander Culture

Like the earlier Wheeler series, Alexander ceramics were first recognized in the middle Tennessee Valley of northern Alabama (J. B. Griffin 1939; Haag 1942). The type site for this pottery, the Alexander mound in Law-rence County, was excavated by Gerard Fowke just prior to the construction of Wilson Dam in the second decade of this century. This site was found to have two major components, a middle Woodland Copena burial mound and an underlying old village midden containing large amounts of sand-tempered pottery bearing a wide range of often complex design motifs (Walthall 1973a). Within the middle Tennessee Valley this Alexander pottery occurs most frequently in the Pickwick Basin area. It appeared in this region be-

Late Gulf Formational Cultures

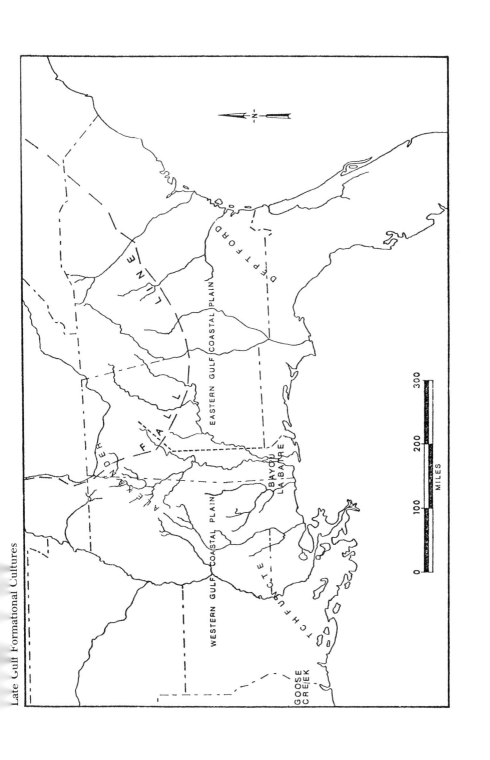

tween 600 and 500 B.C. and was replaced some four centuries later by northern fabric-impressed pottery. Within the Pickwick Basin, Alexander pottery
is commonly found in riverine shell-midden deposits and at upland sites
south of the river. In fact, distribution of Alexander pottery is almost identical
with that of the preceding Wheeler series, a similarity that implies a continuation of the central-based, wandering adaptive strategy in this region.
Like Wheeler fiber-tempered pottery, 90 percent of the Alexander ceramics
recovered during the WPA excavations was found at only two sites, the Bluff
Creek and Perry shell middens (Haag 1942).

More recently, a third major Alexander site has been reported in the
Pickwick Basin area. This location, the Mingo site, was on a knoll on the left
bank of Little Bear Creek in Tishomingo County, Mississippi, to the south of
the basin (Jolly 1971). This site consisted of a middle Woodland burial
mound and an underlying, encapsulated village midden. The old midden
zone was found to contain a large number of Alexander sherds and Flint
Creek projectile points. The association of the Flint Creek projectile-point
cluster (or theme) and Alexander ceramics has been substantiated by three
other studies: correlation by Joseph Benthall (1965) of pottery and
projectile-point forms from a sample of Tennessee Valley sites; Fletcher
Jolly's excavations at the Buzzard Roost Creek rock shelter (1974); and work
by DeJarnette, Walthall, and Wimberly (1975a) at the Crump site to the
south in Lamar County.

David Dye of Louisiana State University has studied the Alexander culture as it is manifested in the middle Tennessee Valley. On the basis of this
research, Dye (1973) has defined a phase (the Hardin phase) for the Alexander culture in that region. He has also divided this phase into three subphases on the basis of type-frequency variation and geographical position. The
Hardin Subphase I is composed of three components located in Hardin
County, Tennessee, just downriver from the Pickwick Basin. The Hardin
Subphase II includes the Alexander components in the Pickwick, Wilson,
and lower Wheeler basins and is considered the core area of the Alexander
culture in the Valley and Ridge region. This subphase includes the Bluff
Creek, Perry, and Mingo sites, three of the largest Alexander sites yet
discovered. The Hardin Subphase III extends from the upper portion of the
Wheeler Basin in Morgan County upriver into the Guntersville Basin. Components of this subphase, the largest of which is the Flint River shell midden
(Webb and DeJarnette 1948a), contain large amounts of undecorated ware
and are considered to represent a marginal extension of the Alexander culture.

To the south, in the upper Tombigbee drainage area, DeJarnette, Walthall, and Wimberly (1975a) have identified a second Alexander phase, the
Henson Springs phase. Their survey of archaeological sites in the Buttahatchee Valley, which lies on the northern boundary of the Henson
Springs phase, revealed seven sites with Alexander components, including

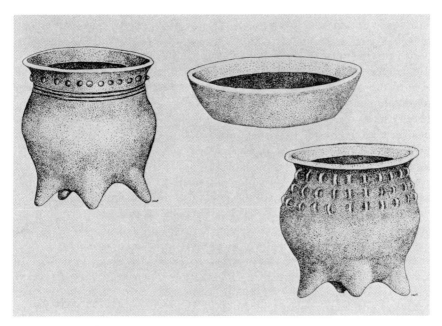

Alexander Vessels

Flint Creek Projectile Points (Brock 1969)

both open-air and bluff-shelter sites. One of these, the Crump site, proved to be a major Alexander base camp on an upper terrace of the Buttahatchee. Large numbers of Alexander pottery sherds, Flint Creek projectile points, and chipped-stone tools were recovered. The southern boundary of the Henson Springs phase is in the Gainesville Reservoir area, where other Alexander components have recently been discovered (Nielsen and Jenkins 1973; Jenkins 1975). Alexander ceramics have been reported farther down the Tombigbee, south to Mobile Bay, but the rarity of these materials suggests that their presence in these areas can be attributed to trade with contemporary Bayou La Batre peoples.

Significant amounts of Alexander pottery have also been reported from habitation sites in Noxubee and Clay counties, Mississippi. At the Broken Pumpkin Creek site, a major Henson Springs phase base camp, large quantities of Alexander sherds were collected. Richard Marshall's excavations at the Metzger site near Starkville have revealed what may be an early variety of Alexander pottery, a brown-to-reddish-buff ware that has large amounts of sand mixed with fiber tempering. This pottery is thick and undecorated but has podal supports. These Mississippi sites appear to mark the western boundary of the Henson Springs phase. Although no major Alexander components have been found to the west of these sites, small numbers of Alexander sherds, perhaps representing trade vessels, have been reported from Poverty Point, Tchefuncte, and Tchula sites in the lower Mississippi Valley. It is likely that the eastern perimeter of the Henson Springs phase is along the Sipsey River in Walker County, where other Alexander components have also been reported (Griffin 1946:51).

The genesis of the Alexander ceramic complex is unclear at present. The structural attributes of the Alexander ware appear to combine modes from several preceding or contemporary Coastal Plain ceramic complexes, including the Tchefuncte ceramics of the lower Mississippi Valley, the Bayou La Batre series of the Mobile Bay area, the Orange–Saint Johns complexes of northeastern Florida, and the Wheeler series. The major Alexander modes—sand tempering; globular and vertical-sided, cup-shaped vessels; tetrapodal supports and annular bases; and rim bosses and decorative motifs such as incising, zoning, punctating, pinching, rocker stamping, and dentate stamping—are not universally present in any one of these possible ancestral ceramic complexes. It seems likely that such a distinct combination of ceramic modes as exhibited in the Alexander complex is the product of diffusion and culture contact with several distinct Coastal Plain ethnic groups, probably over a period of several centuries. These new modes were recombined and innovatively assimilated by the Alexander potters into the local ceramic tradition.

While the question of the origin of the Alexander ceramics remains a problem, the origin of the Alexander people and their culture is better documented. Alexander ceramics temporally and spatially overlap the

Wheeler series. Wheeler sherds are found in significant amounts at every maj-
or Alexander site. (Most examples of both the Wheeler and Alexander sherds
recovered from the Pickwick Basin occur at only two sites, 1Lu⁰59 and
1Lu⁰25.) There are also structural ties between the two complexes (vertical-
sided cups and decoration by punctation and dentate stamping). These observations, combined with continuities in the Wheeler and Alexander lithic
assemblages, indicate that the introduction of Alexander ceramics into the
northwestern Alabama region was not accompanied by population movement or replacement. Rather, it appears that indigenous ethnic groups incorporated traits from other ceramic technologies into their own. If the gradual
shift from the crude Wheeler ceramics to the highly sophisticated Alexander
wares is comparable to the ugly duckling developing into a swan, strong
continuity nevertheless is implied between the cultures of which they were a
part.

6: The Woodland Stage

The first widespread usage of the term "Woodland" in North American archaeology began with the formulation of the Midwestern Taxonomic System during the 1930s. During that era, Woodland was conceived as representing one of two major cultural patterns then recognized in the region encompassing the eastern states. Since then, as dating techniques have been improved and the overall data base expanded, Woodland has come to have varied meanings to archaeologists. "Woodland" has been used to denote a tradition with considerable temporal depth, a period, and a cultural complex. "Woodland" has also been used widely to describe a developmental stage in eastern North American prehistory, and that usage will be employed in this discussion.

The beginnings of the Woodland stage are not to be found in the Southeast. The major characteristics first appeared farther north in an area extending from the upper Mississippi Valley to southern New England. Three major traits have been cited by many authorities in defining Woodland development: pottery, burial mounds, and agriculture. Beyond these specific traits it may be noted that the inception of the Woodland stage was marked by major changes in adaptive strategy, technology, social organization, and ceremonial life. Some of these cultural additions and changes began to coalesce in the East by 1000 B.C. while others made their appearance at different intervals over a span of some two millennia.

Woodland technology differs from that of the Archaic in a number of ways, but most importantly by the introduction and use of pottery and the bow and arrow. The earliest pottery in the northern regions of the East was a grit-tempered cord or plain ware commonly taking the form of a simple subconoidal base jar. It should be emphasized that this northern pottery had a different origin from that of the earlier Gulf Formational ceramics of the Southeast. During the course of Woodland development major diffusion routes were north to south, and the introduction of this northern ware resulted in a stylistic blending of ceramic modes between these two pottery complexes. One of the earliest southeastern ceramic traditions to exhibit northern characteristics was the Deptford pottery, which was finished with a carved wooden paddle. In other areas of the Southeast, where northern stimulus was weak or late, Gulf Formational ceramics continued to be produced—especially in the lower Mississippi Valley and surrounding areas.

The ultimate origins of the northern Woodland pottery are currently a topic of debate. One viewpoint that appears to be shared by members of all conflicting schools of thought is that this ceramic complex was not a product of local independent invention. Here the agreement ends. Some yet unidentified Old World source for this pottery is now thought to be best supported by the available data. It has been noted that both Siberian and Scandinavian wares are similar to early Woodland complexes and that the appearance of pottery in these areas predates North American ceramics. However, such diffusion theories are difficult to support given the lack of intermediate sites or positive evidence for such far-flung contacts.

The bow and arrow may also have Old World origins. This weapons system was developed in response to forest hunting requirements during late Pleistocene times in Europe, where it is well documented by 10,000 B.C. However, there is no evidence of the bow and arrow in eastern North America until the middle of the first millennium A.D. Why the bow was not introduced at an earlier date is unknown. Once it was adopted by eastern hunters it added a considerable advantage to the ambush hunting techniques long employed in this region.

Woodland ceremonial life was highly elaborate compared to that of earlier peoples. An integral part of this ritual was the construction of earthen tumuli (mounds) for the dead. The origin of the burial mounds, like that of Woodland pottery, is shrouded by the presence of several possible sources. Burial mounds were known in northern Asia prior to their appearance in the East, but C. S. Chard (1961) has observed that there is no geographical continuity of this custom across Asia and the intervening regions of North America. Theories of Mesoamerican origins are likewise plagued by the lack of evidence of diffusion in intervening areas.

During the early periods of burial-mound construction in the East, simple earthen tumuli were raised over the dead. As time passed, however, these mounds became increasingly complex, sometimes containing log structures; large, prepared crematory basins; and, in some instances, the remains of scores of individuals. The apex of burial-mound ceremonialism in the East occurred with the development and spread of the Hopewell cultures of the Great Lakes–Riverine region between 300 B.C. and A.D. 500. The most spectacular of these Hopewell societies was that of southern Ohio, centered in the Scioto Valley. Hopewell ceremonialism in this area included the construction of large burial mounds, huge geometric earthworks enclosing from ten to hundreds of acres, and the procurement of exotic materials through long-distance trade networks. These raw materials were manufactured into a wide variety of status-oriented finished products that ultimately functioned as grave furniture upon the demise of their holders.

James B. Griffin (1967:184) has summarized the nature and extent of Ohio Hopewell trade and art as follows:

> The acquisition of nonlocal raw materials by trading parties, which was a significant activity in Late Archaic and Early Woodland times, reaches striking

proportions particularly in Ohio Hopewell. Large amounts of copper were
obtained from pits in the Lake Superior native copper deposits. Silver was
sometimes naturally associated in the copper, but silver was also obtained from
deposits near Cobalt, Ontario. Meteoric iron was combined with copper in
ornaments, and meteoric specimens were found at ten sites in Ohio, at two
sites in Illinois, at one site in west central Georgia, and at Crystal River and
Murphy Island, Florida. . . . Mica, quartz crystal, aventurine, and chlorite
were obtained from the southern Appalachians. Large marine shells such as
Cassis were obtained from the Florida east coast, while *Busycon, Fasciolaria,*
and smaller marine snail shells such as *Marginella, Oliva* and *Olivella* came
from the southeast and the Florida Gulf Coast. Other items used in decoration,
probably from west Florida, include alligator teeth, shark teeth, ocean turtle
shells, and barracuda jaws.

The galena cubes found at Hopewell sites were probably from western
sources, perhaps from northwestern Illinois, or Missouri; nodular flint came
from Harrison County, Indiana, or similar quarries near Cobden in Union
County, Illinois. Recent neutron activation studies at the University of Michigan indicate that obsidian was obtained from what is now Yellowstone Park,
while a mottled brownish chalcedony is said to be from quarries along the
Knife River in North Dakota or from gravel deposits in southern Manitoba. . . .

Ohio Hopewell art was highly developed and is expressed in a variety of
ways. The platform effigy pipes are naturalistically sculptured and skillfully
portray many animal, bird, and fish forms, as well as a few human heads.
Figurines of clay are of a somewhat similar naturalistic style. There are two-
dimensional representations on sheets of copper and mica, of mammals, fish,
and birds, and of portions of these animals. There are also human figures,
hands, and heads. Some of the representations, on this copper, of the turkey
buzzard, parrot, and eagle have feathers, wings, and other features embossed
in the copper. Cut-out designs include the suavastika (a swastika with the arms
extending to the left). Some of the cut-out designs may have been used as
stencils in painting finely woven cloth of native bast fibers. The swastika, also,
was used on a sculptured stone head. Still another art form was a fine engraving
on bone, with highly conventionalized designs, primarily of birds and animals.
Many of these engravings were on human leg and arm bones.

While the ultimate source of Woodland burial mounds in the North is
debatable, no such conflict exists concerning the origin of these structures in
the Southeast. It is well documented that burial mounds in this region were
derived from middle (classic) Hopewell in the Midwest. The development of
Woodland burial-mound practices in the Southeast can be viewed in a series
of three periods, which can be termed Burial Mound 1, 2, and 3. Arabic
numerals are used in the names of these Southeastern periods to avoid
confusion with Ford's and Willey's earlier conceptual units, Burial Mound I
and II, which have a pan-eastern application.

The Southeastern Burial Mound 1 period (A.D. 1–300), which encompasses
the earliest phases of Woodland burial-mound construction in this region,

corresponds to middle Hopewell in the Ohio area. This mortuary custom reached the Southeast shortly after the beginning of the first millennium A.D., probably via Hopewell trade. Mounds dating to this period exhibit strong similarities to northern Hopewell structures, and the grave goods found within them are usually classic Hopewell in style. Artifacts such as copper panpipes and earspools, anthropomorphic figurines, elaborate platform pipes, and exotic pottery vessels are often characteristic of these early complexes. Mounds or mound complexes that date to this initial period include those associated with the Marksville culture of the lower Mississippi Valley, the Miller I phase of northeastern Mississippi, the early Porter phase of the Mobile Bay region, the Yent complex of northern Florida, portions of the Mandeville mounds in southwestern Georgia, and the Tunacunnhee mounds of northwestern Georgia.

The Burial Mound 2 period in the Southeast (A.D. 300–600) corresponds to terminal Hopewell in the north. During this time, the once vigorous Hopewellian trade systems declined in both volume of exchange and in areal extent. Southeastern mound complexes dating to this period exhibit increasing regional differentiation. Midwestern Hopewell trade goods are relatively rare in these manifestations and were largely replaced by locally produced substitutes of widely varying styles. Ethnic groups once involved in the northern Hopewell exchange systems apparently created a series of smaller, often localized trade spheres with surrounding ethnic groups as influence from the north waned. Mortuary ceremonialism also evolved into diverse forms. In the highland areas certain peoples began to utilize caves as natural tombs for the dead, and customs of burial preparation varied widely from tribe to tribe. Major long-distance trade goods found in some of these Burial Mound 2 complexes include copper beads, earspools, reel-shaped gorgets, galena, Gulf coast shell cups and beads, and greenstone implements. Mounds or mound complexes associated with this period include Copena in the middle Tennessee Valley, the Miller II structures, the Porter phase McQuorquodale mound, and the Green Point complex of Florida. The Connestee folk of western North Carolina and eastern Tennessee also participated in this interaction sphere, as did the Swift Creek peoples of southwestern Georgia.

The Burial Mound 3 period (A.D. 600–1000) was a post-Hopewell development characterized by a cessation of mound building over wide areas, a sharp decrease in trade, further regional specialization, and by the rise and spread of the Weeden Island mortuary system along the Gulf coast. Small conical earthen mounds, often containing the remains of less than a dozen individuals, are characteristic of this time. Layers or pavements of stone or shell were constructed over individual burials or over the entire structure. Marine shell cups and ornaments were the only traditional long-distance trade goods exchanged during this period, although, rarely, copper ornaments and elbow pipes are found. Weeden Island mortuary pottery also appears to have been traded widely, and small amounts of this ware are known as far as four hundred miles inland. Mound complexes dating to the Burial Mound 3 period include those of the Weeden Island cultures of northern Florida, southern Georgia, and southern Alabama, the Hope Hull phase of the Alabama River, the Coker Ford phase of the upper Coosa Valley, and the Hamilton culture of eastern Tennessee.

Pipes first appeared in the East during late Archaic times. However, it was during the Woodland stage that pipes and a smoking ritual became an integral part of ceremonial life. Among northern groups the elaborately carved stone platform pipes were popular, while southern tribes preferred the large elbow variety made of clay or stone. In both regions pipes are rarely, if ever, found in habitation refuse. Almost universally, they were carefully placed with the deceased in burial mounds, attesting to the ceremonial nature of the pipe. Indian tobacco (*Nicotiana rustica*), thought to be native to South America, may have been used at this time, but as yet there is no direct evidence. However, by the historic period tobacco, as well as the leaves, bark, roots, and flowers of over twenty-seven indigenous species of plants, were smoked. Mixtures, called "kinnikkinnik," were popular. The most common mixture of this type included tobacco, sumac leaves, and dogwood bark (Knight 1975).

Concomitant with these Woodland technological and ceremonial developments was the pan-regional diffusion of the tropical cultigen maize. This crop was added to a complex of plants whose use dates back to late Archaic times in some areas of the East. These domesticates consisted of squash and certain indigenous pioneer annuals notable for their hardiness, for their high potential productivity, and for their adaptability to disturbed soil conditions (Struever and Vickery 1973). This latter complex of cultigens or possible cultigens includes pigweed (*Amaranthus*), lamb's quarter (*Chenopodium*), knotweed (*Polygonum*), marsh elder (*Iva*), giant ragweed (*Ambrosia trifida*), may grass (*Phalaris caroliniana*), and sunflower (*Helianthus annua*). Sunflower seeds have been identified by Richard Yarnell from botanical remains from the Higgs site in the upper Tennessee Valley, radiocarbon dated to 900–1000 B.C. (McCollough and Faulkner 1973), and remains of squash have been reported at several sites in the Southeast on a late Archaic time level.

While food production may have been of economic importance among some Woodland societies, hunting and gathering continued as major economic activities over broad areas. Woodland subsistence represents a continuation, on a modified basis, of the Archaic limited spectrum economy. Certain foods, such as acorns, were utilized on an unprecedented scale, especially after the introduction of ceramic vessels for processing and cooking. Acorns, as well as hickory nuts and walnuts, were collected by the ton to be processed into food and vegetable oil. These crops were especially valuable because they could be stored for use during the lean winter months.

In aboriginal times acorns were often cracked and boiled to remove the tannic acid, but other techniques of preparation were widely known and practiced. One major process involved grinding the nut meats and placing the meal into shallow pits dug near a stream. Water was then poured over and through the meal in the manner of making drip coffee. This leaching process was repeated until the bitter taste was eliminated. The meal was then added to stews or dried and baked (Driver 1965). Modern connoisseurs of natural foods may likewise prepare acorns for use as snacks or breads by following these procedures:

1. Shell the kernels.
2. Leach out the tannic acid by boiling the acorn meats in water, changing the water each time it becomes light brown. This is best accomplished by pouring the kernels into fresh, boiling water. Leaching in this manner takes about an hour of boiling to remove the bitterness.
3. Remove the kernels, drain, and place on a cloth in the sun, or dry in an oven turned to its lowest heat. When dried, the meats are ready to salt and eat like peanuts or grind in a food chopper for making bread meal.

Hickory nuts and walnuts were also used as staples, but their oil was considered to be of primary importance. These nuts were ground, shell and all, and boiled slowly in water. In boiling, the fragments of shell would sink to the bottom, the oil float to the surface, and the meats swim slightly above the shells. The oil was skimmed off first, sometimes with a large feather, to be stored for use as cooking oil or hair or skin lotion. The meats were then collected and were often dried in cakes and preserved for winter use. When needed, these nut-meat cakes were soaked in warm water and cooked (Fernald and Kinsey 1943).

Woodland village life was characterized by community self-sufficiency. Each ethnic group controlled access to all of the resources needed to sustain its members throughout the year. Thus these groups did not have to rely upon other peoples to provide essential goods and services. As a consequence, these economically autonomous groups were forced to space themselves efficiently throughout their territory to acquire needed resources.

These organizational requirements and demographic pressures resulted in changes in sociopolitical systems during the Woodland stage. The most common form of sociopolitical organization during this time was the tribe, although in rare instances certain groups, such as Ohio Hopewell, may have attained more complex levels of organization. Probably the most widespread type of tribal society in the forested East during Woodland times was the segmentary tribe. E. R. Service (1962) and M. D. Sahlins (1968) have summarized the salient characteristics of this level of tribal society. It can be inferred that many Woodland cultures shared a number of the general traits these two describe.

The segmentary tribe was divided into small, local communities that rarely included more than a hundred members and most commonly claimed no more than a few square miles of territory. These communities were generally organized through a single descent group or lineage or, at times, by an association of several lineages. Each communal group was politically equal. While these primary political segments constituting the tribal whole might ally for a time and purpose, such as warfare or ceremony, the union was episodic. As soon as the objective of the alliance was accomplished, the tribe returned to its normal state of disunity.

The social organization of segmentary tribes was egalitarian in nature. Fried (1960) defines an egalitarian society as one in which there are as many positions of prestige in any age-sex grade as there are persons capable of filling them. While among segmentary tribes certain individuals, such as the official community spokesman, might hold office through ascribed authority (birthright), their distinction and power were slight. Usually, real authority was acquired, at least for brief periods of time, by individuals with special skills. Thus, if such a tribal group had five big men who were strong— successful hunters, shamen, or war leaders—then there would be five "strong men." If there were three or six or one, there would be that many "strong men."

The economy of the segmentary tribe was small-scale, with enough man-power available in each community to carry out the main tasks of livelihood. Each settlement produced much the same thing. The economy was not integrated by a localized division of labor nor by exchange of complementary goods and services. The local economy reflected the tribal economy in miniature. Each community's territory incorporated the full range of environments and natural resources to which the technology was adapted. The community had access to collecting and hunting grounds and, in some instances, to agricultural lands as well.

While exchange among the local communities of the segmentary tribe might develop in the form of social or kin obligations, trade with foreign groups was more common. Among some Woodland societies exotic goods, obtained from trade partners or through systems of barter, often ended up as grave offerings. In these tribal groups such offerings might have been indicators of achieved status (Binford 1962) or might have reflected incipient concepts of ranking that were emerging from contacts with societies on a more complex level of socioeconomic integration (Flannery 1968b).

In the various regions encompassed by present-day Alabama, Woodland cultures were diverse and widespread. The remainder of this chapter will be devoted to the nature and development of these societies, as we can now reconstruct them from archaeological data. These summary statements have

Table 3: Woodland Chronology: Alabama Region

	Tennessee Valley	Coosa	Tombigbee	Mobile Bay	Alabama River	Chattahoochee
A.D. 1000 Late Woodland	McKelvey Flint River	Coker Ford	Miller III	Tates Hammock McLeod	Autauga Hope Hull Henderson Dead River	Weeden Island Late Swift Creek
A.D. 500 Late Middle Woodland	Copena	Yanceys Bend	Miller II	Porter	Calloway	Early Swift Creek
A.D. 100 Early Middle Woodland 300 B.C.	Colbert	Cedar Bluff	Miller I		Cobbs Swamp	Deptford

been organized by major culture areas in order to trace the specific evolution of Woodland manifestations.

The Middle Tennessee Valley

Colbert: 300 B.C.–A.D. 100

Beginning about 300 B.C., new artifact forms appeared at certain archaeological sites in the middle Tennessee Valley. The most diagnostic of these, a fabric-impressed, limestone-tempered pottery, is a marker for the emergence of the Woodland stage in highland northern Alabama. This type of earthenware first appeared to the north during early Woodland times but did not diffuse southward to the Alabama area until the beginning of the subsequent middle Woodland period. Thus in Alabama and some surrounding regions earlier developmental stages temporally paralleled the emergence of Woodland culture in the Northeast and Midwest. In the middle Tennessee Valley, the initial Woodland sequence can be divided into two segments: (1) the early middle Woodland characterized by fabric-impressed, limestone-tempered pottery; and (2) the late middle Woodland typified by carved paddle-stamped, limestone-tempered ceramics and the emergence of Hopewellian mortuary ceremonialism.

The archaeological sites yielding attributes of the early middle Woodland development in this region can be placed into a single unit, the Colbert culture. The term "Colbert" was first applied to archaeological manifestations in this area by James B. Griffin (1946:52), who included both fabric- and check-stamped wares in what he termed the "Colbert Focus." Joseph Caldwell (1958) continued this usage but appears to have modified the concept to include only the fabric-impressed pottery. Caldwell's modified usage will be followed here, but the term "focus" is dropped in favor of the designation "culture" in keeping with more recent classificatory terminology.

Colbert ceramics are drab and do not compare aesthetically to the earlier work of the skillful Alexander potters. However unpleasing to the eye, Colbert pottery was nonetheless highly utilitarian and well suited for a forest existence. This ceramic complex comprises two finish types, the Long Branch series (Sears and Griffin 1950): Long Branch Fabric Impressed and Mulberry Creek Plain. The exteriors of Long Branch vessels were commonly finished with a fabric-wrapped wooden paddle that left wickerlike impressions in the soft clay. A cord-wrapped stick or dowel was also at times carefully applied in imitation of the fabric impression.

The weave pattern imprinted on Long Branch ware varies from a tight, intricate design to a loose, almost netlike simple weave. Only a single vessel form is known, a wide-mouthed globular jar with a conoidal base. The rim form is often flared, and in later times tetrapodal supports were added.

Colbert Village Sites in Northern Alabama

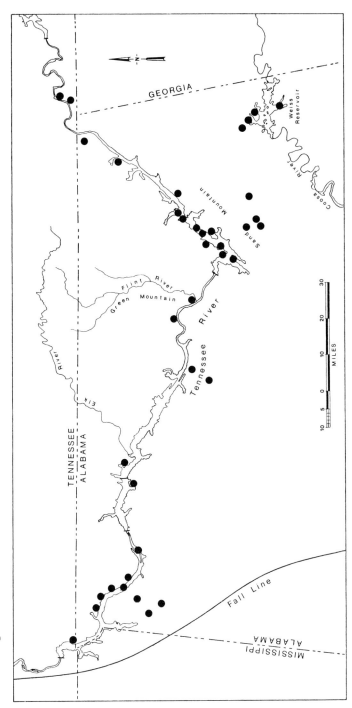

Several radiocarbon determinations have been made on organic samples found in association with Long Branch pottery. These suggest that this ware diffused down the Tennessee River to the Guntersville Basin around 300 B.C. and continued to be produced through the first century A.D. in some areas.

The number and distribution of Colbert habitation sites indicate substantial population expansion, a shift in settlement patterns, and the emergence of a new perception of the environment. During late Archaic and Gulf Formational times, the Pickwick Basin area was the center of major population concentration in the middle Tennessee Valley, while the Guntersville Basin was only sparsely inhabited. This pattern was due in large part to the availability of such resources as shellfish, which were easily procured in the Pickwick Basin area where shallow shoal waters provided an ideal environment for dozens of species. However, the low gradient and high bluffs that characterize the river in the Guntersville Basin produce a deep, relatively sluggish stream, both unfavorable conditions for shellfish.

During Colbert times the shell middens of the Pickwick Basin continued to be extensively occupied, and, in fact, there is evidence of increased exploitation of riverine resources at this time. In the preceding late Gulf Formational period only two of these shell middens appear to have been heavily occupied, while substantial evidence of Colbert settlement has been recovered from nine localities. Upstream in the upper Wheeler Basin, two additional large Colbert shell middens have been located, Ma10, the Whitesburg Bridge site, which contains an almost pure Colbert component, and Ma48, the Flint River site (Webb and DeJarnette 1948a, b). However, with the inception of the Colbert occupation of the middle Tennessee Valley, the most dramatic evidence of population increase is found in the Guntersville Basin. Here, almost a dozen major Colbert villages were established in or near the bottomlands, and rock shelters in the surrounding highland forests were intensively utilized. The new economic orientation reflected in this demographic pattern appears to have been centered around access to the floodplain. Villages were at times established near shellfish beds when they were present but were often located in or along the edge of the floodplain. Although at present there is a lack of good ethnobotanical data, we do have sufficient evidence to postulate a settlement model for the Colbert occupation of the Guntersville Basin.

The highland plateau of the Guntersville Basin region is dissected by the Sequatchie Valley, through which the Tennessee River flows southward until it reaches Guntersville, where its direction is altered westward, forming the Great Bend. This topographical situation created two major environmental zones. The Plateau subregion, bordering both sides of the valley, has an average elevation of 1,000 feet above sea level with a maximum elevation of 1,800 feet. The descent to the valley floor is abrupt, forming a sharply defined ecotone. The average difference in elevation between valley and plateau is 500 feet, with a maximum of 1,000 feet in some areas. Many small streams flow out of the plateau, creating deep gorges that add to the ecological diversity of the region. The plateau forest contains nine species of oak and three species of hickory. In the fall, when forest seeds ripen and drop, deer, turkey, and bear congregate in the uplands. Below these plateau forests, the Sequatchie Valley supports a mixed mesophytic woodland, a remnant of a plant community that once extended over much of the northern hemisphere. In these bottomlands, especially on the moist slopes and in the cool ravines of the valley border, are found eight species of oak, two species of hickory, and one species each of walnut and chestnut. The valley floor was flooded annually in prehistoric times, leaving large areas of barren silt deposits—an ideal environment for annual grasses and floodplain horticulture.

During the WPA investigations of archaeological sites to be inundated by the construction of Guntersville Dam, eleven major Colbert components were found in the bottoms or on the many low islands in the river (Webb and Wilder 1951). Several of these sedentary or semisedentary villages were situated on the riverbanks, but others were back from the river on upper terraces near small tributary streams. This situation is paralleled in areas to the west in the Wheeler Basin region, where villages were often established well back from the main river channel (Nielsen 1972). These valley settlements, at times covering almost two acres, contain many storage pits, fire hearths and earth ovens, and post holes. Milling equipment is also commonly found at these sites, attesting to the importance of seed foods in the Colbert diet. During the warm months deer and other game concentrate in the valley, where greens and other floodplain flora provide abundant food. It appears likely that during the warm season Colbert peoples living in these settlements practiced floodplain horticulture, hunted, fished, and gathered greens and seeds from bottomland annuals. Miller's (1960) report of a charred basket containing *Chenopodium* seeds in an early middle Woodland deposit at Russell Cave adds some support to this reconstruction. Nut foods were collected in the valley and along the plateau slopes in the fall and were stored in subterranean pits, at times lined with mats of woven plant fibers or bark. Work parties left the villages in the fall and winter, perhaps for extended periods of time, to hunt and collect in the upland forests, occupying highland rock shelters. In the nine small shelters excavated by Clayton (1965, 1967) on Sand Mountain, Colbert ceramics were by far the most common pottery found. Clayton observed that this pottery was associated at these sites with numerous mortars and milling stones, probably used for nut processing. Male-related artifacts such as projectile points and butchering tools were proportionately numerous in the Colbert zones, suggesting that these shelters also functioned as hunting camps; deer constituted a high proportion of all faunal remains recovered from these sites. To the northwest across the valley, Russell Cave was also utilized by Colbert foraging parties for much the same purposes as these Sand Mountain shelters (J. W. Griffin 1974).

One of the Colbert valley settlements excavated during the WPA investigations has recently been studied (Walthall 1973a). This site, the MacDonald village, is in Marshall County on the upland valley edge immediately east of the present shoreline of Guntersville Lake. The occupied area encompassed some 1.5 acres along the summit of a ridge paralleling a small tributary stream. The southern portion of the site was extensively excavated, revealing large numbers of storage pits, earth ovens, and hearths. Some of the pits measured almost three feet in depth and two to five feet in diameter. There were many scattered post holes, indicating the former presence of timber structures. Major pottery types in the ceramic sample were Long Branch Fabric Impressed (62 percent) and Mulberry Creek Plain (30 percent). A small amount of check- and simple-stamped pottery was also recovered, but these types were less than 1 percent of the total sherd count. The lithic assemblage included straight-stemmed and medium, triangular projectile points; biface knives; drills; scrapers; greenstone celts; and milling equipment. Vessels of steatite and sandstone were also associated with the Colbert occupation. This occurrence represents the final use of stone containers in the middle Tennessee Valley, for they have not been found in association with later assemblages.

The burials found at the MacDonald site are of special interest. Two major types of interments were found in the village area—flexed and extended burials exhibiting traits of the later Copena mortuary system. The flexed burials can be related to the Colbert occupation. Some of these were associated with steatite vessels or vessel fragments and with Long Branch Fabric Impressed sherds. Steatite vessels have also been reported in association with Colbert burials at the Robinson village in Morgan County (Walthall 1973a) and at the Whitesburg Bridge shell midden in Madison County (Webb and DeJarnette 1948b). The MacDonald village burials indicate that substantial changes in mortuary ceremonialism occurred during the first centuries A.D. During Colbert times burial preparation was comparatively simple: The individual was placed into a small pit, at times an abandoned storage chamber, with his legs bound to the body. Only rarely were grave goods placed into the burial pit. Grave associations were generally confined to stone vessels, but on occasion, utilitarian objects such as projectile points or bone tools were also deposited. Later Copena mortuary ceremonialism was much more elaborate and the burial of the dead played a much more significant role in Copena ideology.

Copena: A.D. *100–500*

The term "Copena," coined during the 1930s as the name for a complex of burial mounds discovered in the Tennessee Valley region of northern

Alabama, is derived from the first three letters of "copper" and the last three of "galena," minerals frequently found in these mounds as burial furniture. In more recent times the usage of this term has been expanded to apply to the entire cultural system of which the mounds were a part. Copena sites now include the original burial mounds, related habitation sites, and a complex of associated burial caves.

The Copena mortuary complex was first formally defined by William S. Webb in his report on the Wheeler Basin survey of 1934. During this depression decade two additional hydroelectric dams (Pickwick and Guntersville) were built by the Tennessee Valley Authority in the Alabama region. The archaeological surveys in the areas to be inundated by their construction resulted in the discovery of more Copena mounds, the rediscovery of a Copena burial cave, and ultimately the recognition of a Copena habitation site (Webb and DeJarnette 1942; Webb and Wilder 1951). During the final stages of the WPA-TVA survey project (1940–1941), archaeological teams were allowed to investigate sites along or outside the reservoir areas. Some fifteen Copena burial mounds and two additional villages were located and excavated. The outbreak of World War II halted the compilation of the results of this final effort, and it was not until 1973 that reports on these sites were made public in the form of a doctoral dissertation by John Walthall (1973a).

The Copena mortuary sites excavated in conjunction with the TVA projects were not the first such sites to have been discovered. In 1890 Cyrus Thomas, Bureau of American Ethnology archaeologist, reported the discovery of two caves in northern Alabama in which burials were found in association with artifacts later interpreted as diagnostic of Copena. It was not until some twenty-five years later, however, that Copena burial mounds were located and excavated by Clarence B. Moore (1915). In his career, Moore investigated archaeological sites along every major waterway in the southeastern United States. While in light of modern standards Moore's excavation techniques were crude, his results were nothing less than spectacular. He began an investigation of the Tennessee Valley in January 1914, and before his explorations of this region were completed he and his crew had traversed the 652-mile-river no less than three times. Moore located seven Copena mounds and mound groups and was the first investigator to link specific Copena artifacts with Ohio Hopewell.

Recently, Walthall and DeJarnette (1974) have reported the existence of five more Copena burial caves in northern Alabama in addition to the two previously reported by Thomas. The burials in these latter caverns demonstrate the diversity of Copena burial preparation. Hampton Cave in Marshall County was rediscovered and investigated as part of the Guntersville Basin survey (Webb and Wilder 1951). It was located on the side of a steep bluff some two hundred feet above the valley floor, a position that made it unsuitable for habitation. One of the interior rooms was found to contain a deposit of ash and charred human bone four feet deep, although the original depth may have been greater, in view of Thomas's reports that local farmers had hauled away much of the deposit for use as fertilizer. Numbers of artifacts were recovered from the extant deposit, which must have contained the remains of scores of the Copena dead. All of the grave goods exhibited evidence of firing, indicating that they had been placed with the deceased before cremation. Among the objects discovered were copper reel-shaped gorgets, cut sheets, beads, and earspools; marine-shell cups and beads; galena nodules; a pearl bead; and stone projectile points, one a stemmed form of quartz crystal.

The second cavern originally reported by Thomas, Cramp's Cave, located to the south in Blount County, has been the subject of more recent discussion by Walthall (1974). The interior rooms of Cramp's Cave were dry, preserving normally perishable associations. Burials were found deposited in long wooden troughs or canoe-shaped coffins, a practice also noted at one of the Wright mounds. Grave goods found in and around the troughs included copper ornaments, marine-shell cups, and wooden bowls and trays that may have once contained offerings of food. The deceased were wrapped in bark or cane matting bound with withes or bark. The burials found within these

Wooden Troughs from Cramp's Cave, Blount County, AMNH 356 CAL

caves compare favorably with those recovered in burial-mound context. Estimates of the numbers of individuals contained within these natural tombs suggest that caves played an important part in the Copena mortuary system. To date, only seven of these caves have been located and verified by professional archaeologists; however, over a dozen others have been reported but upon investigation proved to have been looted or vandalized to such an extent that verification could not be made.

Over the years, some fifty Copena burial mounds have been discovered in the middle Tennessee Valley region. These mounds are typically low, relatively small conoidal structures made of sand or clay, constructed over subsoil burial pits and usually containing numbers of secondary burials within the mound fill. The most typical burial position is extended on the back, but flexed and bundle burials are also known. Cremation was also commonly practiced. Burial preparation was at times elaborate, including specially prepared pits lined with foreign puddled clays and logs or bark. Burials were occasionally placed into log or bark troughs and wrapped in bark matting.

The most characteristic artifacts associated with the Copena mound burials were copper reel-shaped gorgets, earspools, bracelets, breastplates, celts, and beads; marine-shell cups and beads; long stemless projectile points; ground galena nodules; greenstone celts and digging implements; and large steatite elbow pipes, the earliest pipes of this form in eastern North America. Pottery vessels were not placed into the burial pits, and only rarely are ceramic vessel fragments found in the mound fill—perhaps remnants of jars brought to the mortuary site to be used in the preparation of the specialized puddled clays. In fact, only two ceramic artifacts have been recovered in direct association with Copena burials, a limestone-tempered elbow pipe and a pottery disk. Pottery disks have also been recovered from Copena village middens. Some have a central perforation and may have been used in weaving or as game pieces, although their actual function is unknown. Disks of this type are usually thought characteristic of later Mississippian cultures, and their association with Copena marks their earliest recorded appearance in the East.

Radiocarbon tests run on samples of charred bark from subsoil burials found in two Copena mounds resulted in dates of A.D. 320 and A.D. 375 (Walthall 1972). Based upon these determinations and relative dating calculations, a time span of A.D. 100 to 500 can be postulated for the Copena culture, although it seems probable that Copena mortuary ceremonialism reached a peak around A.D. 300, during late Hopewell times.

David DeJarnette in his 1952 summary of Alabama archaeology provided a generalized description of the construction techniques utilized in building the Copena mounds.

> Before beginning the actual mound construction, Copena adherents usually buried separately several individuals (precedent burials) in long, oval pits.

Copena Burial Mound Partially Excavated at Colbert Creek Site, AMNH 14 Lu 54

Copena Burial with Copper Reel at Columbus City Landing Site, AMNH 65 Ms 91

Copena Projectile Points from Fisher Mound, AMNH 98 Hn 4

Steatite Dog Pipe from the Harris Copena Mound, AMNH 25 La 37

Copena Elbow Pipes, AMNH 498 CAL. *Left to right*, Steatite, Ceramic/Limestone-tempered, Sandstone

They would shape each pit with care and make the bottom level; then they would floor the bottom with a layer of clay, spreading the clay by puddling it. Sometimes they would shape a low clay "pillow" and foot rest. They would then lower the body (in an extended position, face upward) into the grave, and after placing with the body carefully arranged burial offerings, they would often completely seal both body and offerings with another layer of clay. Sometimes they would place small logs on either side of the body; at other times they might cover the body with bark.

Leaving piled beside the grave the earth they had thrown up in digging it, they would bring sand and clay from elsewhere to refill the grave. After they had made in this manner a number of closely grouped burials the Copena people began the actual mound construction, bringing sand and clay to cover all the graves in the group, and covering also the heaps of earth that had been piled up in digging the precedent graves. As they deposited the sand and clay, and before any definite mound had been formed, they would add other burials (inclusive burials). In making these inclusive burials they sometimes flexed the body fully, sometimes extended it, sometimes laid down lone heads or skulls, or disarticulated body members or bones. Sometimes they laid down fragments of bodies that had been cremated.

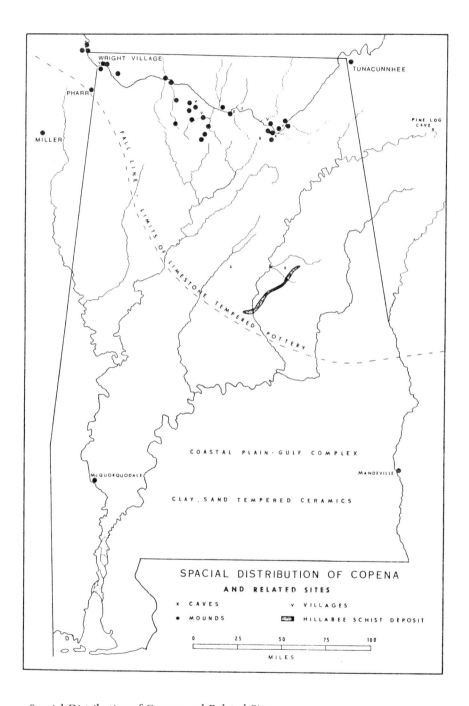

Spacial Distribution of Copena and Related Sites

When their deposits of sand and clay had accumulated to a moderate size, mound construction was completed with a final capping of sand and clay, after which no further burials (no intrusive burials) were added. [1952:278]

The mortuary sites the Copena peoples left behind reveal the full spectrum of construction stages. They range from precedent burial areas upon which no mound was yet raised to incipient mounds containing only a few subsoil burials to intermediate stages containing small numbers of both primary and secondary burials to completed mounds sometimes containing over a hundred primary and secondary burials and capped with a final layer of clay and sand.

Variations in mound size are most probably the result of two major factors, the length of time in which the mortuary site was utilized and the size of the social unit participating in the funerary activities. Charles Faulkner of the University of Tennessee compared Copena to the Illinois Havana Hopewell and Ohio Scioto Hopewell manifestations and made the following observations concerning mound size, distribution, and social organization.

It has been recently suggested that Hopewellian complexes were on different levels of societal organization (Struever 1965:212–214). For example, Havana Hopewell mounds are distributed over long stretches of river valley and are grouped into small clusters containing few status burials, whereas Scioto Hopewell mounds are restricted to certain areas within planned earthworks and the mounds contain numerous status burials and elaborate artifacts made by specialized craftsmen. Copena mounds are scattered along the Tennessee River between three and five miles apart and contain simple tombs with few burials that have been provided with exotic grave goods (Butler 1968:18). Struever's (1965:213) suggestion that the Illinois mounds served small local communities and were constructed by kin groups rather than a regional work force probably applies as well to the Copena mounds. It is likely that the level of societal organization in Copena was closer to that found in the Havana tradition than that characterizing Scioto Hopewell. [1970:109]

These observations are further supported by comparisons of labor requirements necessary for the construction of the Ohio and Tennessee Valley mounds, by the clear evidence of ranking and individual accumulation of wealth in the former, and by the equally lucid evidence of a more egalitarian social system in the latter. Copena burial mounds range in height from three to ten feet, with an average of six feet. They average fifty feet in diameter at the base with a maximum range of from thirty to ninety feet. Using the average dimensions as a base, it can be estimated that Copena mounds commonly contain some 24,000 cubic feet of earth. On the other hand, Ohio Hopewell mounds, which average about one hundred feet in basal diameter and thirty feet in height, usually contain almost half a million cubic feet of earth. Rough calculations indicate that some four thousand man-hours would be required to construct a typical Copena mound, while over two hundred thousand man-hours would have been necessary to raise a common Ohio Hopewell mound. Thus the energy expenditure ratio for the construction of these tumuli would be on the order of 1:50. Considering the enormous number of man-hours required to build the huge Ohio Hopewell earthworks, it is vividly apparent that a vast difference exists in the magnitude of labor requirements for such projects. Some sort of corvée labor system and a large work force were certainly required for the construction of the monumental Hopewell structures, while the efforts of a small work party of kinsmen were all that was required to raise a Copena mound.

The Ohio Hopewell mounds also contain evidence of wide divergence in energy expenditure in preparation of burials and accumulation of wealth by certain individuals. Many burials contained few or no grave offerings, while others are known to have contained huge caches of goods. For example, one Ohio Hopewell burial was accompanied by over one hundred animal effigy pipes, another contained several hundred pounds of rare obsidian, and another over one hundred thousand freshwater pearls. The egalitarian nature of the Copena society is demonstrated by the fact that the most elaborate burial ever discovered in this mortuary complex contained only eight objects. Many Copena burials were accompanied by one or two objects, while most were barren of grave goods. These data indicate two widely varying societies, suggesting that Ohio Hopewell populations were organized on a chiefdom level of socioeconomic complexity, while the Copena society favored the segmentary tribe with its more egalitarian status system.

Copena mortuary offerings can be classified into two major categories on the basis of source. The first of these contains objects that could have been obtained locally or that could have been obtained from adjoining regions by either direct procurement expeditions or through exchange with kinsmen. Such objects as greenstone celts and hoes, steatite pipes, projectile points, and perhaps some copper could have all been obtained in either the Copena territory or from neighboring regions. Artifacts of this nature constitute the most common grave goods found at Copena mortuary sites. The second category of artifacts consists of those not locally available and not obtainable except through long-distance trade. Only three major classes of such goods are found in Copena. Copper ornaments have direct stylistic antecedents in Ohio Hopewell, and a large number must have had their ultimate source in that culture. The second artifact class derived through long-distance trade consists of marine-shell cups and beads. It appears likely that these objects were obtained from ethnic groups to the south and not through trade with Ohio Hopewell, since the majority of the large shell cups from the Ohio mounds belong to the Atlantic coast genus *Cassis* while only the genus *Busycon* has been found at Copena sites. Galena was obtained from sources in the Upper Mississippi Valley, perhaps also via Ohio Hope-

Woven Fabric Preserved by Copper Salts from a Copena Burial, AMNH 492 CAL

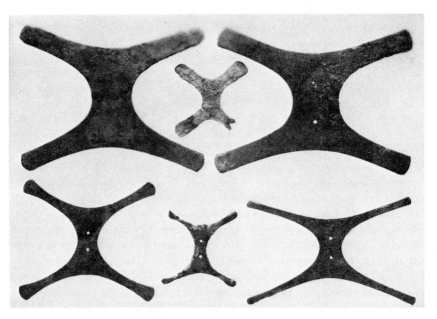

Copena Copper Reels, AMNH 497 CAL

well. Rocker-stamped, cord-marked, and brushed pottery sherds from vessels perhaps ultimately derived from the Ohio Valley have been found in ceramic collections from two Copena villages, but they are rare (not more than five or six vessels are represented).

Not counting beads (of which about 1,000 are known) some 154 copper objects have been recovered from the fifty Copena mounds, an average of about 3 per structure. The Copena copper sample includes 55 reels, 25 celts, 4 breastplates, 29 cut sheets (for bead manufacture?), and 41 earspools. While this total is greater than the sum of *all* of the other Hopewellian-style copper objects found in the entire Southeast, it does not suggest extensive exchange if we take into account that one Ohio tumulus, the Seip mound, contained some 188 copper objects, including 24 celts, 46 breastplates, and 52 earspools.

The number and distribution of Copena copper objects and their stylistic homogeneity raise the possibility that all of the copper artifacts found in Copena context could conceivably represent the result of a single exchange transaction. The discovery of a cache of Hopewell copper at the Ohio Fort Ancient site suggests the nature and size of trade bundles. Recovered in 1898, this find contained 59 copper specimens, including reels, breastplates, celts, earspools and bracelets, a sheet of mica, and 54 pieces of galena—all typical of trade goods found in Copena graves. An exchange transaction consisting of only three bundles of this size could have supplied all of the copper ever recovered in Copena context. If we consider that Ohio Hopewell and Copena coexisted for as long as four hundred years, the data presently available do not support either intensive or continuous trade between these populations.

Two major types of Copena habitation sites are known—open-air villages in or near the bottomlands and upland rock-shelter camps. Copena occupations at both are characterized by high percentages of limestone-tempered plain and carved paddle-stamped ceramics, and by minor-to-rare amounts of fabric-impressed, cord-marked, brushed, and rocker-stamped wares. Variations in the proportions of the major stamped-finish types (check, simple, and complicated varieties) appear to have both spatial and temporal significance and will probably serve as major markers for future subdivisions of Copena into finer developmental units.

The cord-marked, brushed, and rocker-stamped types are confined to the Copena territory east of Green Mountain, from the Flint River upstream into the Guntersville Basin. It was in this area that plain and brushed limestone-tempered pottery became the major finish treatments during late Woodland times. That brushing was introduced during the late middle Woodland is clearly demonstrated by the recovery at the Flint River site (Webb and DeJarnette 1948) of smoothed check- and simple-stamped sherds with overbrushing on their surfaces. All three of these eastern Copena types were recovered from the midden deposit at the Walling I village near the confluence of the Flint and Tennessee rivers (Walthall 1973a). The presence of these types at this site is important in tracing their introduction into the Tennessee Valley from northern Hopewell sources.

The Great South Trail, a major aboriginal artery leading northward into the Nashville Basin where it connects with a series of trails running farther north into the Ohio Valley, converges with the Tennessee Valley near the mouth of the Flint River. This trail may have been the route of diffusion of these northern pottery types into the Copena territory. Their absence or rarity in the western Copena region (Wheeler and Pickwick basin areas), and the late Woodland division of pottery industries in the middle Tennessee Valley—clay-tempered ware in the western region and limestone-tempered in the eastern—suggest that Copena may have been composed of two autonomous yet related segmentary tribes.

The Copena habitation sites are also characterized by the presence of medium, triangular projectile points; a large and varied assemblage of chipped-stone implements; and greenstone celts and large, slab-digging implements. In the Guntersville Basin area, where the valley is narrow, the Copena settlement pattern appears to resemble that of ancestral Colbert populations. Major base camps containing subterranean storage facilities and evidence of timber structures are found on bottomland ridges, and winter camps are found in highland rock shelters. Two major changes in subsistence and settlement can be identified in the middle Woodland continuum in this area. First, there appears to have been a trend, culminating in late Woodland times, that involved a shift in the function of the upland occupations from temporary camps used by work parties consisting of entire nuclear family units to male-oriented hunting camps.

This settlement shift may mark the introduction of maize into the local economy. Cultigens like squash and sunflower were already being raised in the Tennessee Valley bottomlands, and the addition of maize to the established horticultural system may not have precipitated any major shifts in warm season scheduling activites. Such an addition of storable produce may have allowed a more sedentary occupation of valley settlements by large segments of the local communities. Only hunting parties would have been required to range out into the hinterlands in search of game. In times of poor harvests, however, entire families would probably have been forced into upland camps to fend for themselves through the lean winter season.

It should be noted that, throughout the prehistoric occupation of the southern deciduous forests, food production may have never surpassed food collection in economic importance. However, the addition of effective cultivation systems to the local economies may have produced a sufficient quantity of storable food to allow increased sedentism, an overall rise in the nutritional level of regional populations, and an increase in population density in favored environments. The culmination of these processes produced sizable, stable late Woodland societies that served as the demographic base of the later flowering of the Mississippian culture.

The second major shift in subsistence activities during the Woodland centered around shellfish collection. Both Colbert and late Woodland Flint River peoples gathered large amounts of shellfish, but during the intervening Copena period this food source does not appear to have played an important economic role. A typical pattern at stratified Guntersville Basin Woodland sites is a lower Colbert zone containing an extensive shell layer, an intermediate Copena earth midden devoid of shells, and an upper late Woodland stratum again containing large amounts of shell refuse. The situation in the Pickwick Basin is even more dramatic. During Colbert times no less than nine of the great shell mounds were occupied, but only two exhibit any evidence of substantial occupation in later Copena times. Instead, Copena villages were more commonly back from the riverbanks on upper terraces near the valley edge.

Climatic change, producing increased rainfall and flooding of shallow shellfish beds, has been offered as one plausible explanation for the decrease in shellfish consumption during Copena times. However, factors other than an environmental prime mover may have been involved. One other possible explanation is overexploitation of shellfish beds in certain areas, leading to a decrease in productivity to a point that shellfish collecting would not have been economically viable. If this was indeed the case, then a three- or four-century moratorium on intensive shellfish harvesting during Copena times may have allowed the beds to reach a productive level again.

Another factor in at least some areas may have been conflicts in scheduling of procurement activities. The addition of new subsistence techniques in areas where the floodplain was broad may have required the abandonment of riverbank settlements in favor of village locations back from the river in the interior bottomlands near both rich soils and upland collecting grounds. Such a shift appears to have occurred during late middle Woodland times in the western Copena region. One of the best known Copena settlements, the Wright village and mounds (Webb and DeJarnette 1942; Walthall 1973b), was located more than half a mile back from the river near the valley edge.

The habitation area at the Wright village covered some 1.5 acres. Numerous pits and scattered post holes were discovered, indicating the presence of both storage facilities and timber structures. One such complete structure pattern was located during the excavation of the site, representing a circular dwelling twelve feet in diameter, with a central fire basin. Plain and check-stamped limestone-tempered pottery sherds comprised some 88 percent of the total ceramic collection from the Wright village. The bulk of the remaining 12 percent consisted of simple-stamped, complicated-stamped, and fabric-impressed pottery. Only 14 cord-marked sherds (out of a total of 4,000 specimens) were found, probably representing a single trade vessel. Brushed or rocker-stamped pottery were not present.

Limestone-tempered Complicated-stamped Sherds, AMNH 31 CAL

Although the evidence recovered from the Wright village attests to a long, intensive occupation of this locality, only two burials, both of unclear context, were found in the habitation area. From this and similar situations, it is clear that Copena ideology prescribed the spatial segregation of the living and the dead. The inhabitants of the Wright village buried their deceased kinsmen in two mounds raised some six hundred feet to the west of the settlement. One of these structures, Lu 63, was built over an old village midden containing only plain- and check-stamped sherds. Some sixteen burials were identified within this mound, although many more may have been present at one time and were perhaps lost through deterioration. Reconstructible skeletal material has been recovered from only a small number of Copena mounds, probably due to the exposure of the remains to water and highly acidic soil. The complete crania that have been found in these structures indicate that the Copena peoples practiced both frontal and occipital head deformation, at times extreme.

Some of the burial pits in Lu 63 were lined with bark or wooden slabs, and some individuals were placed into wooden troughs. The companion structure, Lu 64, was found to contain thirty-seven burials accorded similar treatment. Many of the burials found in both mounds were accompanied by typical Copena artifacts. The most elaborately furnished Copena burial known is Burial 37 in Lu64, which contained six copper bracelets, a copper celt, and a galena nodule.

Two particularly intriguing areas of speculation concerning Copena are its origins and decline. Connections between Hopewell and Copena were recognized early in this century, and for a considerable time Copena was viewed as one of several southeastern Hopewellian expressions. In 1945, with the publication of the first major synthesis of the midwestern Adena manifestation, William S. Webb suggested that deplaced Adena migrants were responsible for the rise of Copena in the Tennessee Valley. Since that time the debate between an Adena or a Hopewell origin has swung back and forth as various archaeologists made their own interpretations. Recent research by Charles Faulkner (1970) and John Walthall (1973a) has questioned any Adena involvement. These authors, continuing a line of argument first put forward by James B. Griffin during the 1940s, interpret Copena as essentially a local development stimulated by what has been termed the Hopewellian sphere of interaction.

As noted in the foregoing discussion, there is little evidence of intensive or continuous trade ties between Ohio Hopewell and Copena. Instead, Hopewell influence on southeastern populations appears to have been intermittent, mainly concerned with the diffusion of specialized artifact styles and mortuary ideology. The origin of Copena can be traced from an early middle Woodland Colbert base, with the addition of both secular and ceremonial traits mainly derived through culture contact situations (barter, marriage alliance, etc.) with surrounding indigenous ethnic groups. The process of assimilation of these traits into the local cultural system produced the distinctive Copena manifestation. Similarly, the breakdown of the dominant Hopewell culture in the Midwest around A.D. 300 and the resultant loss of influence on southeastern populations brought about a widespread decrease in mortuary ceremonialism and interregional diffusion. Thus the decline of Copena can be viewed as part of a regional trend producing isolationism, new local economic adjustments, and less elaborate ritualism. In the middle Tennessee Valley, this trend resulted in the development of two distinct local late Woodland cultures, Flint River and McKelvey.

Flint River: A.D. 500–1000

At some point around A.D. 500 a fission occurred among the indigenous Woodland populations of the middle Tennessee Valley. This development corresponded to the old Copena territorial division and reflects increasing external influence from developing societies in other regions. Peoples in the western area, encompassing both the Pickwick and Wheeler basins, adopted clay-tempered ceramics ultimately derived from the lower Mississippi Valley, while groups in the eastern Guntersville Basin area continued to produce a modified limestone-tempered ceramic complex. The boundary between these two culture areas appears to have been Green Mountain, a highland ridge running perpendicular to the Tennessee River. On the western side of Green Mountain, a large McKelvey settlement, characterized by clay-tempered ceramics, was located during the Wheeler Basin survey on Hobbs Island. This site represents the last major McKelvey settlement going upstream in the middle Tennessee Valley. On the eastern side of Green Mountain, where the Flint River flows into the Tennessee WPA archaeologists (Webb and DeJarnette 1948a) excavated the largest late Woodland settlement encountered during their investigations. This occupation was characterized by enormous amounts of plain and brushed limestone-tempered pottery, a marker for the Flint River culture. Brushed pottery of this type (Flint River Brushed) was most frequently made into a round-bottom jar. Only rarely found downstream from this site, it occurs in high frequencies at sites upriver to an area just north of the Alabama state line in Marion County, Tennessee.

During the Guntersville Basin survey, some fifteen major Flint River components were investigated in the valley bottoms. In these zones, plain limestone-tempered pottery sherds ranged in frequency from 11 to 76 percent and brushed sherds ranged from 13 to 86 percent, while cord-impressed sherds, a marker for the contemporaneous and related Hamilton culture upstream in eastern Tennessee, were absent at six sites and had a high frequency of less than 1 percent at the others. Although the Flint River and Hamilton cultures shared a number of characteristics (for example, small, triangular arrowpoints and long-stemmed ceramic elbow pipes) and probably a similar economic base, their distinctive ceramic industries suggest two autonomous cultural systems. Madeline Kneberg (1961:Figure 5) has compiled ceramic data from six Hamilton components in the upper Tennessee Valley. Plain ware constituted from 10 to 50 percent of the ceramics from these components, cord-marked sherds ranged from 11 to 57 percent, while brushed sherds were absent at two components and had a high occurrence of 10 percent at another. Thus, during late Woodland times there was an inverse frequency ratio between brushed- and cord-marked ceramics in the upper and middle segments of the valley. Upstream from the Guntersville Basin, brushing decreases while cord marking increases.

This distribution can be further demonstrated by comparing the Hamilton ceramic sample from Hiwassee Island with that of the total sample of Guntersville Basin–Flint River components. Lewis and Kneberg (1946:88) reported the recovery of some 11,000 limestone-tempered sherds from Hamilton components at Hiwassee Island. Of this total, 30 percent had a plain finish, while 69 percent were cord impressed. Marion Heimlich (1952) in her summary of Guntersville Basin ceramics reveals that 63,287 brushed sherds were recovered, while a total of only 547 cord-marked sherds were found at the twenty sites yielding limestone-tempered pottery.

Late Woodland Flint River Brushed Sherds, AMNH 30 CAL

Plain Limestone-tempered Vessels, AMNH 41 CAL

More recently, Major McCollough and Charles Faulkner (1973) of the University of Tennessee have investigated a small Hamilton shell midden, the Doughty site, in the Watts Bar Reservoir. This component was small, measuring some 45 by 30 feet. No structural remains were noted and only four features were recorded. A sample of 1,697 sherds was recovered, including 50 percent limestone-tempered plain, 40 percent cord impressed, and no brushed sherds. Based upon research at the Doughty site and upon earlier investigations by Lewis and Kneberg, McCollough and Faulkner have formulated a new settlement model for the Hamilton occupation of the upper Tennessee Valley. They postulate that during the warm summer and fall seasons these late Woodland populations lived in large settlements in the river floodplain, where they practiced maize horticulture, collected mussels, fished, and hunted and gathered. In the winter, the extended families dispersed to small base camps on upper terraces, and temporary camps were established in the uplands. The small winter base camps yield considerable evidence of female-related economic activities and little evidence of male-related tasks. On the other hand, the upland camps yield large numbers of chipped-stone tools comprising hunting and butchering tool kits and only small proportions of pottery and other female-oriented implements.

From the data presently available, it appears that this Hamilton settlement model can be applied, with only a small amount of modification, to the Flint River occupation of the middle Tennessee Valley. Several extensive shell middens that have been excavated in this region appear to correspond to the summer floodplain settlements of the Faulkner-McCollough model. Two of these components are represented by the upper zones at the Harris site (Ms 80) and at the Flint River site (Ma 48).

At the Harris site, a shell layer 1.3 to 2 feet thick was found to overlie a Copena earth midden. Only two midden pits and three roasting pits filled with fire-cracked rock were found in this zone. However, large numbers of post holes were noted, some in association with burned cane walls. Several lines of these post holes formed curves, suggesting circular timber and cane dwellings. Interspersed among these dwellings were several flat, fire-burned areas. The cultural material recovered from this Flint River zone included plain and brushed limestone-tempered pottery, ceramic disks and elbow pipes, small Hamilton-like triangular points, and limestone and greenstone celts. The shape and size of the stone projectile points suggest that they functioned as arrowheads and provide the first good evidence for the use of the bow and arrow in the Tennessee Valley.

At the Flint River site, the upper layer, Zone A, is a large shell midden containing extensive evidence of late Woodland occupation. In this zone, fire pits, midden pits (some filled with shell), and hearths were uncovered. Over 36,000 brushed sherds were recovered from this upper layer alone. Large numbers of triangular and spike-shaped points, blades, knives, and scrapers suggest hunting and butchering kits. A large bone assemblage was also preserved. Bone awls, needles, pins, and fishhooks were common.

A third component, representing a Flint River summer-fall settlement, has been investigated in Marion County, Tennessee, by Charles Faulkner and J. B. Graham (1966). This midden, the Westmoreland-Barber site, is important because it yielded the first radiocarbon date on Flint River ceramics (A.D. 625 ± 110) and the first direct evidence that these late Woodland populations practiced maize cultivation.

Several small shell middens representing the winter-spring base camp settlement-type have been reported in the Guntersville Basin. One of these, the Cartwright site on Pine Island (Webb and Wilder 1951:155), compares strongly to the Doughty occupation. This site consists of a small shell midden (50 by 60 feet) atop a high natural levee rising some 35 feet above the river. Ten similar sites were located on Pine Island but were not excavated. No structural remains were found in the Cartwright midden, but eight pits were recorded that contained village refuse, animal bone, and burned hickory nuts. No human interments were found, but the remains of a dog burial were discovered. Bone awls, a bear humerus handle, an antler tool, and a bone bead were recovered. Small numbers of chipped tools and triangular points were found, as were a few limestone and greenstone celts. However, a large sample of pottery was recovered; of some 12,637 sherds, 33 percent were plain and 66 percent were brushed. No cord-impressed sherds were found. The high ratio of female- to male-related artifacts suggests a division of labor during the winter-spring. Domestic family units appear to have camped on high ridges in the valley, while males ranged into the upland in search of game. Russell Cave (J. W. Griffin 1974) and the small Sand Mountain rock shelters excavated by Clayton (1965,1967) yielded large numbers of male-related implements and few female-oriented artifacts, suggesting that these localities were used as temporary hunting camps by male hunting parties during Flint River times.

Small caves in the limestone escarpment of the valley edge were also apparently used as base camps in the cold months. Three of these were excavated during the Guntersville Basin survey (Webb and Wilder 1951). The largest, Dispennett Cave, contained two small rooms with dry, powder-like deposits containing mussel shell and cultural debris. Only the front room was large enough for habitation. A fire basin was found in the deposit in this chamber. Bone awls, turkey-bone pins, an antler flaker, and 13 pieces of worked flint (including a few triangular and spiked-shaped points) were recovered. The 264 sherds found in this deposit are interesting because they reflect a recurring ceramic association at terminal Woodland sites in the upper half of the Tennessee Valley. This collection contained 104 brushed and 89 plain limestone-tempered sherds. The remainder were 5 plain clay-tempered sherds and 57 plain shell-tempered sherds notable because they also contained a large quantity of grit and clay as tempering agents. Several sites in the Tennessee Valley, including the Doughty site, have yielded both limestone-tempered Woodland pottery and Mississippian shell-tempered pottery, suggesting acculturation of indigenous populations rather than total replacement by Mississippian invaders. (See chapter 7.)

Little is known about Flint River mortuary practices. A few flexed burials without grave goods have been found in village middens, but these surely represent only a small fraction of what must have been a large population. It is possible that cremation or some other type of mortuary preparation not conducive to preservation was practiced. It is curious that Hamilton peoples upstream and related Coker Ford phase groups to the south in the Coosa Valley constructed mounds for their dead, yet no late Woodland mounds have been reported in the Guntersville Basin. Recent salvage archaeology in the upper portion of the basin may provide data to illuminate the problem.

During these investigations, conducted by personnel from The University of Alabama and the University of Tennessee at Chattanooga, three low, conical burial mounds were discovered that contained flexed subsoil burials with no grave goods. Although these structures have yet to be dated, it can be predicted that they will ultimately be associated with the Flint River culture. Mounds of this type have probably not been previously reported because they contain no mortuary furniture, few burials, and are so small only a trained eye can distinguish them from natural knolls.

The Flint River culture, although drab in comparison to Copena, represents a large, stable society well adapted to the Tennessee Valley environment. These people lived in large, semipermanent riverbank settlements over a long period of the year, practiced floodplain horticulture, and claimed the surrounding uplands as their hunting territories. The small numbers of subterranean storage facilities, especially when compared to the Copena villages, suggest new storage techniques, perhaps raised timber cribs like those of later farming peoples. Smoking appears to have developed into a more secular activity during this time. Copena pipes are never found in village middens and were always carefully placed into burial pits as mortuary offerings or were buried by themselves in the mound fill, which suggests that smoking was part of ceremonial life. However, broken ceramic pipes have been found in several Flint River middens, implying a more careless attitude towards these objects and their function.

Little or nothing is known about Flint River ceremony and religion. Not a single artifact that can be interpreted as solely ceremonial in nature has survived at their settlements. However, for all we know, Flint River life may have been richly ceremonial, perhaps centered around the use of wooden or other perishable objects now lost. Perhaps excavation of additional dry, protected deposits like that found in the Dispennett Cave will one day shed light on this problem. There is an increasing amount of data suggesting that these late Woodland peoples formed the population base for the later, more flamboyant Mississippian occupation of the Tennessee Valley, with its temple mounds and renewed mortuary ceremonialism. Perhaps some of the ceremonialism attributed to Mississippian development actually had its origin in the obscure ritual life of these late Woodland ethnic groups.

McKelvey: A.D. *500–1000*

The Copena occupation of the western portion of the middle Tennessee Valley was succeeded by the McKelvey culture. Continuity between the two is evident in the material remains of these manifestations, suggesting in situ development stimulated by culture contact with ethnic groups to the west and south. Although a genetic relationship is implied in such industries as ceramics, major changes did occur. Perhaps most dramatic were a decline in mortuary ceremonialism, cessation of mound construction, and a shift in settlement pattern involving the establishment of riverbank villages.

McKelvey pottery was tempered with *grog* (pulverized potsherds) and was made into a single major vessel form, a globular pot with a slightly flaring mouth. Straight-sided cup forms were also made but are rare. Added rim strips are common and decorations include pinched nodes, ridges, and incised lines below the vessel lip. The major finish types are check-stamped, cord-marked, and plain ware. Rare surface treatments include patterns of single cords, textile impressions, and zoned punctations within incised lines on straight-sided cups (Haag 1942:517–18). While archaeologists agree that temporal change in the McKelvey development is marked by frequency variations in the major finish types, the correct sequence of development is open to debate, due in large part to the lack of well-stratified late Woodland sites in the Pickwick Basin region, the McKelvey core area. The developmental model proposed below should be considered hypothetical and subject to future modification as more information becomes available. The sequence proposed here is the reverse of that hypothesized by other researchers (Jenkins n.d.), and a good case can be made for either viewpoint in light of present data.

In this discussion, McKelvey will be divided into two temporal units termed McKelvey I and McKelvey II. McKelvey I is characterized by large percentages of plain and check-stamped ware and by a minority of cord-marked pottery. During McKelvey II times, probably after A.D. 700, cord marking replaced check stamping as a major finish treatment. Toward the end of this latter period, the proportion of plain ware appears to have increased substantially. Check stamping is placed into an early temporal position in this sequence for two major reasons: (1) the Pickwick Basin appears to have been a center for check stamping during late Woodland times, and (2) plain and check-stamped wares represent the dominant pottery types of the local ancestral Copena ceramic complex. At the Copena Wright village, plain ware constituted 50 percent of the total ceramic sample, while check-stamped sherds comprised 33 percent. In comparison, the three major McKelvey settlements in the same area have the following frequencies of these two finish types (Haag 1942):

	Plain	Check
Lu 92	50%	25%
Ct 27	50%	34%
Hn 1	60%	30%

During the late Woodland period, groups in the nearby Tombigbee Basin (Miller III) began to produce clay-tempered plain and cord-marked pottery. Marriage alliances between these peoples and Pickwick Basin populations to the north may represent the vehicle for the diffusion of these traits into the middle Tennessee Valley. The addition of these two modes, clay tempering and cord marking, to the late Copena ceramics would have produced the major attributes of our proposed McKelvey I pottery complex. Other major traits shared by the Copena and McKelvey ceramic complexes are the globular pot with slightly flaring mouth and added rim strips. If we postulate that the two Copena shell-mound components found during the Pickwick Basin survey represent late occupations, and there is no indication that they are not, then it may be that the settlement pattern shift back to riverbank villages may have begun in later Copena times.

McKelvey I settlements appear to have been concentrated in the floodplain of the Tennessee River. Later, in McKelvey II times, there appears to have been a shift in this settlement distribution, as many of the small tributary stream valleys to the south were occupied. Sites in these areas are characterized by high percentages of the McKelvey II plain and cord-marked wares. A radiocarbon test on charcoal samples from one of these interior settlements in the Bear Creek Reservoir produced a date of A.D. 1010 ± 200, which probably represents a good terminal date for McKelvey II (Oakley and Futato 1975). That check-stamped vessels continued to be produced in some areas during McKelvey II times is supported by a date of A.D. 900 ± 65 from a feature containing sherds of this type at site Je 32 in Jefferson County (Jenkins and Nielsen 1974).

As will be further discussed in chapter 7, there is evidence of Mississippian influence on late Woodland cultures in the upper portions of the Tennessee Valley and in the Black Warrior Valley region to the south. This latter manifestation, the West Jefferson phase, is characterized by a clay-tempered plain ware with Mississippian vessel forms and attributes. West Jefferson appears to have its origin in the McKelvey development, yet there is no evidence of this coalescence of late Woodland and Mississippian traits in the Pickwick Basin core area. Although West Jefferson-like sites were not found during the Pickwick Basin survey, they may yet be discovered by employing intensive, problem-oriented surveys. However, current data suggest a

large-scale abandonment of the Pickwick Basin around A.D. 900–1000 as
McKelvey populations filtered southward into upland tributary valleys. This
abandonment corresponds to the emergence of Mississippian settlements in
western Tennessee and in the upper Tennessee Valley. The following major
occupation of the Pickwick Basin took place during the mature Mississippian
period (A.D. 1200–1500), as a fully developed Mississippian culture, the
Kogers Island phase, appeared in the area. After this occupation, the Pickwick Basin was abandoned until the arrival of European settlers in the
early nineteenth century. During the intervening protohistoric and historic
periods, the Pickwick Basin area appears to have served as an unpopulated
buffer zone claimed by competing Chickasaw groups to the west and Creek
settlements to the east. If it did indeed occur, the abandonment of this area
during terminal Woodland–early Mississippian times may have been the
result of such competition between coalescing ethnic groups in surrounding
regions.

Two major types of McKelvey settlements are known, nucleated floodplain villages and upland camps. While there is yet no direct evidence of
cultigens from McKelvey sites, maize and squash were probably grown by
these peoples. In fact, the McKelvey settlement pattern almost duplicates
that of later Mississippian peoples. At nearly every site in the Pickwick and
Wheeler basins where McKelvey ceramics are found, shell-tempered Mississippian pottery is also present. It appears reasonable to infer a similar
economic base for both groups. The McKelvey floodplain settlements, both
in the Tennessee Valley proper and in upland tributary valleys, appear to
have been small farming villages or hamlets, while upland rock shelters,
such as Stanfield-Worley and Buzzard Roost Creek, served as temporary
hunting and collecting camps.

One of the McKelvey floodplain settlements is represented by the type
site, the McKelvey village (Hn 1) in Hardin County, Tennessee, just across
the Alabama state line (Webb and DeJarnette 1942). This site is on a riverbank terrace in an area where the rich bottomlands are almost two miles
wide. The McKelvey midden was encapsulated by a later mature Mississippian platform mound. The late Woodland stratum contained large amounts
of mussel shell, fire-burned areas, clay-lined fire basins set in prepared clay
floors, scattered post holes, and a few midden pits. No definite structure
patterns were noted, but timber and cane dwellings were probably constructed over the clay floors. A striking aspect of the cultural material recovered from this component is the enormous sample of pottery found (some
20,000 sherds) in respect to the minute amount of lithic material: only ten
small, triangular points; two drills; a few biface knives; and several stone
discoidals. This suggests that the production of stone implements was conducted away from the main settlement, perhaps at specialty camps near
sources of lithic materials, and that hunting parties butchered game at kill
sites or at work camps and brought dressed meat back to the village. The

small number of possible storage pits and the recovery of only a few milling stones may imply the use of timber cribs for storage and wooden implements for food processing.

The easternmost McKelvey settlement was established on Hobbs Island in the Wheeler Basin (Webb 1939). This site, Ma 4, was very similar to the McKelvey village, Hn 1. The major occupation of this locality occurred in later Mississippian times, but the Mckelvey shell midden was substantial. Burned clay floors were found, suggesting the former presence of structures. Only 64 projectile points were recovered and, as with Hn 1, a large sample of pottery and a wide range of bone tools—including awls, needles, gouges, and pins—were present.

Little is known about McKelvey mortuary practices. The best evidence available concerning this aspect of the McKelvey culture comes from the Robinson site (Mg 64), a large village on the banks of the West Flint Creek in Morgan County, some nine miles south of the Tennessee River (Walthall 1973a). The ceramic sample recovered from the Robinson site suggests a late McKelvey II occupation. Of the 1,463 clay-tempered sherds, 91 percent had a plain finish and 9 percent were cord marked. The only evidence recognized that suggests contact with early Mississippian peoples, perhaps living in Guntersville Basin settlements, consists of a single plain shell-tempered globular jar with loop handles. One artifact recovered from this site is unique thus far in the McKelvey assemblage, a clay-tempered elbow pipe.

The McKelvey burials found at the Robinson village are flexed interments occurring singly or in groups of up to five individuals. No grave goods were found with these village burials, and little else can be said concerning McKelvey mortuary practices except that these people appear to have expended as little effort as possible in disposing of their dead. Old midden pits were at times utilized, or graves were dug just large enough to contain the deceased. The group interments appear to represent flesh burials. Perhaps related individuals who died over a brief period of time were interred in a common grave that was reopened when necessary.

In summary, the McKelvey culture appears to have direct antecedents in the preceding Copena manifestation and exhibits evidence of contact with regional Baytown–Coles Creek-related ethnic groups. McKelvey peoples occupied permanent riverbank or creek-bank settlements, where they collected mussels, fished, and practiced floodplain horticulture. Upland hunting territories were extensively utilized by the inhabitants of these settlements and temporary camps were established in convenient rock shelters. The single ceramic pipe recovered in McKelvey association suggests that smoking was practiced, although it is not known in what context. There is little information concerning McKelvey mortuary practices, and the available data do not support the presence of elaborate ritual treatment of the dead. Mounds were not constructed, and at least some of the dead were buried in occupied village areas. The extant data also do not support local

Mississippian acculturation of these peoples and, in fact, suggest an abandonment of the major Pickwick Basin floodplain villages prior to Mississippian occupation of the region.

The Coosa Valley

The Coosa River, flowing southwestward from headwaters in northern Georgia, constitutes the major drainage system for the lower Appalachian Valley or, as it is sometimes called, the Valley and Ridge province. The river skirts the western edge of the Piedmont province, important in aboriginal times as a source of such raw materials as greenstone and steatite. Major excavations were conducted in the late 1950s in that area of the Coosa Valley to be flooded by the construction of the Weiss Reservoir in Cherokee County. Some thirty archaeological sites were investigated by personnel from The University of Alabama and Florida State University (DeJarnette, Kurjack, and Keel 1973). Well over half of these sites produced evidence of major Woodland occupations. It is thus possible to construct a Woodland sequence for this area divided into three sequential phases, each characterized by strong influences emanating from either the Guntersville Basin forty miles to the northwest or from the northern Georgia region upriver.

The earliest known Woodland occupation of the Weiss Basin area, the Cedar Bluff phase, dates to the early middle Woodland period and can be considered to represent a spatial variant of the Tennessee Valley Colbert culture. While these early middle Woodland components exhibit evidence of strong cultural ties with the Tennessee Valley, the following late middle Woodland occupation, the Yanceys Bend phase, is characterized by a northern Georgia ceramic complex and can be considered a phase of the Cartersville culture of that region. During succeeding late Woodland times, Tennessee Valley ethnic groups again appear to have exerted a dominant influence on their Coosa Valley neighbors, and the components of this manifestation, the Coker Ford phase, represent a variant of the Flint River culture. Outlined below are each of these Coosa Valley phases as they are now known.

The early middle Woodland Cedar Bluff phase is characterized by limestone-tempered plain and fabric-impressed pottery; medium, triangular projectile points; steatite vessels and bar gorgets; and by base camp settlements containing large numbers of storage facilities. There is little evidence of substantial earlier occupation of this portion of the Coosa, and we can speculate that these Cedar Bluff camps represent the habitation sites of settlers from the Tennessee Valley who broke from the parent Colbert population to occupy the rich bottomlands and upland forests of the Valley and Ridge province. Cedar Bluff groups probably maintained ties with Tennessee Valley peoples through marriage alliances, shared common hunting and collecting territories on Sand Mountain, and participated in a system of reciprocity that included the exchange of steatite vessels and ornaments from Piedmont quarries to the south.

Four major Cedar Bluff components were investigated during the Weiss Reservoir project. The Watson Ford site (Ce 194), on the right bank of the Little River, a tributary of the Coosa, contained evidence of a major early middle Woodland occupation. Over 100 midden pits were discovered in the area excavated. Some 78 post holes were also found, and, though no structure patterns were noted, their presence implies the existence of timber dwellings. No burials were discovered. Five steatite gorgets, ovoid to rectangular in shape, were recovered, as were 7 steatite vessel fragments. Limestone-tempered, fabric-impressed pottery was the dominant ware associated with this Cedar Bluff occupation, and medium, triangular Camp Creek–Greenville-type projectile points were common.

Another Cedar Bluff component was discovered at the Coker Ford village (Ce 200), also located on a knoll overlooking the Little River. Six complete steatite vessels, all with lug handles and notched rims, were recovered from this site. Large numbers of scattered post holes were noted and 79 midden pits were recorded. Other important Cedar Bluff phase occupations were found at the Yanceys Bend (Ce 12) and Forks (Ce 215) sites. At the Forks site two flexed burials were discovered, one in association with a steatite vessel. Two more steatite vessels and 11 fragments were also found in the village area. Excavation records reveal that 116 post holes and 66 pits were recognized in the midden at the Forks site.

These four valley sites suggest that Cedar Bluff peoples occupied the bottomlands during a substantial portion of the year. The large numbers of midden pits suggest storage of plant foods, most probably acorns and annual seed produce. Upland territories were probably utilized during the fall and winter months for hunting and gathering. The two burials recovered at the Forks site suggest that the deceased were at times buried in the village area, although it is not at all clear how the majority of the dead were prepared or interred since so few burials are known. However, current evidence does suggest that during early middle Woodland times this portion of the Coosa Valley was occupied by a sizable, semisedentary population of hunters and gatherers.

The following late middle Woodland occupation, the Yanceys Bend phase, is marked by the diffusion of sand-tempered, carved paddle-stamped ceramics into the Weiss Reservoir area. The appearance of these northern Georgia forms suggests two possibilities: (1) that resident Cedar Bluff peoples entered into marriage alliances with Cartersville ethnic groups upriver and that the ceramic techniques of the foreign wives became dominant, or (2) that Cedar Bluff populations were expelled from the Coosa Valley by Cartersville settlers pushing downriver from their homeland. While a certain amount of evidence is available to support both hypotheses, the problem is compounded by the fact that the parent culture of the Cartersville population, the Kellog manifestation described by Joseph Caldwell (1958), was characterized by an almost identical material culture as that of the Cedar Bluff phase. The only major distinction is the use of sand as a tempering agent in Kellog ceramics and limestone in Cedar Bluff pottery. The recovery of a few sand-tempered, fabric-impressed sherds at Cedar Bluff sites may represent either trade vessels or transitional forms as sand tempering became popular in the Weiss Reservoir area. I favor the marriage-alliance hypothesis, mainly because of a personal bias against the use of migration as an easy means of accounting for any and all culture change. Also, if a related resident population in the Coosa Valley was producing carved paddle-stamped pottery, existing marriage alliances between these groups and Colbert populations in the Tennessee Valley may explain the diffusion of this ceramic complex northward to form the Copena assemblage. Small numbers of limestone-tempered, cord-impressed, and carved, paddle-stamped sherds in Yanceys Bend phase pottery samples and sand-tempered, carved, paddle-stamped sherds in Guntersville Basin Copena ceramic collections may represent evidence of such contact situations.

Major differences between the Cedar Bluff phase and the succeeding Yanceys Bend phase, other than the appearance of these new ceramic forms, include the cessation of steatite vessel production and trade, the total absence of village burials, and the presence of a new settlement type consisting of small habitation sites without underground storage facilities. Continuities include the production of medium triangular projectile-point forms and other types of chipped-stone tools and the continued occupation of some valley ridges as base camps with subterranean storage pits.

Two major types of geometric patterns were impressed onto the outer surfaces of Yanceys Bend phase vessels, a checked-grid design and a simple-stamped motif consisting of series of parallel lines. There is a certain amount of stratigraphic data suggesting a temporal difference in the popularity of these patterns, with the check-stamped type representing the earlier form. Charles Fairbanks (1955a) has reported his excavations at a deeply stratified Cartersville site, 9 H 164, some one hundred miles due east of the Weiss Reservoir, on the upper Chattahoochee River in Hall County, Georgia. At this site Fairbanks found numerous pits and post holes; numbers of greenstone celts and hoes; medium, triangular projectile points; and a large sample of sand-tempered pottery sherds. Of the total of 8,787 sherds recovered, 79 percent were check stamped, 19 percent were plain, and less than 2 percent were simple stamped. The relatively small numbers of simple-stamped sherds found were recovered mainly from the upper zones, suggesting that the major occupation of 9 H 164 took place before this finish technique became popular.

In terms of material culture, site 9 H 164 would not be out of place in the Weiss Reservoir. Of the four sites in this area that were found to contain substantial Yanceys Bend phase occupations, two have high percentages of plain and check-stamped sherds and minor amounts of simple-stamped ware, while the remaining two are characterized by reversed percentages. At one of these latter sites, Ce 200, plain ware constituted 42 percent of the ceramic sample, simple-stamped 56 percent, and check-stamped only 4 percent. If the ceramic sequence recorded by Fairbanks is valid, it is possible to subdivide the Yanceys Bend phase into two temporal subphases. The Yanceys Bend I subphase is characterized by large percentages of check-stamped ware and by minor numbers of plain, fabric-impressed, and simple-stamped sherds. Conversely, the Yanceys Bend II subphase is marked by the rise in popularity of simple-stamped and plain wares, by the disappearance of fabric impressing, and by the decline or cessation of check stamping.

A radiocarbon date of 150 B.C. ± 140 years was obtained by Fairbanks on organic samples recovered from the lower strata at 9 H 164. This date suggests that carved paddle-stamped ceramics may have reached the Weiss Basin area by the beginning of the first century A.D.

Three of the Yanceys Bend sites, Ce 12, 18, and 29, were found to contain a total of only four midden pits. No evidence of structures was noted, but large amounts of village refuse—including sherds; medium, triangular points; and greenstone celts—suggest substantial occupations. While the dearth of subterranean facilities may imply the use of other means of storage, it is also possible that these sites represent summer riverbank occupations by extended families involved in fishing, hunting, and in gathering nonstorable vegetable produce. One Cedar Bluff-like base camp is known. At site Ce 200, the Coker Ford village, a large Yanceys Bend II component was found. This site is on a ridge overlooking the Little River. Eighteen midden pits found in the excavation units can be associated with the late middle Woodland occupation.

These Yanceys Bend habitation sites have yielded little information about ceremonial aspects of the local late middle Woodland culture. One observation appears valid, however. The Yanceys Bend population, like their Copena neighbors, believed that the dead should be segregated from the living. Habitation sites in both areas characteristically yield only purely secular artifacts of a utilitarian nature. While we know that the related Copena and Cartersville people constructed burial mounds for their dead or placed the deceased in natural cave tombs, the question remains: How did the Yanceys Bend people dispose of their dead? Though low conoidal earthen mounds have been reported in this area, the three such structures excavated during the Weiss Reservoir project were found to date to the late Woodland period. Thus we have burial mounds in surrounding areas and in the Weiss Basin by A.D. 700. I suspect that earlier Yanceys Bend burial mounds do exist, perhaps on the upland ridges outside of the reservoir survey area.

While evidence for the use of burial mounds is presently circumstantial, the use of cave tombs by Yanceys Bend peoples is more definitely known. To the north of the Weiss Basin, on Red Mountain above the west fork of the Little River, local residents have reported the discovery of two small burial caves in DeKalb County near the present town of Sulphur Springs. The larger cave contained one intact adult burial and other human osteological material scattered—probably by rodents—throughout a 10-inch-deep floor deposit. Associated with the human skeletal material were a cut and polished bear canine pendant, a cut and ground deer mandible, four polished stone beads, one shell bead, some galena nodules, and two medium, triangular projectile points. A nearby second cave contained a single extended burial that included a small string of copper beads. The medium, triangular points, galena fragments, and other materials found in these caves indicate a late middle Woodland context and suggest that geographically intermediate Yanceys Bend peoples participated in a regional Copena-Cartersville mortuary system that is unique in eastern North American prehistory in its intensive use of cave tombs as well as mounds.

Another type of ceremonial site may be associated with the Yanceys Bend phase, the DeSoto Falls earthworks. This site is upstream from the Yanceys Bend settlements on the Little River. The earthworks were first reported in 1823 and have been the subject of more recent descriptions by R. G. Roberts (1949) and P. E. Smith (1962). These earthworks consist of two walls, each 4 feet high and 4 to 8 feet wide, spanning the open end of a horseshoe-shaped plateau bounded on three sides by steep bluffs dropping about 100 feet to form the Little River gorge. The outer wall, constructed of earth and stone, is 600 feet long, running from bluff to bluff. The inner wall measures 500 feet in length and has an outside parallel ditch at its base 2 feet deep and several feet wide. The DeSoto Falls earthworks are structurally similar to Hopewellian hilltop enclosures in Ohio. Other such enclosures have been reported in Tennessee, in northern Georgia (P. E. Smith 1962), and in the highlands above the middle Tennessee Valley. Only one structure of this nature has been systematically investigated in recent times, the Old Stone Fort near Manchester in Coffee County, Tennessee, which was reported in 1966 by Charles Faulkner of the University of Tennessee (1968). The stone and earth walls of this enclosure were similar to those at DeSoto Falls, and the primary use of both structures appears to have been to form a barrier accross the open end of a horseshoe-shaped area bounded by the steep gorges of small streams—Little River in Alabama and the Duck River in Tennessee.

Cultural material at both sites is virtually nonexistent, a factor that does not help in attempting to associate these structures with known archaeological complexes. The absence of village refuse also does not support the hypothesis that these were defensive works. Faulkner's inquiry into the origin and function of the Old Stone Fort makes interesting reading, having some elements of an Arthur Conan Doyle mystery. Faulkner believes that the evidence currently available suggests a ceremonial function for these earthworks. Radiocarbon dates on charcoal samples from the fill of some of the walls suggest that the Old Stone Fort was constructed over a period of several centuries, dating from A.D. 30 to A.D. 430. These dates indicate that the Old Stone Fort was built by local late middle Woodland peoples closely related to Copena and other neighboring cultures. The dates, distribution, and known association of such enclosures in eastern North America suggest that they appeared during the first half of the first millennium A.D. in a Hopewellian-related context. These data further suggest that for the present the DeSoto Falls earthworks can be associated tentatively with the Yanceys Bend phase.

There is further evidence that Coosa Valley peoples participated in the regional Hopewellian interaction sphere. Downstream, in Talledega and Coosa counties, Copena-like artifacts and sites have been discovered. C. B. Moore (1915) reported that a copper reel was recovered during the late nineteenth century from a site in Coosa County, and in the Alabama Historical collections I have counted some fifty large Copena-like steatite elbow pipes in surface collections from Coosa and Talledega counties. Fundaburke and Foreman (1957) have illustrated a remarkable owl effigy pipe found in a plowed field in Talledega County. The eyes of the carved bird were filled with mica. This pipe is very similar to an owl effigy pipe recovered from the Hopewellian Seip mound in Ohio.

Walthall and DeJarnette (1974) have also reported the presence of a substantial late middle Woodland habitation site and related burial cave in Talledega County. The village site, 1 Ta 9, was located on the left bank of the Coosa near its confluence with Talledega and Tallaseehatchee creeks. A large surface collection suggests a single component site. Plain grit-tempered pottery constituted 74 percent of the ceramic sample, followed in frequency by check-stamped ware (25 percent). Of the 49 projectile points found, 40 were medium, triangular forms. Greenstone polled celts and slab hoes were also recovered.

In 1964, Fred Layton, owner of nearby Kymulga Cave, discovered two burial areas within this large cavern. Associated with these interments were two medium, triangular projectile points and masses of foreign puddled clay. Walthall and DeJarnette have suggested that the presence of these Copena-like traits in this particular area is due to the existence of sources of greenstone and steatite in the bordering Piedmont highlands. The large number of Copena-like pipes found in this area indicates that indigenous peoples may have turned from manufacturing steatite vessels to the production of pipes, celts, and hoes for trade with groups to the north. Indications of strong contact with Copena groups further suggest that these Tennessee Valley peoples were major importers of Coosa Valley raw materials and finished products.

The Coker Ford Phase

The beginnings of the late Woodland Period in the Weiss Basin area are marked by the appearance of Flint River pottery, which diffused southward after A.D. 600. The major ceramic types associated with the local manifestation, the Coker Ford phase, are limestone-tempered plain and brushed wares. Rare types are represented by limestone-tempered, cord-marked, and red-filmed sherds, and by plain ware tempered with sand, clay, or shell. If the trend toward an increase in the proportion of plain ware noted in the late Woodland continuum in the Guntersville Basin is also valid for the Coosa Valley, then most of these Weiss Basin sites were occupied late in time. The small amounts of clay- and shell-tempered pottery found at most of the known Coker Ford phase sites support such a placement. Comparison with archaeological sequences in other areas suggests a temporal range of A.D. 700–1100 for the Coker Ford phase components reported in the Weiss Basin.

The type site for the late Woodland expression in the Weiss Reservoir is the Coker Ford site, consisting of a village area and two associated stone-capped burial mounds. Mound A at this site measured 5.5 feet high and 35 feet in diameter, and the bulk of the fill was composed of dark humus littered with village refuse from the surrounding habitation area. A layer of river boulders was added to the top of the mound as a final act of construction. Of six burials found sealed within the tumulus, four were flexed, one was extended, and one consisted of an isolated skull. No artifacts were found in direct association with these burials. However, a large amount of cultural material was found in the mound fill raked and collected from the surrounding village. A sample of 3,400 pottery fragments contained 3,100 plain and 92 brushed limestone-tempered sherds, 7 plain shell-tempered; and 154 plain sand-tempered sherds. The presence of 10 small, triangular projectile points in the mound fill suggests use of the bow and stone-tipped arrows.

Mound B at Coker Ford was 3.5 feet high and 35 feet in diameter, and in all respects was almost an exact duplicate of Mound A. Seven fragmentary burials, one partially flexed, were found in the mound fill. Again, nonperishable grave goods did not accompany the dead. The ceramic sample from the fill of Mound B consisted of 1,438 plain, 210 brushed, and 27 red-filmed, limestone-tempered sherds; 26 plain clay-tempered; and 2 plain shell-tempered sherds.

An exploratory trench, extended from Mound B, 105 feet across the village area in a northwesterly direction, was dug after the completion of the mound excavations. Three features and two burials were located, the features consisting of fire pits found to contain a total of 87 plain and 42 brushed limestone-tempered sherds. Burial 1 in the village midden was flexed and had no associations. Burial 2 was also flexed, and, unlike the other Coker Ford interments, included a mortuary offering—a Hamilton-like limestone-tempered pipe, an elbow form with a long tapering stem. Six fragments of similar ceramic pipes were found in the fill of the Coker Ford mounds. Pipes of this type have also been reported in Flint River and Hamilton context in the Tennessee Valley and serve as a horizon style marker for the late Woodland in the Middle South. Twelve limestone-tempered brushed sherds were found in the fill of Burial 2. Of a total of 200 sherds found during the excavation of the exploratory trench, 68 percent were limestone-tempered plain and 31 percent were brushed. The homogeneity of the village pottery suggests a single component site. The presence of rare ceramic types in the fill of the two mounds suggests that trade vessels may have been purposefully deposited in the mound or that the mounds were built at a later time, when contact with early Mississippian groups in the Guntersville Basin was accelerating.

A second major Coker Ford phase habitation site has been reported by B. C. Keel (1960). This locality, the Moneys Bend site, on the south bank of the Chattooga River, exhibited evidence of two major occupations—a Coker Ford settlement and a later occupation dating to Mississippian times when a village surrounded by a ditch and wooden palisade was constructed on the site. Charcoal samples taken from the old stockade line have yielded a radiocarbon date of A.D. 1410 ± 150, suggesting a mature Mississippian association for the fortification. The pottery sample recovered from the site is, however, an almost pure Coker Ford assemblage. Small, triangular projectile points and limestone-tempered ceramic pipe fragments were also recovered.

The evidence presently available suggests that the known Coker Ford phase habitation sites represent small nucleated villages probably supported by maize horticulture and hunting and gathering. Deceased kinsmen were placed into graves dug into the village midden or into small, stone-capped burial mounds, the last such structures to be raised in the Weiss Basin area. The material culture of these Coker Ford settlements suggests such strong ties with Flint River groups in the Guntersville Basin area that the Coker Ford phase may best be viewed as a local expression of the Flint River culture. There is some evidence to suggest Coker Ford contact with early Mississippian peoples to the north, but the minute amount of data available concerning later prehistoric occupations of the Weiss Basin does not allow even speculation about the fate of these peoples. It does, however, appear fairly certain that by A.D. 1400 fortified Mississippian villages were being occupied on sites of previous Coker Ford settlement.

The Upper Tombigbee Region

The headwaters of the Tombigbee River are in the fall line hills above Tupelo in extreme northeastern Mississippi. From there the river flows southward into Alabama, where it crosses the Black Belt region, eventually emptying into Mobile Bay on the northern Gulf coast. For the purpose of this discussion, the Tombigbee drainage area will be divided into two sub-regions: (1) the upper Tombigbee, extending from the headwaters to its confluence with the Black Warrior River on the southern edge of the Black Belt, and (2) the lower Tombigbee, flowing from the Black Warrior confluence to an area just north of Mobile Bay where it joins the Alabama to form the Mobile River. Archaeological investigations suggest a cultural basis for this division. Prehistoric sites along the upper reaches of the river share a common material culture, while sites below the Warrior confluence exhibit greater affinity with Mobile Bay manifestations. These lower Tombigbee sites will be included in a later section on Mobile Bay Woodland groups.

The Woodland sequence in the upper Tombigbee region is characterized by the Miller ceramic tradition, originally defined by Jesse Jennings (1941) based upon information recovered during his excavation of the type site and from surface collections from other sites in Lee County in northeastern Mississippi. Jennings's seriation of these pottery samples resulted in the recognition of three sequential periods defined on the basis of frequency variations of major ceramic types. Miller I, the earliest of the three units (later designated "phases" by Peter Bohannon), was thought to have been characterized by the presence of fiber-tempered pottery and a sand-tempered, fabric-impressed ware. The appearance of sand-tempered plain and cord-marked pottery was thought to mark the beginning of Miller II, while Miller III was differentiated by the use of clay particles as a tempering agent. More recent studies (Bohannon 1972; Jenkins 1975b; Jenkins, Curren, and DeLeon 1975) have modified the sequence while retaining Jennings's basic framework.

It is now recognized that the cessation of production of fiber-tempered pottery predates the appearance of sand-tempered, fabric-impressed ware by half a millennium. Jennings's association of these two ceramic complexes had been based upon surface occurrences and not upon stratigraphic context. Therefore, fiber-tempered pottery had now been dropped from the Miller sequence. Late Gulf Formational Alexander pottery is occasionally found in Miller I ceramic samples and probably represents a true association, for the temporal position of these two wares overlaps. Cord-marked pottery appeared in the upper Tombigbee region during late Miller I times as local ethnic groups began to participate in Hopewellian exchange systems. Based upon these considerations, the Miller I ceramic series now consists of two major types: Saltillo Fabric Impressed and Baldwin Plain. Minor-to-rare frequencies of Alexander pottery also occur at early components and cord-marked pottery at late components. Occasional finds of lower Mississippi Valley Marksville trade ceramics have been noted, especially at mortuary sites; along the southern areas of the upper Tombigbee early Mobile Bay Porter ceramics were found at Miller I sites. These rare finds of foreign ceramics have been valuable in establishing the temporal parameters of the Miller sequence, which, unfortunately, has not yet been confirmed by absolute dating techniques.

Although these minority types are found at many sites, there are indications that in some areas a pure Miller I ceramic complex was produced. The existence of this pre-cord-marked–post-Alexander Miller I assemblage is best demonstrated at the Bynum site in northeastern Mississippi (Cotter and Corbett 1951). Here, pure plain and fabric-impressed ceramic assemblages were sealed beneath four burial mounds. Two of the Bynum mounds contained only plain and fabric-impressed sherds, while the remaining two yielded a few cord-marked sherds from their upper zones. In the adjacent habitation area at Bynum, several features were found to contain only plain and fabric-impressed sherds. A surface collection from another site in this area, Le 53, was also found to contain a pure Miller I ceramic sample. Jennings (1941) reported that this site yielded 29 percent of Baldwin Plain sherds and 71 percent of Saltillo Fabric Impressed sherds.

The ceramic division between Miller I and Miller II is now believed to be less distinct than first postulated. Jenkins (1975), who has recently made considerable refinements in the Miller sequence, believes that Miller II is best defined as beginning when both Baldwin Plain and Saltillo Fabric Impressed ceramics start to decline in frequency and Furrs Cord Marked increased. For early Miller II times, fabric-impressed sherds are the third most frequent type found but decrease in proportion as cord marking reached a peak in popularity. An example of a good Miller II ceramic assemblage was reported by Jennings (1941:205) from a village locality, Le 56, near Tupelo. A pottery collection of 1,161 sherds from this site contained 32 percent Baldwin Plain, 67 percent Furrs Cord Marked, and less than 1 percent Saltillo Fabric Impressed.

The late Woodland Miller III phase is represented by the clay-tempered Tishomingo series. Plain and cord-marked ceramics were the dominant finish types during this time, although minor amounts of fabric-impressed, check-stamped, incised, and brushed pottery are occasionally found. The use of clay as a tempering agent appears to have had its origin in the lower Mississippi Valley. This ceramic technique diffused eastward from regional Baytown settlements as the Tombigbee cord-marking treatment was being introduced to western potters. Similarly, cord marking spread among northern communities and became a popular finish type among the Tennessee Valley McKelvey peoples. Rare finds of McKelvey check-stamped ware at Miller III village sites reflects this diffusion process.

Miller I: 100 B.C.–A.D. *300*

The Miller I occupation of the upper Tombigbee region is perhaps best summarized by describing three of the major components dating to this time, the Craigs Landing village and the Bynum and Pharr mound groups. The Craigs Landing site, designated 1 GR 2, was excavated as a part of The University of Alabama archaeological salvage program in the area of the Tombigbee Basin to be inundated by the construction of the Gainesville Lock and Dam, a Tennessee-Tombigbee Waterway project. This site was originally discovered by C. B. Moore (1901) and was later rediscovered during a preliminary survey of the Gainesville area by John Walthall in August 1970. The deposits at Craigs Landing proved to be deeply stratified and two field seasons were spent investigating this locality (Nielsen and Jenkins 1973; Jenkins 1975b).

In the Miller I stratum at this site, which appears to have been the first base camp established in the Gainesville area of the Tombigbee, a large lithic assemblage was recovered, including the Gary projectile-point type, a stemmed variety with a contracting base; biface blades; scrapers; and milling equipment. Curren (1975b) has reported that the major mammals exploited by Miller I hunters were deer, turkey, rabbit, squirrel, and raccoon. Shellfish were also collected from nearby riverbeds. A fragment of a ten-row maize cob was found in the Miller I stratum (C. E. Smith 1975). Although a later Mississippian component was present in the upper strata, no intrusive features were recognized in the area of the maize find. If this cob fragment was indeed associated with the Miller I component, it represents the earliest evidence of maize cultivation in the Middle South. Some credence is lent to this association by the recovery of maize in contemporary Marksville context in the lower Mississippi Valley (Struever and Vickery 1973). It has already been noted that Marksville trade vessels have been recovered in Miller I components, establishing proof of contact between these ethnic groups. Thus from available data, it appears that the Miller I economy was centered around hunting, shellfish collecting, and the gathering of wild plant foods, perhaps supplemented by maize horticulture.

At some time around the beginning of the first millennium A.D., Miller I groups began to participate in the Hopewellian interaction sphere. Diagnostic trade materials suggest trade with both northern Hopewell peoples and Marksville groups to the southwest. The proximity of known Miller I burial-mound groups to the Natchez Trace suggests that this aboriginal trail may have served as a major north-south trade route during middle Woodland times. C. B. Moore reported the existence of several burial mounds and mound groups in the Gainesville area. Although several of these sites have been recently relocated, none are in the project area and there are no immediate plans to investigate them. However, two major mound groups have been excavated upstream in northeastern Mississippi and have yielded significant information about Miller I mortuary customs.

Cotter and Corbett (1951) investigated one of these mound groups, the Bynum site, during the late 1940s. Bynum is located on the Natchez Trace Parkway, a few miles east of Houston, Mississippi. The site consists of six conical burial mounds and an associated village area. Of the three structures excavated, Mound B is perhaps the most intriguing. Fourteen feet high and 80 feet in diameter, this tumulus was raised over a large central feature—a huge oval pit—46 feet long and 38 feet wide, dug to a depth of 4 feet below the old ground surface. Within this feature, a second smaller pit was dug an additional 1.5 feet into the subsoil. The floor of the central feature was covered with a deep bed of ashes that was found to contain the remains of three cremations. Associated with these deposits of calcined human bone were 29 stone celts and a cache of 9 spearpoints, specimens recently identified as belonging to the Snyders type, which is found in the Illinois Valley in early-to-middle Hopewell context, circa 100 B.C. to A.D. 100 (Jenkins 1975b). The Snyders projectile-point form was not locally produced in the Tombigbee region, and these Bynum specimens appear to represent trade items from northern Hopewell sources. The small subpit in the floor of the central feature was found to contain a fourth cremation in association with a second cache of Snyders points. The lip of the central feature was lined with parallel logs that perhaps served to impede erosion. Large and deep post holes in the feature floor suggest that a timber structure was constructed over the crematorium. This structure appears to have been burned before mound construction began. Also found in Mound B were copper earspools, galena fragments, and two fragments of marine shell.

The Pharr mound group, located fifty miles from the Bynum site, was also on the Natchez Trace (Bohannon 1972). This site consists of eight conical burial mounds and an extensive village area. Four of the mounds were investigated. Mound H, damaged by recent cultivation, was only 2 feet high at the time of excavation. The major feature discovered within this structure was a central crematory basin, 4 feet wide and 5 feet long, which had been sunk about a foot into the subsoil. Within the basin fill, a greenstone platform pipe and some flakes of mica were found. Mound A, which was 7 feet high and 60 feet in diameter, contained a low clay platform built over the old ground surface. Just to the side of this mantle a major feature, a large subsoil burial pit 6.5 feet wide and 11 feet long, was found to contain calcined human bone, charcoal, and fragments of what may have been a copper-covered wooden panpipe. Another of the mounds investigated, Mound D, was 15 feet high and 90 feet in diameter and had been constructed in three stages. On the old ground surface a large burned area was found, as was a pavement of stone slabs. Bone fragments and copper earspools were recovered from this paved area.

The data recovered from the Bynum and Pharr sites suggest that Miller I mortuary customs centered around the use of prepared depositories, the construction of mounds as an important ceremonial event, and the relatively common inclusion of Hopewellian trade goods as mortuary offerings. Both cremation and inhumation were commonly practiced during mortuary ritual. It should be noted that Marksville trade vessels have also been found in burial context in these Miller I mounds. This association and the relatively large number of similarities between the Marksville and Miller burial complexes suggest that these two cultural manifestations were contemporary and closely related. The nature of this relationship will constitute a major problem for future research into the development of Hopewellian-inspired mortuary ceremonialism in the Southeast.

Miller II: A.D. *300–500*

The Miller II phase represents a cultural continuum of the Miller I development, with continuity demonstrated in both material culture and mortuary ceremonialism. Miller II peoples constructed burial mounds and practiced a modified form of Miller I burial ritual. Sand-tempered globular jars with rounded or conoidal bases were still produced, although, as previously stated, cord marking replaced fabric impressing as a major finish type. The Gary projectile-point type continued to be produced during Miller II times, and there appears to have been little change in the form of other lithic implements. However, in the Gainesville Basin area there is evidence of increasing population density. While in Miller I times only a single base camp was occupied along this portion of the Tombigbee, during the Miller II phase five base camps were settled. Four were established in areas of fine sand soil, while the fifth, 1 Pi 19 in Pickens County, was situated in an area of fine sandy loam one mile north of the Blubber Creek mound group first discovered by Moore.

A major Miller II mortuary site, the Miller mound group in Lee County, Mississippi, was investigated by Jesse Jennings in 1940 (Jennings 1941). This site consists of a pair of conical burial mounds separated by a village area 600 feet wide. Mound A, the larger of the two structures, was 15 feet high and 85 feet in diameter, constructed over an old ground surface that exhibited evidence of numerous fires. The remains of some 32 individuals were found within the structure; two burials had been placed onto the old ground surface while the others were incorporated into the mound fill. Most of the Mound A burials were extended, but a few flexed inhumations were also recognized; cremation was apparently not practiced at this site. Grave goods were rare—only a single burial was accompanied by mortuary offerings. Burial 28, unique at this site in that the body had been sandwiched between layers of pure clay, was associated with a conch-shell cup and a limestone platform pipe.

Mound B, 13 feet high and 80 feet in diameter, was built over an old extension of the village midden. Inhumations were found in subsoil pits beneath this structure as well as in the mound fill. Only six burials were discovered—three in subsoil pits (one of these in association with a Furrs Cord Marked vessel), while three others were found clustered in the central portion of the mound fill five feet above the old ground surface. In the fill of a historic treasure hunters' pit, Jennings found fragments of two copper-covered wooden earspools. Also found in Mound B was a globular, round-based jar, decorated with random fingernail punctations. Jennings originally classified this jar as an Alexander Pinched type, but the vessel shape and context suggest that it was a local, albeit unusual, Miller II product.

Miller III: A.D. 500–900

The inception of the Miller III phase in the upper Tombigbee region is marked by the introduction of clay as a tempering agent. Cord marking appears to have reached a zenith in popularity during early Miller III times and decreased in later centuries as plain ware became the dominant form (Jennings 1975b). Major developments occurred during the Miller II and Miller III continuum. Large-stemmed points, probably hafted to atlatl darts, gave way to small, triangular types, which probably marks the introduction of the bow and arrow into the Tombigbee region. A microtool assemblage—containing flake perforators, bipointed perforators, shaft drills, and expanded base drills—has been recognized in the Miller III lithic assemblage. Small chert flakes were frequently utilized as knives, and pebbles were chipped into scrapers.

Major changes also occurred in local mortuary ceremonialism: Burial mounds were not constructed during Miller III times. While some individuals were buried in village areas, the disposal of the majority of the deceased is not known.

The spatial extent of the Miller III phase is better understood than that of Miller I or II. North and east Miller III components are bordered by McKelvey settlements in the Tennessee and Warrior valleys. To the west, Miller III overlaps with the Deasonville and Coahoma phases of the Yazoo drainage area (Phillips 1970). Downstream, Miller III sites are known to exist below the Tombigbee-Warrior drainage area, where they are bounded by northern settlements of a regional Weeden Island manifestation.

In the Gainesville Basin area, there is evidence of a dramatic population increase. A much larger number of Miller III base camps have been identified and the areas inhabited were more extensive, suggesting both higher population density and larger resident segments. Some nineteen Miller III base camps have so far been found in the Gainesville survey area, an increase of almost 500 percent over Miller II. Most are located on loam soils, in contrast to the settlement of sandy soil areas during earlier times. The loam soils are prime areas for cultivation, and this shift may reflect an increasing dependency on food production. It is probably not too speculative to identify these Miller III components as farming hamlets. They are often found grouped together near shellfish beds, a resource that appears to have been extensively exploited, so much so that there is evidence of depletion of the beds (Curren 1975b). Curren has noted a greater number and variety of faunal remains in Miller III components than in previous occupation zones, possibly the result of new technological developments such as the bow and arrow, which made hunting more efficient.

The Miller III component at the Craigs Landing site has yielded the only available data concerning late Woodland mortuary customs in the Tombigbee region. At this site a large burial pit, measuring some 3.4 feet in diameter and 3.5 feet in depth, appears to date to the Miller III occupation. At the base of this feature, the skulls of sixteen individuals were found, some exhibiting evidence of burning. Two other individuals were represented by small deposits of calcined bone that appear to have once been contained in individual bags or baskets (Hill and Smith 1975). Age and sex determinations indicate that men, women, adolescents, and children are all represented in this ossuary sample. These data suggest that Miller III peoples commonly practiced cremation and reburial of the dead, which may explain the absence of Miller III burials at most known components.

In summary, the data presently available suggest that the Miller III phase represents the remains of an expanding, vigorous population whose economy centered around patterns of intensive hunting, gathering, and food production reminiscent of later Mississippian cultures. In fact, as pointed out in other sections of this chapter, there is increasing evidence that such late Woodland ethnic groups in the Middle South represent the demographic base for regional Mississippian development.

Mobile Bay and the Lower Tombigbee

The Porter Phase

Following the decline of the Bayou La Batre culture in the Mobile Bay–lower Tombigbee region, a new cultural manifestation, the Porter phase, emerged. Porter was first defined on the basis of southwestern Alabama ceramic types exhibiting what was considered a "Hopewellian look" (DeJarnette 1952). Originally this complex was referred to as "Porter Hopewell" and later as "Porter Marksville" (S. B. Wimberly 1960). Walthall (1975) in a recent synthesis continued the use of the "Porter Hopewell" designation. However, the current consensus of regional specialists appears to favor the deletion of both suffixes, for recent ceramic analysis suggests that there is actually little evidence of Marksville influence in the Porter ceramic assemblage, and it is now recognized that Porter ceramics are no more

"Hopewell" than those of contemporary southeastern middle Woodland cultures.

In the following discussion, the term "Porter phase" will be used in referring to this local middle Woodland manifestation; the taxonomic designation "culture" does not appear to be applicable. Strong similarities in cultural material between Porter and northwest Florida Gulf Coast Santa Rosa settlements suggest that these southwestern Alabama components are best viewed as a regional expression of the more geographically widespread Santa Rosa culture. The Porter phase had considerable time depth, extending through the first five centuries A.D., and frequency variations in the major ceramic types will in the future serve as temporal markers for division into a series of subphases.

Porter pottery is sand tempered, although clay tempering sometimes occurs. Vessel forms include beakers or cups with outslanting sides, jars with high shoulders, and open bowls sometimes with an incurving rim. Exterior surfaces commonly have a plain finish but were also decorated with incised, rocker-stamped, and punctated motifs or patterns. Minority types include cord-marked and complicated-stamped vessels. William Sears (1964) has characterized the Porter assemblage as a "thorough" mixture of lower Mississippi Valley early Troyville and eastern Coastal Plain early Swift Creek pottery forms. While the major Porter ceramic modes appear to have originated after Marksville, the presence of a few fragments of Marksville trade vessels at some settlements (Porter and Coden Bayou) suggests that the beginning of the Porter phase at least partially overlapped with Marksville. The recovery at Mobile Bay region sites of certain classic Hopewell artifact types (such as copper panpipes) definitely places the beginnings of Porter participation in Hopewellian interaction sphere exchange systems on a Marksville–Yent–early Swift Creek horizon.

At least two functional types of habitation sites were present in the Porter cultural system. The first was centered around littoral economic activities and is represented by small shell middens along the coast and bay areas. Trickey and Holmes (1971) have reported their investigations of two small Porter group middens on the south bank of Tensaw Lake in Baldwin County. Both of the middle Woodland zones were shallow, indicating brief occupations. All of the cultural zones contained large quantities of shells of *Rangia cuneata*, a species of brackish-water clam. A sample of shell from one of the Porter zones was submitted for radiocarbon analysis and produced a date of 79 B.C. ± 150.

North of Tensaw Lake, on the lower Tombigbee in Clarke County, several Porter sites—both habitation localities and burial mounds—have been discovered and investigated. Steve Wimberly (1960) reported the excavation of five habitation sites with Porter components. Two of these, the Porter and McVay villages, revealed evidence of major Porter settlements. The McVay village was located some four miles northwest of the present town of Salitpa on the crest of a low ridge paralleling the right bank of Kintusha Creek, a tributary of the Tombigbee. The surface material at this site covered an area 400 by 650 feet. Excavations were conducted during the winter of 1940/41 by a WPA crew under the direction of Harry A. Tourtelot. The investigation of the village midden revealed "8 shallow, bowl-shaped refuse pits containing animal bone, charcoal, pottery sherds and a few shells. Both freshwater mussel and gastropod shells were scattered in small amounts through the site" (S. B. Wimberly 1960:14).

The Porter village, discovered a few hundred yards north of the McVay site, was excavated in the spring of 1941. The village midden, ranging from .5 to 1.5 feet in depth, contained scattered lenses of shell, mainly freshwater gastropod. Several circular midden pits were recorded and nine burials were exposed. The midden pits, which ranged from 2 to 3.5 feet in diameter and from 1 to 3.5 feet in depth, contained animal bone, pottery sherds, and occasionally deposits of shell. Of the nine burials, six were flexed, one was extended, and one consisted of an isolated skull. The remaining inhumation was found within the midden and had been disturbed. Only one of these burials was accompanied by a mortuary offering, a child burial (Burial 3) associated with a bone awl and some opossum bones.

Both village sites contained proportionately large amounts of Porter ceramic types, Alligator Bayou Stamped, Crooks Stamped, Basin Bayou Incised, Santa Rosa Punctate, and Franklin Plain. These two villages differed from other nearby habitation sites dating to preceding or later periods by the presence of a relatively large amount of lithic material and by the absence of large amounts of mussel shell. Both the McVay and the Porter villages yielded significant numbers of stemmed projectile points of similar types made from Tallahatta quartzite (Josselyn 1960). Of the 240 stemmed projectile points recovered from eight Clarke County habitation sites excavated during the 1940/41 investigation, 197 were recovered from the McVay and Porter villages.

The data recovered from these two habitation sites indicate that they represent a functionally different type of settlement from the aquatic-oriented collecting stations on Tensaw Lake or along the coastal shores. Both sites contained only small amounts of naiad or gastropod remains. Although quantitative data are lacking, it appears likely that the subsistence activities at these dispersed, interior settlements centered around hunting and the collecting of lowland floral resources. The swamplands surrounding both sites support several varieties of oak, black walnut, chestnut, and several other types of plants utilized by historic Indians as a source of food (C. Wimberly 1960:3). Whether the coastal sites and these interior villages were a part of a seasonal settlement pattern or whether they represent separate adaptations to diverse ecological zones cannot be determined at present.

However, it does appear that the Porter economy was based primarily on the intensive collecting of coastal and estuarine fauna and indigenous coastal-plain flora.

Several burial mounds associated with the Porter tradition have been investigated in southwestern Alabama. C. B. Moore explored a group of these small mounds on the lower Tombigbee River around the turn of the century. These mounds were located some ten miles south of the McVay and Porter villages, near present-day Jackson, Alabama. In the center of one of these low mounds, Moore's crew discovered several burials, near which they found a Hopewellian copper panpipe (Moore 1905a:259).

Another Porter burial mound investigated in the same area is the McQuorquodale mound (1 Ck 25), excavated by a WPA crew under the direction of Harry Tourtelot in the summer of 1941 (Wimberly and Tourtelot 1941). This structure was located some two miles down the Tombigbee from the McVay and Porter villages and some eight miles north of the Jackson mound group.

The McQuorquodale mound is a low, conoidal structure some 60 feet in diameter and approximately 3 feet high. The structure was apparently built in two construction stages. Ten burials were recovered, six lying on top of the first mound stage and four included in the fill of the second or upper stage. These interments consisted of seven reburials, two extended burials, and one unassociated skull. Among the exotic goods recovered were a copper bead, a copper earspool, galena nodules, mica, a siltstone cup, greenstone celts, hematite and limonite nodules, quartz discoidals, stone gorgets, and a mass of black asphaltic material (Wimberly and Tourtelot 1941:8–13). Many lithic artifacts, pottery sherds, and other village debris were found in the mound area and in the mound fill, indicating that the structure had been built on or near an abandoned habitation site.

Farther south, near the old town of Blakely in Baldwin County on the northeastern shore of Mobile Bay, Moore investigated a shell midden containing Porter burials. In association with these burials, Moore's workmen found another copper panpipe.

> In one hole, not far from the surface, were parts of four skulls, and other scattered bones. At a depth of 16 inches was a circular deposit of fragments of cremated, human bones, 10 inches in diameter, 4 inches deep. No sign of fire marked the immediate vicinity of this deposit. Just above the bones lay a tool with a blunt point, made from an antler of a deer, showing no mark of fire. Thirty-two inches from the cremated remains, in the same hole, at about the same level, was a mass of fragments of calcined shell, including, however, a number of shells showing no trace of fire. No charcoal was present in this deposit. About 1 foot below a skeleton which lay near the cremated remains, was another skeleton, flexed on the left side. One hand resting on the neck was in contact with an ornament of sheet-copper that had imparted a green color to some of the bones of the hand and to at least one of the cervical vertebrae. This

Stone Gorgets and Copper Earspool from the McQuorquodale Mound, AMNH
32 CK 25

Siltstone Cone from the McQuorquodale Mound, AMNH 29 CK 25

ornament, 3 inches long by 1.5 inches wide, is corrugated on one side and belongs to a type common to the mound at Crystal river, northwest Florida; the larger mound at Murphy Island, St. John river, Florida; and other localities. With the copper lay two mussel shells. One (Lampsilis anodontoides) shows a perforation at one end; the other was broken to fragments in digging. Near the skull of the skeleton on which was the copper ornament lay an isolated calvarium. [Moore 1905b:284–85]

The information presently available indicates that the Porter communities utilized two types of mortuary systems: burial in contemporary habitation areas and interment in burial mounds spatially removed from living areas. A number of burial techniques were practiced; in some cases the corpse was flexed, extended, reburied, or cremated. Isolated skull burials also have been noted.

It has been suggested that in Mesoamerica groups were brought into the Olmec exchange system because they had, or controlled, access to scarce raw materials and commodities desired by the lowland Olmec elite group (Flannery 1968b). Groups whose territory contained nothing of value to the Olmec were bypassed. An analogous situation probably existed in the eastern United States during the middle Woodland period. Communities that participated in the Hopewellian transaction systems more than likely controlled access to certain goods valued by other groups in other areas.

This raises the question: Why did the Porter ethnic group participate in the Coastal Plain transaction systems? Several reasons can be offered. First, the geographical location of their territory appears to have been of primary importance. The Porter peoples inhabited both the eastern and western shores of Mobile Bay and the surrounding Gulf Coast plain area, placing them directly between the Santa Rosa–Swift Creek peoples to the east and the Marksville-Troyville groups to the west. Extensive coastal trade and contact among these groups is exhibited in their material cultures. Besides the Hopewellian interaction sphere concepts and artifacts common to their traditions, they shared similar ceramic styles and motifs, and their lithic assemblages are almost identical.

Exchange between these Mobile Bay region communities and the Santa Rosa–Swift Creek and related cultures to the east seems to have been especially important. The Santa Rosa–Swift Creek tradition in northwestern Florida was originally defined by Gordon Willey (1949:336–96) and later divided into two sequential phases (Yent and Green Point) by William Sears (1962). Porter appears to have been more closely associated with the earlier Yent phase. Sears has placed the Yent mound, Pierce Mound A, and the central mound of the burial complex at Crystal River into this complex.

Hopewellian trade with groups in the Florida area has been substantiated by the recovery of Hopewellian copper artifacts (panpipes, breastplates, and earspools) and other exotic materials from Yent phase burial mounds. Conversely, artifacts that had their ultimate origin in the Florida region have been recovered from Midwestern tumuli. Examples of these latter trade items include marine helmet shells *(Cassis)* from east Florida, whelk *(Busycon)*, tulip *(Fasciolaria)*, olive *(Oliva)*, and dwarf olive *(Olivella)* marine shells from the Florida Gulf coast. Shark teeth, alligator teeth, barracuda jaws, and marine turtle shells from west Florida have also been reported in this context (J. B. Griffin 1967:184). Hopewellian interaction sphere artifacts have also been found at a number of sites in the northern Saint Johns River area and at the recently reported Fort Center ceremonial site in south-central Florida (Sears 1971). All of these sites appear to have been linked through the pan-eastern exchange system that flourished during middle Woodland times.

The Mobile Bay area was of considerable economic importance during this period because of the major river systems that flow southward into the bay and Gulf of Mexico. The bay was strategic to the early European settlers in the region because by controlling access to the area they could dominate the interior trade flowing up and down the Tombigbee and Alabama river systems. Likewise, the Porter communities would have enjoyed differential access to interior trade because their territory included the strategic confluence of these major river systems.

The Alabama River system, of which the Coosa and Tallapoosa rivers are a part, was apparently a major route to the interior highland crystalline area (so called because it contains greenstone, steatite, mica, graphite, and other minerals) covering the west-central counties of Alabama (Mosley 1958:13). It is known that this area was exploited as early as the Archaic period and that the Tennessee Valley middle Woodland Copena peoples obtained, either through trade or direct procurement, scarce raw materials from this source (Walthall and DeJarnette 1974). This crystalline area is only a short distance northwest of the Mandeville site on the Chattahoochee River. It is likely that, besides controlling the interior trade along this river system, the peoples inhabiting this community also acquired raw materials and finished products as well. The recovery of a Hopewellian figurine fragment from a small site on the Tallapoosa River in the heart of the crystalline area probably reflects trade with the coastal Hopewellian groups or the Mandeville peoples. The cultural material collected from this interior site consisted of "greenstone celt fragments, steatite vessel sherds, large and medium sized projectile points, clay-grit and sand tempered plain ware pottery sherds and the ceramic figurine fragment" (Cottier 1970a:126).

Within the Porter territory, several types of goods were available that could have been used in exchange for exotic finished products. Alligator and shark teeth as well as marine shells could have been procured from the coastal areas. Inland, there were three major natural resources over which the Porter group could have had economic control. First, the Tallahatta geological formation, most extensive in Clarke County, produces three major types of lithic materials utilized during the middle Woodland period:

Middle Woodland Alligator Bayou Stamped Vessels from the Northern Gulf Coast (After Moore 1901)

Middle Woodland Alligator Bayou Stamped Vessels from the Northern Gulf Coast (After Moore 1901)

quartzite, chalcedony, and siltstone. The Tallahatta formation was extensively quarried in this area during the prehistoric period, and several quarry workshops have been located (Dunning 1964).

It has already been noted that the two Porter village sites—McVay and Porter in Clarke County—produced more lithic artifacts (stemmed projectile points, blades, and drills) than any of the other six sites dating to other periods investigated in the area. The major materials used in the production of these implements were Tallahatta quartzite and chalcedony. The low debitage: tool ratio (2:1) suggests that, while some lithic implements were manufactured at these localities, many tools were "roughed out" or finished at the quarry workshops.

Projectile points made from Tallahatta quartzite have been recovered as far north as the Tennessee Valley and are commonly found over a radius of more than two hundred miles from their source, especially in the Coastal Plain area where good lithic materials are rare (Dunning 1964:50–60). Siltstone artifacts (a cupstone and gorget) were among the mortuary goods recovered from the Porter McQuorquodale mound (Wimberly and Tourtelot 1941). Similar artifacts made from identical material have been reported from middle Woodland Copena burials in the Tennessee Valley (Walthall 1973a; Walthall and DeJarnette 1974).

A second natural resource within the Porter territory was ocher. Major deposits of siliceous iron ores, both hematite and limonite, yield yellow, orange, and brown varieties. According to Barksdale (1930:8), the pigments are "permanent," the colors remaining unaltered even when exposed to the atmosphere for an indefinite period of time. Three ore bodies occur in Clarke County, all having exposed outcrops that are easily quarried. The common occurrence of minerals of this nature in many middle Woodland burial mounds throughout the eastern United States indicates that ocher was widely traded during this time period.

Only the nonperishable goods that could have been controlled by the Porter communities have been mentioned. However, it is quite likely that a perishable natural resource found in Porter territory was procured by these peoples for use in the exchange network: salt. Salt may have been a major exchange item in the interior highland Hopewell transaction systems (Walthall 1973a). Two salt springs are in Clarke County, some ten miles south of Jackson, in the center of Porter territory. Both saline springs exhibit evidence of extensive exploitation by both Woodland and Mississippian groups (Barksdale 1929:8, Wentowski 1970:22). According to Wentowski (1970:22–23), who studied salt as an ecological factor in the prehistory of the southeastern United States, the Spanish complained that there was no salt in the provinces of Coza and Tascaluza (in central and northern Alabama). "Swanton (1946:303), in surveying sources of salt along the Gulf Coast between Florida and the Mississippi River, finds only one aboriginally known source other than the sea. This was the salt springs of Clarke County, Alabama."

Porter can thus be defined as the middle Woodland phase of the southwestern Alabama region, comprising both the lower Tombigbee and Alabama river systems as well as the Mobile Bay area. Subsistence activities were apparently centered around the procurement of indigenous Coastal Plain and marine flora and fauna. Several types of cultural traits—including burial of the dead in mounds and the presence of exotic items (copper ornaments, galena, a ceramic figurine, etc.) at sites belonging to this cultural manifestation—indicate that this group participated in the Hopewellian sphere of interaction.

Late Woodland Phases

Archaeological evidence recovered from late Woodland sites in some areas of the Southeast suggests a cultural decline from former middle Woodland florescence. However, while mortuary ritual and accompanying ceremonialism may have been modified drastically or curtailed in certain regions, new religious systems emerged in others. This is particularly true of the northern Gulf Coast. Between A.D. 400 and 1000, in an area from central Florida west to Mobile Bay and extending for over a hundred miles into the interior, a new vigorous cultural manifestation emerged as Hopewellian influence in the Southeast was on the wane. This development, referred to as Weeden Island, was originally defined by Gordon Willey (1945), based upon excavations of villages and burial mounds in northern Florida.

The term "Weeden Island" has been used in a number of ways over the years. William Sears (1964) has noted that Weeden Island has been used as the name of a ceramic complex, a culture, and a cultural period. To this list, Jerald Milanich (1974) has added a ceremonial system and a sociopolitical-economic complex. He goes on to say "Once it is recognized that Weeden Island ceramics are not the only definitive characteristic of Weeden Island culture, these concepts become extremely compatible, and Weeden Island takes on a meaning similar to Hopewellian or to Mississippian, e.g. an economic and sociopolitical ceremonial complex, a general evolutionary stage or level defined by various combinations of culture traits and culture processes" (1974:39).

The Weeden Island ceramic complex contains two basic classes of ware: (1) a ceremonial pottery decorated with incised lines or by painting, ultimately derived from the Gulf Formational ceramic tradition, and (2) a utilitarian pottery consisting of plain and carved paddle-stamped forms. Of these latter types, complicated-stamped and check-stamped surface finishes are the most common. The distribution and relative frequency of these utilitarian types, varying through both time and space, have been used to define both local developmental sequences and regional phases. Simple-stamped pottery commonly occurs as a minority type in some areas and occurs as a major finish type in at least one, the lower Tombigbee.

Weeden Island ceremonialism is best documented from evidence recovered from burial mounds. Weeden Island burial mounds are commonly low, conoidal structures built of sand and were usually constructed as a continuous event beginning with the interment of a single individual on the old ground surface or in a subsoil pit. Other burials were at times added to the mound as construction progressed. William Sears (1958) believes that some of the secondary inhumations represent individuals who were sacrificially slain as part of the mortuary ceremony. Bundle burials, single-skull burials, and flexed inhumations are the most common form of interments found within these mounds. Pottery and other mortuary offerings are often found in these structures. Ceramic vessels were frequently deposited in a cache on the east side of the mound. These ceremonial wares were sometimes made into elaborate anthropomorphic and zoomorphic effigies. Pottery vessels found in mortuary context usually have been deliberately ruined or "killed" by punching a hole in the bottom. Some forms were at times "prekilled" by neatly cutting holes into the vessel before firing. Other mortuary offerings include projectile points, caches of biface blades, shell cups, shell beads, clay elbow pipes, sheets of mica, and copper ornaments.

Weeden Island economy reflects a basic sociopolitical pattern centered around a hunting, gathering, and horticultural adaptation. Variations have been noted among specific Weeden Island cultures and have been attributed to the potential of the diverse ecological settings of these communities. This economic pattern appears to have been reinforced by an often elaborate set of religious beliefs involving mound raising, ceremony, and ritual. Sears (1964) believes that the mounds indicate a highly stratified, theocratically oriented society, with an upper class related to a solar deity. While this model may be applicable to some Weeden Island cultures, it does not appear to be valid in others. Evidence from certain areas, such as the Mobile Bay region, suggests local societies on a much less complex level of political organization. Mound construction and ritual appear in these latter cultures to be confined to kinsmen inhabiting single communities or a group of closely related villages forming a tribal neighborhood.

During the late Woodland period, diffusion emanating from both the east and west brought about considerable change in local Mobile Bay region cultures. These developments are clearly documented in terms of both material culture and mortuary ideology. Contact between Weeden Island ethnic groups to the east and Mobile Bay peoples is evident in the appearance of Weeden Island utilitarian and ceremonial wares at sites in southwestern Alabama. Burial mounds exhibiting typical Weeden Island traits also appear in the area during this time. From the opposite direction, influence from

Coles Creek settlements along the Mississippi Gulf coast is demonstrated by the presence of significant amounts of Coles Creek clay-tempered ceramics at late Woodland shell middens along the extreme southwestern Alabama coast. The result of this acculturation was the emergence of two contemporary, yet distinct, Weeden Island cultures in the Mobile Bay region. One of these, the McLeod phase, was centered around the lower Tombigbee in Clarke County, north of Mobile Bay. McLeod (pronounced "Ma-cloud") peoples produced a sand-tempered pottery often finished with check- or simple-stamped designs. Clay-tempered ceramics are not found in their village middens. To the south, in the coastal salt marshes of Mobile County, a second manifestation, the Tates Hammock phase, emerged as the result of contact with both Coles Creek and Weeden Island settlements. Tates Hammock pottery is confined to two major finish types, plain and check-stamped. Simple-stamped vessels were not produced. While sand was a common tempering agent, clay was also frequently used. The differences in pottery types between the McLeod and Tates Hammock phases suggest that these manifestations represent distinct ethnic groups occupying diverse ecological zones in the Gulf Coast lowlands.

The McLeod Phase

McLeod was originally defined ceramically as "an assemblage of decorative types" found at archaeological sites concentrated in southwestern Alabama (DeJarnette 1952). This ceramic complex was later formally described by Steve Wimberly (1953b), who gave it the appellation "McLeod Deptford" because of its supposed close relationship to the Georgia Deptford series. In this discussion, the term "Deptford" will be deleted. While it is recognized that McLeod pottery shares at least one major trait with Deptford, check stamping, it shares more traits with the Weeden Island type, Wakulla Check Stamped. Differences in rim form between McLeod and classic Weeden Island pottery are not of a sufficient magnitude to constitute separate types. Ceramic samples from Weeden Island villages in northern Florida consistently display a range of rim forms, of which the classic Weeden Island type is only a minority (Milanich 1974). McLeod check-stamped vessels fit comfortably into this range and can be considered a variety of Wakulla Check Stamped.

Unlike the Deptford type, the McLeod simple-stamped finish was not produced with a grooved wooden paddle. Two varieties are recognized: Some McLeod Simple Stamped surfaces appear to have been brushed, while others appear to have been produced with a paddle wrapped with thongs or roots (N. J. Jenkins: personal communication). The major McLeod finish types—plain, check-stamped, and simple-stamped—are found on straight-sided or globular bowls and on jars. Exterior rim folds are common on both vessel forms. Sand was used to temper the potter's clay. Based upon a seriation study of pottery sherds from southwest Alabama sites, E. Bruce Trickey

(1958) placed McLeod into a temporal position postdating Weeden Island, while Wimberly (1960), on the basis of limited stratigraphic evidence, placed this complex into a pre–Weeden Island context. However, Wimberly also noted that "late" McLeod forms merge into Weeden Island types. The constant association of McLeod ceramics with Weeden Island pottery at both village sites and burial mounds suggests that, alternatively, McLeod is perhaps best considered to represent a local Weeden Island manifestation that developed over a period of several centuries as diffusion from eastern Weeden Island settlements intensified.

Five McLeod phase components were excavated during the WPA investigations in southern Clarke County. Four of these—the Deas, McLeod, James, and Beckum sites—were villages, while the fifth—the Rockey Ford site—was a small mound (Wimberly 1960). The type site, the McLeod village, was located on a natural levee running parallel to the southern banks of Horseshoe Lake, an old meander channel of the Tombigbee River. The occupation area at this site covered a quarter of an acre and consisted of a shallow midden deposit containing scattered mussel shell lenses. A number of post holes were exposed; three distinct groups appear to represent the remains of crude structures. One of these structures was rectangular with an open end and interior dividing walls, while the other two were open, semicircular structures perhaps representing windbreaks. Several midden pits were found in the area of these structure patterns. One burial was encountered, a partially flexed adult female. A sample of 8,094 sherds was recovered from the McLeod village, including 21 percent plain ware, 26 percent check-stamped, and 53 percent simple-stamped. Nine sherds of the classic Weeden Island series were found, including five Carabelle Incised, one Carabelle Punctate, one Keith Incised, one Mound Field Net Impressed, and one Tucker Ridge Pinched. Only one chipped-stone tool was recovered, a biface drill, which again raises the possibility that prehistoric Mobile Bay area groups utilized projectiles of wood or cane with sharpened tips rather than some stone points.

Another major McLeod habitation site was discovered at the James village locality three miles upstream from Horseshoe Lake. This extensive village was situated some 800 feet from the Tombigbee River on a natural levee. Between the present river and the village is an area appearing to be an abandoned riverbed, suggesting that the habitation site was once nearer the river than at present. In the shallow midden deposit at James village, two structure patterns were discovered. One was elliptical in shape, measuring some 20 by 15 feet, while the other represents an open-end, rectangular structure with a central hearth. Both structures are reminiscent of those found at the McLeod site. Twenty-six midden pits were found around these post-hole patterns. Twelve human burials and five dog burials were also exposed in the habitation area. One large pit, 4.5 feet in diameter and 3 feet deep, contained the remains of five individuals—an adult male, an adult

Human Effigy Vessel from a Weeden Island Mound in Clarke County, McLeod Phase (After Moore 1905)

female, an adolescent, and two children—buried at the same time, perhaps a nuclear family struck by some unknown tragedy. Most of the burials found at the James village were partially flexed. Only one was accompanied by mortuary offerings, a string of marine-shell beads.

C. B. Moore (1905a, b) discovered several McLeod burial mounds along this area of the Tombigbee River during his turn-of-the-century explorations. Three merit description. The Paynes Woodyard mound, a structure built of sand and measuring 40 feet in diameter and 4 feet in height, was found to contain typical Weeden Island features (Sears 1958). Moore found a pottery cache in the eastern side of this structure. The four vessels in this deposit represent Weeden Island Punctate, Weeden Island Plain, Carabelle Incised, and Weeden Island Zone Red. All of these specimens had a hole punched through the vessel bottom. In the central portion of the mound base, a partially flexed burial was discovered sandwiched between deposits of sandstone slabs.

A second burial mound, the Carneys Bluff mound, also contained a pottery cache in the eastern side. One vessel was an anthropomorphic effigy, another an Indian Pass Incised bowl, and the third a vessel of the Weeden

Plain and Check-stamped Vessels from a Weeden Island Mound in Clarke County, McLeod Phase (After Moore 1905)

Island Plain type. At the base of the central portion of the mound, a burial was found surrounded by sandstone slabs. Bundle burials and isolated skulls, also at times encapsulated with rocks, were found in the mound fill. Yet another burial, a partially flexed inhumation, was found in a subsoil pit beneath the mound base.

The third burial mound discovered by Moore, the Kimbells Field mound just north of the present town of Jackson, was 5 feet high and 48 feet in diameter. Forty-five burials were found within this structure, including bundle burials, a few cremations, and twenty-three isolated skulls. A mass of mica was found near one skull and a copper earspool near another. Plain, incised, and check-stamped sherds were recovered from the mound fill. Two plain vessels were found in the western side of the mound and a gourd effigy bowl in the eastern side. Near the mound center a cache of five vessels was discovered, among which were bowls and jars of the Weeden Island Incised, Weeden Island Plain, and Wakulla Check Stamped types. At the base of the mound a subsoil burial pit was found that had been capped with sandstone slabs.

The Tates Hammock Phase

Six Tates Hammock phase components—four habitation sites and two sand mounds—were excavated during the WPA investigations of archaeological sites in the salt marshes west of Mobile Bay on the southwestern Alabama coast. One of these sites, the Andrews Place shell midden, was found within the limits of the present town of Coden. This midden, which covered an area 1,000 by 400 feet, paralleled the shore of Portersville Bay. The shell deposits at Andrews Place once stood 10 to 12 feet high but had been considerably reduced by commercial road-building operations. At the time of investigation, the midden was only 2.5 feet thick, except in an area where a large oak tree had preserved an 8-foot-high remnant. The midden was found to contain massive accumulations of oyster shell and fishbone, suggesting littoral economic activities. There was no evidence of structures. Nine burials were exposed, most of which were partially flexed; there was one bundle burial. Only three pieces of chipped stone were recovered—two stemmed points and one small, triangular arrowhead—while over 5,000 pottery sherds were collected from a single excavation unit. The major Andrews Place ceramic types were plain and check-stamped wares. Sixteen percent of this sample was composed of clay-tempered wares, mainly plain and check-stamped vessels identical to the more profuse sand-tempered types. A collection of 101 classic Weeden Island sherds (3 percent) were recovered, including incised, punctated, and pinched varieties.

Three more Tates Hammock phase components were found across Powells Bayou from the Bayou La Batre site to the west of Andrews Place. On the southern bank of Powells Bayou, WPA investigators discovered the Tates

Hammock midden, which covered a 200-square-foot area. No structure patterns were encountered; three partially flexed burials were the only features noted. A sample of 659 pottery sherds was recovered and when analyzed was found to contain 20 percent check-stamped, 49 percent plain sand-tempered, and 26 percent clay-tempered ware. Weeden Island types constituted some 5 percent of the total sample.

One hundred feet to the south of the Tates Hammock midden, the first of two nearby sand mounds was found. One of these, the Powell mound, was 100 feet in diameter and 12 feet high. Three borrow pits were located just west of the mound. The Powell mound had been built in two stages. The first was a layer of gray sand 2 to 2.5 feet thick covering an area 6.5 feet in diameter. The second sand layer was 5.5 feet thick. That no burials were found in this mound is not surprising considering the poor preservation conditions. A sample of 834 sherds was taken from the mound fill, and the types and frequency variations noted within this ceramic sample compare favorably to the Tates Hammock midden collection. Some 150 feet south of the Powell mound, a second structure was raised. This site, the Salt Marsh mound, was 35 feet in diameter and 2.5 feet high. A subsoil pit was discovered under the base of the central portion of the structure and a flexed burial found within this pit. Again, a ceramic sample almost identical to those found at the two other nearby sites was collected from the mound fill.

The Alabama River Region

The Alabama River is formed by the confluence of the Coosa and Tallapoosa rivers at the southeastern edge of the Piedmont uplands, just north of present-day Montgomery. From these headwaters the Alabama flows westward across the Black Belt until it reaches the area around Selma, where it arcs southward through the Coastal Plain to its juncture with the Tombigbee in southern Clarke County. Archaeological explorations in the Alabama River drainage area began around the turn of the century when C. B. Moore (1899) investigated prehistoric sites along the riverbanks. Later, in the 1920s, a group of Montgomery citizens organized the Alabama Anthropological Society, headed by the indefatigable Peter Brannon. Brannon and his associates excavated, in what can only be termed a cavalier manner, dozens of Indian settlements and mounds along the Alabama River. The results of their investigations were reported in the society's publication, *Arrowpoints*, which ran through twenty-one volumes between 1920 and 1936.

James B. Griffin of the University of Michigan visited the Montgomery area in the summer of 1937 to study amateur collections and visit local archaeological sites. The results of this study were included as part of Griffin's 1946 synthesis of eastern North America prehistory. Some thirty years

Powells Mound, AMNH 9 Mb 9

Marsh Island Shell Midden, AMNH 1 Mb 5

lapsed before scientific investigations were again resumed in the area. In the early 1960s David Chase moved to Montgomery and began an unprecedented study of local archaeology that spanned fifteen years and resulted in the location of some two hundred prehistoric sites. Chase has identified almost a dozen regional phases and has published portions of his findings in several reports (1965; 1967a, b; 1968a, b, c). He has generously supplied me with an outline of his forthcoming synthesis of central Alabama prehistory, an act that has greatly facilitated the compilation of this summary.

During the 1960s The University of Alabama also began a series of archaeological salvage projects in conjunction with the construction of three reservoirs along the Alabama River. Two field seasons of investigations were conducted between 1965 and 1967 in the area to be inundated by the Claiborne Lock and Dam in Monroe County. Six prehistoric sites were located and excavated during this project (Graham 1967). Upstream, archaeological surveys revealed twenty-seven sites in the project area of the Millers Ferry Lock and Dam in Wilcox County (Cottier 1968). An additional twenty-nine sites were found along the Alabama in the area of the Jones Bluff Lock and Dam in Autauga and Lowndes counties (Dickens, Prince, and Benthall 1968; Dickens 1971; Nielsen 1970). In 1971, University of Alabama archaeological salvage operations were resumed along the Alabama River prior to the construction of Interstate Highway 10. Of thirteen archaeological sites found in the path of this project, two were extensively excavated, revealing large Woodland components (Futato 1973).

The most recent work in the Alabama River drainage region has been conducted by C. Roger Nance of The University of Alabama in Birmingham. In 1970 Nance (n.d.) began excavation at the Durant's Bend site, located some seven miles east of Selma in Dallas County. The forthcoming report on this multicomponent site should greatly enhance our understanding of the Woodland sequence in this region. Under Nance's direction, Marvin Jeter (1973) summarily conducted a survey of Dallas County that resulted in the location of eighty more sites. Nance has also conducted salvage operations in the Montgomery area in connection with the planning of a flood-control project. These investigations resulted in the first radiocarbon date on the well-known Hope Hull manifestation (Nance 1975).

The cumulative results of three-quarters of a century of archaeological investigations in the Alabama River drainage region have produced a complex Woodland sequence. Largely due to the nature of these research efforts—surface collection and salvage along the immediate banks of the river—some Woodland manifestations are better known than others. For certain phases settlement and subsistence are well documented, while for others information is based only upon ceramic associations. Following are brief summaries of the major Woodland phases in the Alabama River drainage region as they are now understood.

The Cobbs Swamp Phase: 200 B.C.–A.D. *300*

Two major waves of foreign influence, both emanating from cultures to the southeast, can be recognized in the regional Woodland sequence. The earliest of these diffusions occurred during the middle Woodland period and is marked by the appearance of Deptford ceramics at sites along the Alabama River. Later, after A.D. 500, Weeden Island pottery diffused from coastal communities into the interior. The appearance of these ceramic forms in Woodland components in central Alabama denotes the beginning of the late Woodland period.

Deptford-like ceramics have been found at a number of large sites in the Montgomery area. They constituted a sizable component at Durant's Bend and have been found as far downriver as the Claiborne Lock and Dam Reservoir. The grit-tempered Cobbs Swamp check-stamped pottery resembles the Cartersville series of the upper Coosa Valley more than the classic Deptford ware. Bold and linear check stamping is rare in both the Cobbs Swamp and Cartersville assemblages. The similarities noted in these two wares are probably due to their common origin and contemporaneous diffusion into the interior. Cobbs Swamp pottery is often found in association with fabric-impressed sherds in early components and with Swift Creek complicated-stamped sherds in later zones. Tetrapodal bases are common features on jar forms.

Several small Cobbs Swamp phase shell middens have been found along the banks of the Alabama, but more extensive settlements have been discovered up tributary streams. At these sites greenstone celts; medium, triangular projectile points; and stone gorgets are commonly found. Ceramic disks, some with central perforations, have also been reported in Cobbs Swamp context. Chase has reported the recovery of caches of hickory nuts and acorns in midden pits at some of these components, suggesting that gathering, as well as hunting, constituted a major economic activity of these peoples.

The dead were occasionally buried in village areas. Burial mounds have not been found for this period in central Alabama, and little else is known about middle Woodland mortuary ceremony in this area. At one Cobbs Swamp village, Chase did discover what appears to be a ceremonial cache, including a number of ground hematite concretion bowls, three tetrapodal trays with ground edges that were made from broken pottery vessels, and a claystone zoomorphic effigy pipe depicting a bear.

The Calloway Phase: A.D. *300–600*

Calloway ceramics show influence from the Santa Rosa–Swift Creek traditions and display the first evidence of contact with Weeden Island settlements. Calloway pottery, a predominantly plain ware, is grit-mica tempered and takes the form of bowls or conoidal base jars with slightly flaring rims. Small tetrapodes are known but are uncommon; lips are often decorated by notching. Minor ceramic types include Swift Creek complicated-stamped forms; rocker-stamped decorations similar to the Santa Rosa patterns; and a number of Weeden Island types, including Weeden Island Plain, Weeden Island Zone Red Filmed, and Carabelle Incised.

Several small Calloway shell middens have been found along the Alabama shoreline and up small tributary streams. A single burial is known, a flexed adult inhumation found in one of the shell-mound deposits, with no grave associations. The Calloway lithic assemblage is known to include small, stemmed or notched projectile points, similar to the Swan Lake type, and elongated biface blades.

The Dead River Phase: A.D. 500–700

The pottery associated with the Dead River phase forms a typological link between Calloway and the succeeding Hope Hull phase. Two major types are found in the Dead River ceramic assemblage, Kilby Plain and Dead River Red Filmed. Kilby Plain vessels have conoidal bases and excurvate rims, often exhibiting a line of tooled indentations below the lip circumscribing the entire vessel. The red-filmed vessels, which indicate Weeden Island influence, are small, straight-sided, round-bottom bowls.

Dead River phase components have been found only at small riverine shell middens. Greenstone celts and small, Hamilton-like triangular arrowpoints; trade vessels of the Weeden Island Punctate and Keith Incised types; and only a few Swift Creek sherds have been found at these sites.

The Hope Hull Phase: A.D. 700–900

The Hope Hull phase is one of the best known of the Woodland manifestations in central Alabama. The following summary is largely drawn from a synthesis of Hope Hull data by David Chase (1968a). This cultural complex was first recognized as a distinct prehistoric manifestation by R. P. Burke (1933), a member of the Alabama Anthropological Society. Burke referred to what he called a "subculture," which he named the "Orange-Red Pottery People" after the bright orange-colored slip found on bowl-shaped vessels. Burke delineated three ceramic and several lithic types that he thought were diagnostic of the culture. He also noted that, while some flexed burials were found in village middens, mounds were also constructed for the dead. Burke describes some of the artifacts found with burials:

A bone gorget was found at the Ashley Place by E. M. Graves. This was a shallow burial. Small round disc shaped gorgets have been found at the Hope

Hull site. The beads are usually disc or button shaped, and made of shell. These people made round and barrel shaped shell beads. Some of the round shaped beads from the Ashley Place are ¾ inch in diameter. A large drinking cup made of a conch shell was found in a burial at Hope Hull. Marginella shells and a long sea shell were perforated as beads. Hundreds of perforated water-worn pebbles have been found at the Thrasher Place and at the Ashley Place. These may have been strung and used as ornaments.

About 15 beautiful greenstone celts have been found with the burials at Hope Hull. These are of excellent workmanship, highly polished. They may have been used as ceremonial objects, or as implements in preparing hides. Some of those from the Ashley Place are over 11 inches long. [Burke 1933]

James B. Griffin, during his visit to Montgomery in 1937, studied local collections and made surface collections from sites of the "Orange-Red Pottery People," referring to the phenomenon as the "Hope Hull focus." David Chase has more recently conducted excavations at one of these localities, the Hickory Bend site, situated on the south bank of the Tallapoosa River some 20 miles east of Montgomery. This site was a large village that may have been fortified. A 40-foot-long line of post holes was found by Chase along one perimeter of the village area, suggesting a stockade. Nine Hope Hull phase burials were unearthed in the midden zone, two of which contained grave goods. A burial of a small child was associated with a cache of 8 conch-shell cups, and around the neck of an adult burial were found 29 marine-shell disk beads, 50 small shell beads, and 11 marginella beads. Stains of copper oxide on the skull of the adult burial suggest the former presence of a copper burial offering. Six other partially flexed burials were found in a common grave pit that had been capped with clay.

Hope Hull burial mounds are commonly small conoidal structures of sand and clay. Chase found one of these at a pure Hope Hull habitation locality, the Jenkins site, also on the south bank of the Tallapoosa. This mound is 40 feet in diameter and 3 feet high. A test unit excavated in an eroded side of this structure revealed a large amount of Hope Hull pottery.

Hope Hull ceramics, as well as the mounds and marine-shell burial offerings, reflect contact with Weeden Island cultures to the south. Two major types, Adams Plain and Montgomery Red Filmed, constitute the Hope Hull ceramic series. About 90 percent of all Hope Hull pottery found is of the Adams Plain type, a conoidal-base jar form. The Montgomery Red Filmed vessels are usually small, shallow bowls sometimes decorated with engraved rectilinear lines or zoned punctate designs. A radiocarbon date of A.D. 775 ± 55 has been obtained by Roger Nance from a Hope Hull shell midden, Mt 201, near Montgomery. Hamilton-like small, triangular arrow points have been reported frequently from these Hope Hull components.

The Hope Hull phase may represent a link in interior Weeden Island trade with highland ethnic groups. The contemporaneous Hamilton burial-mound complex of eastern Tennessee is also characterized by small earthen tumuli often containing burials associated with marine-shell gorgets and beads. A number of red-filmed, zoned-punctate, and rectilinear-incised sherds, reminiscent of Weeden Island types, may be associated with the Hamilton component at Hiwassee Island (Lewis and Kneberg 1946). Also found at Hiwassee Island was a fragment of a punctate-decorated rim castellation similar to those found on Weeden Island bowls. Red-filmed sherds have been reported from the Guntersville Basin and from Pinson Cave near Birmingham in late or terminal Woodland context (Heimlich 1952; Futato 1973:124).

The Henderson Phase: A.D. 500–800

Downstream from Montgomery, another late Woodland manifestation, the Henderson phase, was first identified by Chase and later formally defined by Roy Dickens (1971) on the basis of cultural materials recovered from four small shell middens in the Jones Bluff Reservoir area of Lowndes County.

Henderson ceramics are sand tempered, and three major types are recognized—check-stamped, plain, and punctated. These appear to represent local versions of the Weeden Island types—Wakulla Check Stamped, Weeden Island Plain, and Carabelle Punctate. The check stamping covers the entire exterior vessel surface on globular or straight-sided bowls and conoidal-base jars. Rim forms are folded, thickened, or unmodified. The punctate decorations are found on bowl forms characterized by rounded or flattened lips and by occasional rim castellations.

The Henderson lithic assemblage is composed of small-stemmed or triangular arrowpoints. Both pitted and unpitted hammerstones have also been noted. Henderson sites are small, one- to two-acre shell middens usually located on the first river terrace, apparently seasonal, riverine camps. No structure remains are known. Two types of features discovered at these sites are: (1) small, basin-shaped pits perhaps used to steam shellfish, and (2) deep, bell-shaped pits used as storage receptacles. Nuts and seeds, including one squash seed, have been found in these latter pits. A radiocarbon date of A.D. 530 ± 100 was obtained by Dickens on a sample of charred nutshells from one Henderson storage pit. This feature contained a large amount of plain ware and only a small number of check-stamped sherds, suggesting that it was used during early Henderson times.

The Autauga Phase: A.D. 800–1100

The last known Woodland manifestation in central Alabama is the Autauga phase, centered in the area between Selma and Montgomery. This cultural complex was originally called the "Bear Creek phase" (Dickens 1971), but the name was later changed by Chase to its present form in order to avoid confusion with the Texas Bear Creek ceramic series. Autauga ceramics are sand tempered and are usually plain or have punctated decorations. Small amounts of incised, check-stamped, and corncob-marked ware are also associated with the Autauga assemblage. The major vessel form is a medium-to-large bowl. The punctated decoration consists of fingernail impressions that begin just below the lip and cover the entire exterior surface. This form is possibly related to the Weeden Island type, Tucker Ridge Pinched.

A single major Autauga component, Au 7 in Autauga County, was reported by Dickens in the Jones Bluff area. This extensive village was situated on the second river terrace and covered some ten acres. One unusual feature was recovered in the village area at Au 7—Feature 1, a large, rectangular, shallow depression measuring 11 by 13 feet, may represent the remains of a semisubterranean structure. A large sample of Autauga cultural materials was found in this depression, including pottery fragments; small, triangular arrowpoints of black chert; and a pebble hammerstone. A radiocarbon date of A.D. 920 ± 105 was obtained from a deposit of charred nutshells associated with this feature.

Richard Yarnell (1971) has analyzed the botanical remains from Feature 1. He reports the presence of corn, hickory nut, acorn, and walnut, suggesting a horticultural economy supplemented by seasonal gathering. In comparison to the Henderson middens, only a small amount of mussel shell was found at Au 7. A few shallow, basin-shaped pits and a number of scattered post holes were also noted. The data recovered from Au 7 suggest a large, stable resident population practicing maize horticulture and using the bow and arrow, prior to Mississippian settlement of the area. The role these Autauga peoples played in Mississippian development in central Alabama remains a topic for future investigation.

The Chattahoochee Region

Archaeological investigations along the Chattahoochee River, which forms Alabama's southeastern boundary, began around the turn of the century when C. B. Moore (1907b) explored the area. Later, in 1947, Wesley R. Hurt surveyed the Chattahoochee floodplain in an area encompassing portions of Russell, Barbour, Henry, and Houston counties. Hurt's project, sponsored by the Alabama Museum of Natural History, resulted in the location of 124 habitation sites and 20 mounds or mound groups. A report on this work is contained in a recent volume on Chattahoochee archaeology edited by David L. DeJarnette (1975). Plans for the construction of a series of dams along the Chattahoochee precipitated intensive archaeological salvage programs in the areas to be inundated. Between 1957 and 1962, investigations were conducted in the Jim Woodruff Reservoir, the Oliver Basin, and in the Walter F. George Basin by personnel from The University of Alabama, Florida State University, and the University of Georgia (Bullen 1950, 1958; McMichael and Kellar 1959; Kellar, Kelly, and McMichael 1962; DeJarnette 1975). These archaeological projects have produced considerable data concerning the Woodland sequence in southeastern Alabama, a continuum represented by three major cultural manifestations: Deptford, Swift Creek, and Weeden Island. This sequence has been most recently reviewed by N. J. Jenkins (1976), and his outline has served as the basis of this present summary.

Deptford: 300 B.C.–A.D. 100

The initial Woodland occupations of the middle and lower reaches of the Chattahoochee Valley are represented by components containing a Deptford ceramic assemblage. This regional expression of the Deptford culture can be divided into two sequential phases. Early Deptford settlements are characterized by three pottery types—check-stamped, plain, and fabric-impressed. This latter finish treatment appears to be related to the Dunlap Fabric Marked type of northern Georgia, and its presence in the southern Chattahoochee Valley can be attributed to diffusion downstream from settlements of the contemporaneous Kellog culture of that area (Caldwell 1958). Although fabric-impressed sherds are rare in these ceramic samples, their presence provides a good temporal marker. Fabric impressing did not become a popular finish treatment in northern Georgia until after 300 B.C., and the recovery of sherds of this type in southern Chattahoochee Valley assemblages suggests that this area was not occupied by Deptford peoples before middle Woodland times.

Late Deptford components in the southern Chattahoochee Valley are differentiated from earlier manifestations by the appearance of simple-stamped, complicated-stamped, and cord-marked wares, and by the cessation of production of fabric-impressed vessels. Both Deptford phases in this region are characterized by a chipped-stone assemblage containing large, square-stemmed projectile points; smaller, triangular points; biface blades; drills; and flake scrapers. Also, during late Deptford times, local ethnic groups began to participate in the Hopewellian interaction sphere, which resulted in the appearance of foreign finished goods and Hopewellian mortuary ceremony.

Three early Deptford components have been identified in the Alabama portion of the Chattahoochee Valley. Two of these settlements are represented by small, transitory camps. Site Ho 19 in Houston County was discovered by Hurt on a small, sandy ridge overlooking a tributary of the Chattahoochee. Cultural materials were found scattered over an area encompassing 150 by 225 feet. The small ceramic collection recovered from the surface of this site consisted of 26 plain, 2 check-stamped, and 4 fabric-impressed sherds. Hurt also found site Ru 16 in Russell County, situated on top of a small ridge above Weolustee Creek some 13 miles west of the Chattahoochee. From the surface 8 plain and 4 check-stamped sherds were collected. However, unlike site Ho 19, a large lithic sample was found at Ru 16. Numerous stone chips, two stemmed projectile points, and a drill were found, indicating that tools were fabricated or repaired during the occupation of this locality.

A major early Deptford component, perhaps representing a base camp, was discovered beneath a platform mound at a third location, the Shorter site in Barbour County (DeJarnette 1975). This mound and an adjacent habitation area were located just north of present-day Eufaula less than half a mile west of the Chattahoochee. The earthen platform appears to have been built by later, protohistoric Lamar peoples. A sample of 1,035 sherds recovered from a premound midden and in the first layer of the mound contained a typical early Deptford assemblage. Check-stamped sherds constituted 65 percent of the sample, plain sherds 32 percent, and fabric-impressed sherds 3 percent. The upper layer of the mound, which was made of earth gathered from the surrounding village midden, also contained a high percentage of check-stamped and plain sherds, but the presence of simple-stamped, complicated-stamped, and cord-marked sherds indicates that this locality was occupied through late Deptford times as well. A sherd collection from the village area was found to contain similar percentages of these later types.

The occurrence of a Deptford component encapsulated by a Mississippian mound was also noted at the Mandeville site, across the Chattahoochee River in Clay County, Georgia (Kellar, Kelly, and McMichael 1962). The Mandeville site consisted of two mounds separated by a large, multicomponent village area. Mound A, the Standley mound, was a truncated earthen pyramid 240 feet long, 170 feet wide, and 14 feet high. Mound B, the Griffith mound, was a conical burial structure 50 feet in diameter and 12 feet high. The Deptford component at this site was designated Mandeville I by the excavators. The Mandeville I assemblage, found concentrated in premound village deposits, in the lower zones of the platform mound, and in the primary core of Mound B, was characterized by a predominance of plain and checked-stamped types and by significant percentages of simple-stamped and complicated-stamped sherds. Evidence of participation in the Hopewellian interaction sphere by Mandeville I peoples is indicated by the recovery of typical Hopewellian artifacts in association with the Deptford cultural material. Included in the sample of the Hopewellian artifacts were large quantities of cut mica, a quartz crystal, copper beads, a platform pipe, galena nodules, greenstone celts, three flint blades, and ceramic anthropomorphic figurines. The figurines are stylistically similar to northern Hopewell forms but were made of local clays.

Early Swift Creek: A.D. *100–500*

The regional early Swift Creek phase, which represents a direct continuum from late Deptford, is best documented at the Mandeville site,
where it was designated Mandeville II. The Mandeville II ceramic assemblage is defined by high percentages of Swift Creek Complicated
Stamped and plain wares, with check-stamped and simple-stamped sherds
constituting minor types. A transition in projectile-point forms also serves as
a marker between the late Deptford and early Swift Creek phases. The large,
square-stemmed type popular in Mandeville I was replaced by a smaller,
expanded-base form during Mandeville II times.

The Mandeville II component at the Mandeville site was concentrated in
the upper layers of the village midden, in the upper layers of Mound A, and
in the final mantle of Mound B. Hopewellian-related materials were recovered in the Mandeville II zones of both mounds. In the occupational zones of
Mound A were found large quantities of mica, a shark tooth, fragments of
ground hematite, and a fragment of a platform pipe. Recovered from the
Mandeville II layer of Mound B were several pounds of galena, 9 greenstone
celts, 5 copper panpipes, 14 copper earspools, a large greenstone spade, a
platform pipe, and a skull exhibiting copper stains, perhaps from a head-
dress. The recovery of sherds from vessels imported from Santa Rosa settlements and from Crystal River suggest an intensification of contact between
Mandeville peoples and Florida groups during early Swift Creek times.

While the distinction between the Mandeville I and Mandeville II components at the Mandeville site appears to have been clearly documented by
the original excavators, a note of caution should be added. Recent studies of
the pottery from Mandeville suggest that at least at this particular site the
differences in the late Deptford and early Swift Creek components are not so
well defined as originally presented. Betty A. Smith (1975) has reanalyzed the
Mandeville ceramics and has suggested that these components represent a
single continuous occupation. Support for her contention is found in an
analysis of the Hopewellian trade goods at the site (Toth 1966). The
homogeneity of these artifact types and the known temporal position of
certain forms indicate that the major traits of the Mandeville ceremonial-
mortuary complex should date to the first two centuries A.D. Many of the
trade goods found at Mandeville, such as the panpipes, are classic Hopewellian types and, in general, serve as horizon markers for middle Hopewell
manifestations.

Late Swift Creek–Weeden Island: A.D. *500–1000*

After A.D. 500, indigenous Swift Creek populations appear to have participated in intensive interregional diffusion with Weeden Island groups to the
south in northern Florida. During late Swift Creek times, complicated-

Vessels from a Weeden Island Mound on the Chattahoochee River (After Moore 1907)

stamped vessels continued to dominate local ceramic industries, but Weeden Island types became increasingly popular. After A.D. 800, Weeden Island ceramics replaced the traditional Swift Creek types in the southern Chattahoochee Valley. This Weeden Island II complex is best documented in the Torreya phase of the Apalachicola River area (Milanich 1974). Jenkins (1976) has suggested that the similarities between the Chattahoochee and Torreya assemblages are of a sufficient magnitude to include these southeastern Alabama components in the Torreya phase. The Torreya ceramic assemblage contains large percentages of Wakulla Check Stamped and Weeden Island Plain pottery and minor amounts of cob-marked, complicated-stamped, punctated, incised, and cord-marked sherds. Red-filmed bowls have also been noted in Chattahoochee Valley Weeden Island burial mounds.

Two of these local Weeden Island burial mounds were excavated by C. B. Moore (1907b). The Fullmore's Landing mound was discovered 1.5 miles east of the Chattahoochee River in Houston County. This structure was three feet high and was found to contain a number of burials in a poor state of preservation; several had been covered with pieces of decomposed chert. In the eastern side of the mound, continuing into the central portion, a pottery cache was unearthed, containing seven complete vessels and many fragments of others. These vessels had been "killed" by punching a hole through the bottom or by deliberate breakage. All specimens described by Moore are typical Weeden Island types.

Moore found a second Weeden Island burial mound at Purcell's Landing upstream in Henry County. No burials were discovered, probably due to poor preservation conditions. However, in the eastern side of the structure, Moore found the diagnostic pottery cache. This deposit consisted of many vessel fragments and two complete "killed" red-filmed and punctate-decorated bowls.

7: The Mississippian Stage

During the two centuries prior to A.D. 1000, aboriginal culture in Alabama began to take on a decidedly different form. Regional archaeologists continue to debate whether this change was initiated through trade and culture contact with resident ethnic groups in surrounding areas or by actual population movement into the Alabama region. The truth may lie somewhere between these two theories. However, the result of this culture change is quite obvious in the archaeological record of late prehistoric times. The resultant prehistoric manifestation is called the Mississippian, a development that produced such impressive civic-ceremonial centers as Moundville in Alabama, Etowah in Georgia, Spiro in Oklahoma, and Cahokia in Illinois. According to Jesse Jennings, "In areal extent of influence, ceremonialism, public works, technology, population density, and general richness, the Mississippian is exceeded by no other aboriginal American culture north of Mexico" (1974:246).

Before tracing the development of Moundville and other Mississippian communities in Alabama, a generalized overview of Mississippian culture will first be presented. This should give the uninitiated some basic background information and provide the serious student with a useful summary. Unless otherwise noted, the major sources used in compiling this descriptive summary are J. B. Griffin (1967), Jennings (1974), Howard (1968), and Willey (1966).

The emergence of the Mississippian stage is marked by the appearance of distinctive forms of pottery, commonly shell-tempered, and by the construction, on or around a central plaza, of large earthen platforms that served as substructures for temples, elite residences, and council buildings. Other important Mississippian traits include the use of the bow; arrows tipped with small, triangular stone points; floodplain horticulture based upon maize, beans, and squash; religious ceremonialism connected with agricultural production and centered around a fire-sun deity; long-distance trade; increased territoriality and warfare; and the emergence of highly organized chiefdoms.

The major development of the Mississippian took place in the central Mississippi Valley, where it is recognized by A.D. 700. Many archaeologists believe that this core area also was the center of origin for Mississippian development, but this has yet to be demonstrated with certainty. It has been suggested that there were three distinct but mutually interdependent centers, all of which were influenced over the centuries by minor cultural increments ultimately radiating out of Mesoamerica. These three major re-

Major Mississippian Sites

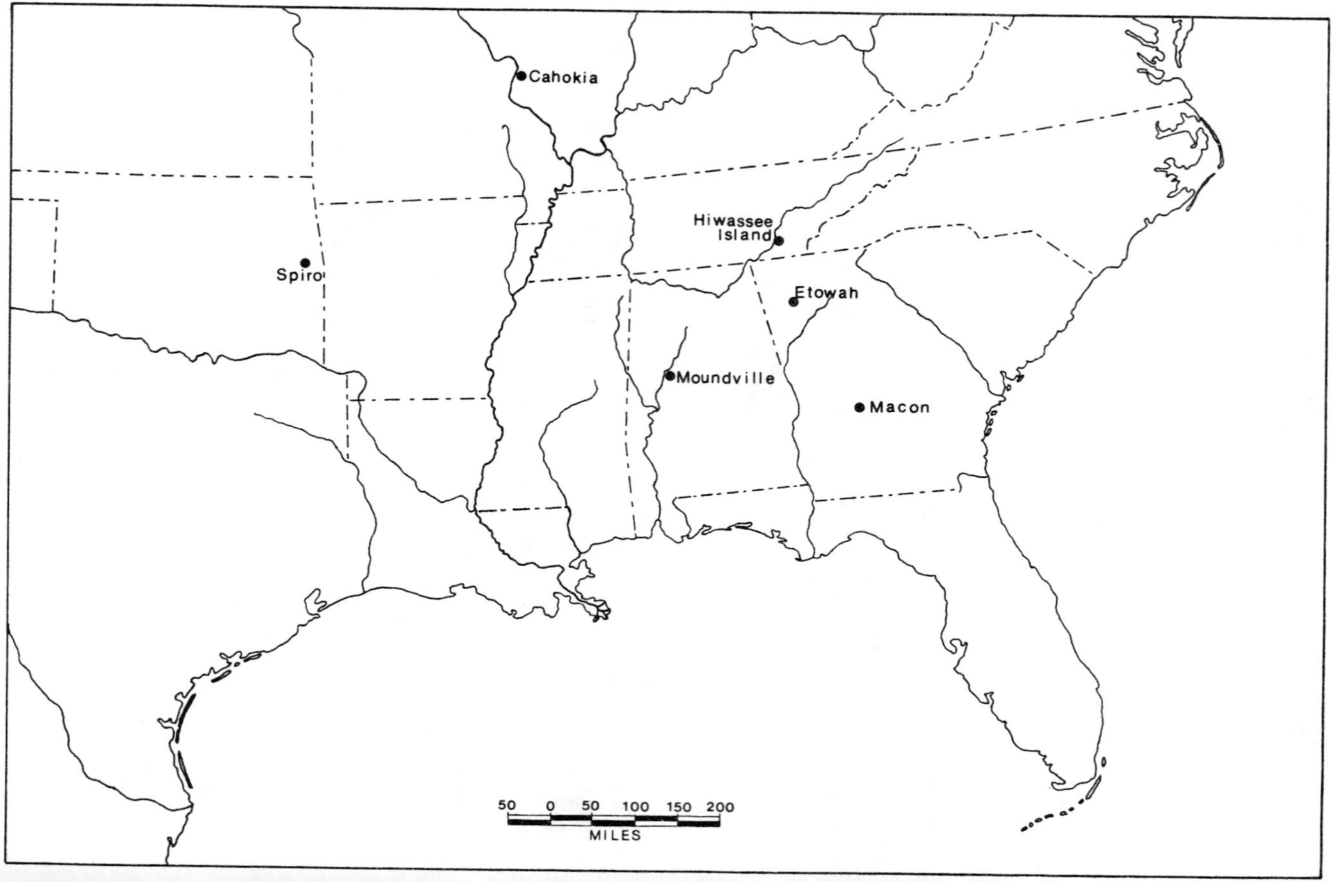

Cahokia

Spiro

Hiwassee
Island

Etowah

Moundville

Macon

50 0   50 100 150 200

MILES

gional centers of the Mississippian were (1) the central Mississippi Valley, which embraces the largest known Mississippian site, Cahokia near East Saint Louis, Illinois; (2) the Tennessee-Cumberland drainage area; and (3) the Caddoan area of eastern Oklahoma, Texas, and Louisiana. The height of this Mississippian development occurred in the period between A.D. 1200–1500, and its final general disappearance took place in the historic period beginning around A.D. 1700.

Mississippian temple mounds served as raised platforms for structures built of timber, mud, and thatch, although, as we shall see, high-status burials and human offerings were also at times placed within them. Charles Wicke (1965) recently summarized the similarities between Mexican pyramids and these southeastern temple mounds and made a convincing case for their common origin. Among the major similarities are truncated (flattened) tops, ramps or stairways leading up one side, evidence of periodic destruction of the temples, and construction of additional layers over the entire pyramid. As many as ten building phases have been recognized in some mounds. Even though these mounds were not the result of a single building event, their size and the amount of human labor expended in their construction is often staggering to the imagination. All were built with basketloads of earth carried on human backs. The largest known Mississippian mound, Monk's mound at Cahokia, stands 100 feet high, has basal dimensions of 700 by 1,080 feet, and covers some sixteen acres. This structure alone is estimated to contain some 22 million cubic feet of earth. While Monk's mound is unique in size, even some of the smaller structures required countless hours of human toil. Each of the largest mounds at Moundville and Etowah, both about 60 feet high, contain over 4 million cubic feet of earth.

Public buildings and elite residences placed on mound summits were generally larger, more ornate versions of ordinary domestic dwellings. Mississippian houses were rectangular to square in shape. Family dwellings were commonly between 10 and 30 feet in length. During the initial stage of house construction, wall posts were set and usually wedged into narrow trenches or placed into deep individual post holes. Canes (wattle) were then threaded between, or tied to, the wall posts and plastered with mud (daub) inside and out. These wattle and daub walls made a thick, insulated shell that was durable but demanded frequent minor repair. The roofs were constructed of wattled rafters topped with thatch, set at a steep angle to allow good runoff during the heavy rains so frequent in the humid Southeast. Dwellings normally contained only a single room, although partitions of cane mats may have been used to divide the chamber. A centrally located fireplace usually was built inside the dwelling to provide warmth in the winter and protection from insects in the summer. Most of the cooking was probably done outside, either in the open or under kitchen sheds. Household

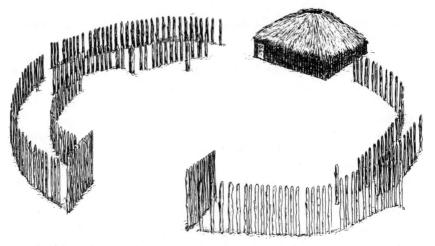

Mississippian Structure and Stockade Enclosure, Bessemer Site, AMNH 114 Je 14

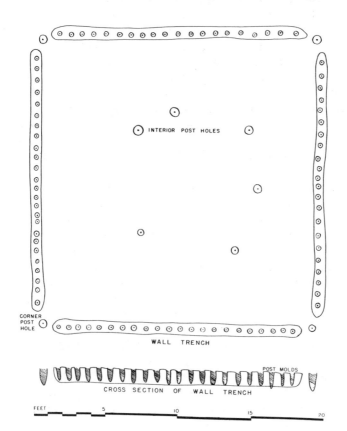

Open-Corner Wall Trench Pattern, Bessemer Site, AMNH 466 CAL

furniture was meager: Wooden stools were probably used, and wooden benches or sleeping platforms were constructed along the interior walls.

Mississippian material culture demonstrates the potential of Stone Age technology. Metals, such as copper, were cold hammered and worked into various forms of ornamental or ceremonial objects. However, smelting was unknown, and clay, fired into pottery, was the only raw material that was structurally altered. Even so, Mississippian craftsmen achieved remarkable results in knapping, grinding, carving, and weaving natural materials. Five primary raw materials were utilized: stone, plant products (wood, cane, and fibers), shell (both freshwater and marine), bone, and clay.

Stone was chipped into arrow points, knives, scrapers, drills, and ceremonial objects and pecked and ground into celts, axes, adzes, manos, mortars, and sharpeners. Bone and antler were worked to make awls, pins, needles, projectile points, fishhooks, hoe blades, chisels, and beads. Shell was used to make hoe blades, gorgets, beads, pins, dippers, bowls, and trumpets.

Because of the humid southeastern climate perishable materials usually have not survived over the centuries unless they were accidentally charred. Much of what must have been elaborate assemblages of wooden, vegetable, and animal-craft products has been lost. Even so, based upon the few such artifacts that have been preserved and upon ethnographic accounts, a glimpse of this part of the Mississippian material culture can be reconstructed.

Timber and cane were major raw materials. Wood was used as a primary building material and was carved into digging sticks, canoes, handles, drums, bows, arrow shafts, and a wide variety of other utilitarian objects. Some wooden ceremonial objects have survived in mounds, including masks of red cedar with shell inlay work, human statues, and a variety of rattles often carved into animal forms. One of the few pieces of decorated wood recovered from Moundville is a five-inch-long wooden plaque of walnut bark with a spider and other designs carved on it. Bark was also used in making cloth, ropes, thread, and dyes.

Cane was used in numerous ways. John Swanton (1946:244–48), the leading southeastern ethnographer of this century, notes that the seeds of cane were used as food and that cane was used in weaving baskets and mats, and in making fish traps, weirs, arrows, beds, knives, torches, boxes, cradles, sieves, fans, hampers, blowguns, shields, fences, rafts, litters, drills, tubes, pipes, and hair ornaments.

Weaving was also practiced, and, although the true loom was not known, a rectangular wooden frame was used to separate the fixed vertical warp strands. The weft was woven across the warp with a needle or bodkin of bone. Although hand weaving was slower than using a loom, it enabled the Mississippian craftsman to produce a variety of woven materials. Garments were made by weaving plant fibers, hair, or a combination of these, sometimes with feathers added to the outer surface. Rabbit hair was a favorite material because it was easily procured, could be readily dyed, and could be spun into yarn by itself or in combination with vegetable fibers. One such rabbit-hair garment was recovered from a Mississippian mound at Spiro. Designs were dyed into garments and capes by a process similar to the batik technique used by contemporary artists. Wax or a similar substance was placed on the garment around the design. Dye was then applied to the uncoated areas, and, after drying, the material was placed into hot water to dissolve the wax, leaving the desired pattern. The few small scraps of such clothing that have survived the elements indicate that Mississippian apparel, especially ceremonial costumes, must have been both colorful and aesthetically pleasing even by modern standards.

Ceramics were the forte of Mississippian artisans. Clay, mixed with crushed shell, grog, or sand, was transformed into an almost bewildering array of forms. According to James B. Griffin:

> The pottery complex is much more diversified than previous complexes. There are clear functional differences of form and quality. Cooking and storage jars and simple bowls are the most common objects, but there are many polished and decorated bowls, bowls with effigy heads, plates, large pans for evaporating salt, and a wide variety of bottles, including animal and effigy forms. There is a considerable use of red filming and of bichrome, polychrome, and negative painting, particularly in the central area of the Mississippi cultures, which also had such exotic forms as the stirrup-neck bottle and human-effigy-head-vases. [1967:190]

Both raw materials for manufacturing and finished craft products were obtained through trade networks connecting regional population centers. Trade was of two major types: (1) long-distance trade of rare products made of materials of limited distribution such as copper, galena, marine shell, and certain types of stone; and (2) localized redistribution of foodstuffs and craft goods. Many of the more rare trade objects (copper celts, marine-shell cups, flint batons, etc.) served as indicators of rank and status in Mississippian society. The rarity of these symbolic artifacts, and therefore their social value, was maintained through cultural rules requiring that they be placed into the graves of their holders as mortuary offerings. Thus elite burials at Mississippian sites are usually accompanied by elaborate goods, while graves of commoners are often bare.

Mississippian subsistence was based upon three major procurement systems: (1) cultivation of crops such as maize, squash, beans, pumpkins, and sunflower; (2) collection of native plant foods, especially nuts and fruits; and (3) exploitation of animal populations. Fields were tilled with digging sticks and hoes. Hunters used the bow and arrow and made traps and snares. Fish were taken on hooks of bone and copper and in traps and weirs. Poisons, made from certain tree roots, were probably also employed in shallow pools to stupefy fish, a widespread custom in historic times. Shellfish were also gathered and baked, steamed, or added to stews.

Subsistence activities followed an annual cycle based upon seasonal availability of both cultigens and native food sources. Bruce D. Smith (1975) recently completed a study of Mississippian hunting activities. He believes that the exploitation of animal populations was based upon the concept of maximization; that is, Mississippian hunters attempted to gain maximum meat yields with a minimum of effort. This was accomplished by concentrating on certain species that were abundantly available on a regular seasonal basis, easily taken, and produced high meat yields. According to Bruce Smith:

> The projected yearly cycle of animal exploitation by Middle Mississippian groups can be divided into two basic seasons: a summer season during which various species of fish were the most intensively exploited, with aquatic species of turtles and perhaps rabbits being of secondary importance, and a winter season of exploitation during which a wide variety of terrestrial mammals, migratory waterfowl, beaver, and turkey were taken. The whitetail deer was the most important animal species taken during this winter hunting period. [1975:122]

Mississippian settlement patterns reflect the diversity of these subsistence activities. Most Mississippian settlements are found within the alluvial valleys of major rivers on or adjacent to stretches of sandy loam or silt loam soils. These locations were chosen, at least in part, to exploit the well-drained, moist, fertile, and easily cultivated alluvial soils. Lewis Larson (1970) recently argued that there were factors other than agricultural requirements that determined settlement location. He believes that proximity to boundaries of major natural areas (ecotones) and access to diverse native floral and faunal resources were of equal importance.

The shift in settlement patterns recognized in many areas during the late Woodland-Mississippian continuum is thought to have coincided with the emergence of chiefdoms. This type of sociopolitical organization differs from tribal societies in several ways. Chiefdoms usually have a higher population density than tribes. While there is a wide range in population among chiefdoms, the mode in the East was probably between 5,000 and 15,000. The chiefdom society is also much more complex and more highly organized (Service 1962:142). As tribal societies evolve into chiefdoms, two major features appear: (1) social organization based upon hereditary ranking, and (2) centers or capitals from which economic, social, and religious activities are coordinated.

That certain Mississippian societies were organized within a social framework distinguished by hereditary ranks has been demonstrated both ethnographically and archaeologically. First, it is known from early European accounts that some of the surviving Mississippian societies, such as the Natchez and Taensa, were characterized by hereditary ranking. Second, studies of mortuary practices at major Mississippian centers such as Spiro (J. A. Brown 1971), Etowah (Larson 1971), and Moundville (Peebles 1971, 1974) clearly indicate differential treatment of the dead, which is indicative of ranking.

The salient characteristics of a chiefdom can be summarized as follows. Lineages were graded on a prestige ladder. Usually one of these lineages reserved the right of tenure for the highest political office, that of chief. Ranking of lineages and individuals was based on a principle of primogeniture, and frequently present was the concept that all members shared common descent from a single ancestor. Within such an organization everyone was related to the chief, and each individual occupied a unique position of rank that was determined by calculating the exact degree of closeness or distance to the chiefdom. In chiefdoms containing several thousand people, and without a system of written records, this type of calculation based upon tradition must have been a herculean task. One result of this type of reckoning is that true stratification into classes, characteristic of states, was absent, as there were no large groups made up of people of equivalent rank. Societies were still primarily based upon kinship, with ranking mechanisms added as new structural principles. In these societies, the person of the chief was almost sacrosanct. He was furnished with a retinue of wives, retainers, and assistants, and contact with him was restricted by elaborate rules of protocol. The life crises of the chief—birth, marriage, and especially death—were usually accompanied by elaborate public ritual.

The chief's economic basis of power lay in his role as a redistributor. Local specialization in craft products and in production of food and raw materials was highly developed in chiefdoms. Surpluses of these goods were periodically produced by local kin groups and paid as kin obligations to the chief. In turn, the chief used these surpluses for maintenance of his household and, importantly, for redistribution to his subjects. Chiefs could also command periodic contributions of labor for construction and maintenance of their houses, public buildings, temples, fortifications, and mound substructures. Such contributions of labor were symbolically rationalized as kin obligations and involved reciprocal payment by the chief in the form of goods, particularly food. Market economies were usually absent or weakly developed in chiefdoms, and full-time craft specialization, when present, was limited to artisans attached to the chief's household.

Chiefdoms were also distinguished from tribal societies by the presence of centers or capitals. The chief and members of his lineage dwelt in such a settlement, in addition to priests, craftsmen, and political assistants. Temples, granaries, the chief's residence, and houses of noble and servant alike were present. It is likely that the major Mississippian settlements such as Cahokia, Moundville, Spiro, and Etowah were centers of this sort. Each of these chiefdoms was situated on an ecological boundary affording access to a wide variety of resources. The utilization of this edge area, or ecotone, differed from previous adaptive strategies. A band or segmentary tribe inhabiting such an area would most likely take advantage of the ecological variation present by moving from one zone to another as part of a seasonal transhumance pattern. However, in chiefdoms, which had both specialized production by localized sectors of the society and redistributive networks, *products,* not people, were moved between zones (Service 1962:145). The location of these chiefdoms on ecotones made a broad spectrum of cultivated and natural foods available. This, plus the presence of redistributive networks, generally provided surpluses that served as the foundation for continued cultural growth and as economic insurance in time of crop failure.

Warfare, or the threat of it, may have been a feature of daily life in the Southeast during late prehistoric times. While violent conflict was probably common among earlier cultures, it is in the Mississippian stage that a major change occurred in the nature of aboriginal warfare. Fortified settlements appeared for the first time. Lewis Larson (1972), who studied this aspect of Mississippian life, believes that many of the settlements in the interior areas of the Southeast were fortified. Mississippian defensive works included one or more of the following features: (1) wooden stockades with bastions constructed of closely set vertical posts, (2) dry moats, and (3) earthen embankments. In Alabama, such sites as Moundville and Gunter's Landing were fortified with palisades, and the Florence mound apparently had an earthen embankment constructed around the three sides not exposed to the Tennessee River.

Larson suggests that one cultural objective of Mississippian warfare was the seizure of a town and the territory it controlled. Because territories containing both agricultural lands and diverse environmental zones were limited, such areas were at a premium. Expanding neighboring populations, themselves inhabiting essentially circumscribed areas, could enlarge their own holdings only by invading and seizing surrounding territories.

Dismissing such maneuvers as siege as not materially feasible and frontal assault as impractical, and noting that houses were often spaced so that an entire town could not be fired upon by flaming arrows from outside the fortifications, Larson thinks that "success was dependent on surprise, surprise that caught the town during a moment of laxity in maintaining the security of its gates, surprise that generated confusion and prevented the organization of an effective defending force" (1972:391). Many of the inhabitants of conquered towns were probably driven off. Those who did not escape were either killed or taken captive. Captive women and children were often adopted by the victorious groups, while others, probably including the majority of captured adult males, were sacrificially slain. Human skulls, often elaborately decorated, have been recovered from Mississippian mounds and may represent grisly symbols of victory over a slain foe.

Another integral part of Mississippian life was ritual and ceremony. The highest expression of Mississippian ceremonialism has been called the Southeastern Ceremonial Complex, or Southern Cult. Associated with this complex was a series of art forms on several media that were widely traded and ultimately ended up as mortuary offerings in the graves of civil, religious, and war leaders. This religious symbolism, often portraying death motifs, was engraved, painted, and sculptured on ceramics, carved on shell and wood, sculptured or chipped on stone, embossed on copper, and dyed on cloth. According to James B. Griffin (1967:190), "Many of the symbols, such as the weeping eye and the bilobed arrow, are difficult to interpret, but others can be interpreted; for example, the cross, the swastika, the sun circle, and the skull, heart, and crossbones symbolize, respectively, the concepts of the four world quarters, the wind, sun worship and the sacred fire, and the sacrifice of captives."

James Howard (1968) has made a detailed study of the Southeastern Ceremonial Complex and believes that it was related to the "Busk" or "Green Corn" ceremony still practiced by many contemporary southeastern Indians. The Busk was primarily an annual ceremony that ushered in the new year. It took place when the maize or green corn had matured sufficiently to be eaten. It was basically an agricultural rite, and one of its main functions was to prepare the people to eat this important food crop without disastrous effect. However, as Howard also notes, this was only one of several important functions of the Busk; the health and welfare of the group, propitiation of animal spirits, and success in hunting and warfare were also important. From his study of both archaeological materials and ethnographic sources, Howard has concluded that: "we have every reason to believe that it was the Busk which climaxed the ceremonial year in Mississippian times. . . . It is more than likely that it was this ritual, central to the agricultural economy, which provided the main impetus for the construction of the massive temple mounds and fostered the production of the beautiful ritual objects of the Southeastern Ceremonial Complex with their attendant, religiously inspired, motifs" (1968:87).

Some of the religious symbolism of the Southeastern Ceremonial Complex may have been derived from post-classic Mesoamerica, although the way in which these concepts spread to this region remains unknown. Objects directly traceable to Mesoamerican origin have not been recovered in Mississippian context, and, conversely, diagnostic Mississippian artifacts have not been found in Mesoamerica. An interesting theory, which has been put forward by a number of archaeologists, is that the cult could have been the result of Mississippian contact with a group of traveling merchants like the Aztec *pochteca*, a group of tough, aggressive, aristocratically organized merchants who are known to have conducted long-range trading expeditions. They frequently settled among local populations and often came to dominate their hosts politically. An important aspect of this theory is that the types of

Table 4: Mississippian Chronology: Alabama Region

	Black Warrior	Tennessee Valley	Alabama River	Mobile Bay	Chattahoochee
A.D. 1700 Protohistoric A.D. 1500	Burial Urn	Crow Creek	Burial Urn	Pensacola	Abercrombie Bull Creek
Mature Mississippian A.D. 1200	Moundville	Henry Island　Hobbs Island　Kogers Island	Local Moundville Variant		Roods Sequence
Early Mississippian A.D. 900	Bessemer West Jefferson	Langston			

traits in Mississippian culture that appear Mesoamerican are precisely those that the *pochteca* would most likely have introduced: religious concepts, notions about rank, and certain sumptuary practices, such as human sacrifice.

There is, besides the factors noted above, a certain amount of data that support such a contention. The earliest recognized appearance of the Southeastern Ceremonial Complex is around A.D. 1000, when the long-nosed-god masks cut from sheet copper appear in burials in several areas of the Southeast and as far north as the Aztalan site in Wisconsin. It has been suggested that this long-nosed-god motif may be connected with the god of the Aztec *pochteca*, Yacatecuhtli, who is at times portrayed with a prominent nose. Yacatecuhtli is also sometimes shown with a group of arrows and a disk, which suggest the bilobed arrow, and with a barred staff suggestive of a serpent, which resembles engravings on shell from Spiro depicting priests holding serpent staffs (J. B. Griffin 1967:190). A large portion of the southeastern ceremonial complex symbolism and ritual appears to have survived into historic times. This also seems to be true of much of Mississippian life. Comparison of Mississippian archaeological sites and material culture with that of historic southeastern tribes shows considerable cultural continuity. A major change during this continuum appears to have been in the realm of social organization—a fission into petty chiefdoms and segmentary tribes. This decline of the major Mississippian chiefdoms appears to have occurred during the latter part of the fifteenth and early sixteenth centuries. Many of the major centers, such as Moundville and Etowah, were abandoned before DeSoto's *entrada* into the Southeast in the 1540s. Why this decline occurred is still unknown, but the reasons must be highly complex. It probably will take many more generations of archaeologists to reconstruct this event or series of events. Like the emergence of Mississippian culture, the nature of the Mississippian decline must have varied from region to region. In the following pages we will trace the emergence, florescence, and decline of the regional Mississippian culture in the Alabama area. To aid in this undertaking, this stage will be divided into three periods: early (A.D. 900–1200), mature (A.D. 1200–1500), and protohistoric (A.D. 1500–1700).

Early Mississippian Development: A.D. 900–1200

The emergence of the Mississippian stage in the Southeast has been traditionally interpreted as a series of invasions by culturally dominant ethnic groups radiating out of the central Mississippi Valley. This movement has been described as "the spread of people in exactly the same sense that the biologist might refer to the dispersion of a species of plants or animals over a domain not previously occupied" (Caldwell 1958:64). However, as clearly illustrated in the archaeological record, numerous native populations, often sedentary and quite large, already inhabited much of the Southeast prior to Mississippian occupation.

Generally, adherents to the invasionist theory dealt with this problem by calling upon another old anthropological model, "hominid catastrophism." The classic application of this model occurred around the turn of this century when the French prehistorian Marcellin Boule dealt with the Neanderthal problem by conjuring up a massive invasion of Europe by modern man, an invasion that swept away the preexisting Neanderthal population and its culture. Similarly, it was thought that late Woodland populations in the Southeast were pushed out of their territories by Mississippian invaders and were driven into the hills or into other marginal regions, where they met an unknown fate.

This expulsion was generally considered to have been so sudden that neither group contributed to the culture of the other. However, in recent years, archaeologists like Charles Faulkner (1971) of the University of Tennessee have reassessed Mississippian development in the Southeast. Faulkner's research has led him to conclude that, while population movement and replacement may have occurred in some instances, in other cases acculturation and internal development by late Woodland populations appear to best explain Mississippian emergence.

The diverse origins of the Mississippian cultural pattern in the Southeast, which are now being traced in several subareas, appear to be related to such factors as ecological potential, cultural-carrying capacity, size and stability of resident populations, and proximity to trade routes and other ethnic groups. To the north and east of present-day Alabama, three areas have been studied where major early Mississippian communities once existed. A review of the data produced may provide some insight into the nature of this development within Alabama.

To the north, early Mississippian sites have been investigated in both western and eastern Tennessee. In the Gulf Coastal Plain (a physiographic province of western Tennessee) two major early Mississippian ceremonial centers have been investigated. These sites, Obion and Pinson, are both on small tributaries of the Mississippi River. Madeline Kneberg (1952:195) described the Obion site, situated near the headwaters of the Obion River, as one of the earliest Mississippian communities in west Tennessee. She believes that this settlement was possibly the source of Mississippian diffusion into the lower Tennessee Valley, some fifty miles to the east.

At its height, Obion was a large ceremonial center with seven substructure mounds grouped around a plaza. Archaeological investigations at this site have been confined to limited testing, once in 1913 and again in 1940. Little is known about the village area except that both open-cornered wall-trench structures and single-post construction houses were built. The ceramics recovered at Obion are Mississippian in form, but both clay-tempered and shell-tempered wares were made—with a possible increase in the use of crushed shell as a tempering agent (Baldwin 1966). Globular pots were the most common vessel forms, and narrow-strap or loop handles were sometimes added. Mushroom-shaped pottery trowels and ceramic and stone discoidals were also recovered. Baldwin (1966) believes that Obion was settled around A.D. 1000 and that this occupation continued for some two to three centuries. Support for this temporal estimate has come from two radiocarbon determinations on charcoal from the old village midden under the largest mound, which produced dates of A.D. 990 ± 150 years and A.D. 1040 ± 110 years.

A similar site that could have also played an important role in the development of the Mississippian in west Tennessee is the Pinson site on the Forked Deer River in Madison County (Faulkner 1971). Preliminary tests conducted in 1961 and 1963 indicate that Pinson was a multicomponent site. At least two mounds were identified as Mississippian. During the 1961 excavations, a burned wall-trench structure was encountered. Clay-tempered pottery was found in association with this dwelling. Two radiocarbon tests on charcoal from this feature confirm the early Mississippian placement of this occupation. These dates, A.D. 850 ± 120 and A.D. 1130 ± 110, indicate that Obion and Pinson were probably contemporary.

To the east, in the lower Tennessee Valley, Lewis and Kneberg (1947; Kneberg 1952) have isolated an archaeological phase that shares some similarities with these occupations. This manifestation, called Harmon's Creek, has produced such characteristic early Mississippian traits as open-cornered, wall-trench structures; pottery discoidals and trowels; triangular projectile points; stone disks; and flint hoes and adzes. However, Harmon's Creek pottery is a clay-tempered ware with plain or cord-marked surface treatments. Substructure mounds have not been reported at Harmon's Creek Sites. The settlement pattern is one of small, dispersed hamlets rather than the nucleated village found at Obion and Pinson (Faulkner 1971).

In east Tennessee, in the upper Tennessee Valley, another early Mississippian group has been recognized. The type site for this culture is Hiwassee Island (Lewis and Kneberg 1946). Hiwassee Island towns were generally fortified with stockades of vertical logs. Within the stockaded settlement zone, substructure mounds, civic and ceremonial structures, and domestic dwellings were built. Houses were generally rectangular, open-cornered, wall-trench structures, although both rectangular and circular single-post construction is also known. Entrances were placed at the corners of the rectangular buildings, and interior features included clay-lined fire basins and clay platforms and seats.

Hiwassee Island pottery was shell tempered. The most common vessel forms were bowls and plain, globular jars, at times with added loop or narrow-strap handles. Minor varieties of surface treatment are represented by cord-marked, complicated-stamped, red-filmed, and red-on-buff vessels. One of the most diagnostic of these minority types is a vessel with a tapering neck often called a blank-faced effigy water bottle. Another characteristic pottery type found at Hiwassee Island is the fabric-marked salt pan—a large, crude, shallow bowl thought to have been used in the production of salt by evaporating brine from salt springs. Many of these pans have been recovered at sites located at considerable distances from such springs, suggesting that in some cases they may have served as communal food bowls like those used in the Southeast during historic times.

Recent excavations in the Little Tennessee River Valley have produced additional information about Mississippian emergence in east Tennessee. At the Martin Farm site, two early Mississippian components were isolated (Salo, ed. 1969). A Hiwassee Island occupation of this site was characterized by shell-tempered jars; loop and narrow-strap handles; red-filmed bowls; fabric-marked salt pans; small, triangular arrowpoints; and wall-trench and single-post construction dwellings. An earlier component exhibited what could be considered a combination of Woodland and Mississippian traits: both limestone-tempered and shell-tempered globular jars with flaring rims and occasional loop handles, triangular points, and wall-trench buildings. Faulkner (1971) has suggested a date of A.D. 900 for this emergent Mississippian component. At the nearby Mayfield site, a Hiwassee Island house was dated at A.D. 1250 ± 95 years, suggesting a local Mississippian development in the Little Tennessee River Valley over a span of some two to three centuries.

To the east of Alabama in central Georgia, another major early Mississippian site, Macon Plateau, has been discovered and investigated. Major excavations were conducted during the 1930s, and the area, along with its restored mounds, has been made into Ocmulgee National Monument. The Macon occupation of central Georgia is confined to two known sites: Macon itself and nearby Brown's Mount. Two earthworks surround the Macon Plateau site. Within this enclosure are large platform mounds, ceremonial structures, and dwellings. Most of the buildings at Macon are rectangular, wall-trench structures. Macon pottery is grit or shell tempered. The dominant vessel shapes are Mississippian forms: flaring-rim globular jars, some with loop or narrow-strap handles; blank-faced effigy bottles; and fabric-marked salt-pan ware.

Two unusual ceremonial structures have been discovered at Macon. One of these, the Earth Lodge, is a circular structure built on ground level rather than on a platform mound. It is about 45 feet in diameter and apparently served as a council chamber. Interior features include a central clay-lined fire basin and a large clay platform fashioned in the shape of an eagle. Around the circular walls, a low clay bench was built with 47 seats, each separated by clay ridges and marked by small depressions or basins at the front. Three similar basins in the back of the raised eagle-effigy platform mark the locations of additional seats. Opposite the eagle platform is a long passage entrance. The walls of the Earth Lodge were built of clay, and the roof was

supported by four large posts, stringer beams, and beams laid out radially
from the stringers to the walls. The entire structure was apparently covered
with cane and earth.

The second unusual structure at Macon is the Funeral mound, a small,
truncated earthen pyramid measuring some 230 feet long, 100 feet wide, and
25 feet high (Fairbanks 1956). Seven construction stages were isolated during excavation. The primary mound was found to have been a low (7 feet
high) earthen platform with a clay-stepped ramp. A formal structure pattern
was not present on this platform; only a single large post penetrated its clay
cap.

Burials, sometimes in log tombs, were made both under and in the
mound. These mortuary activities were accompanied by elaborate ritual
often including bone cleaning and reburial. Bodies were at times buried in
the flesh, but extended deposits of cleaned bones (often rearticulated), bundles, flexed burials, and cremations were also common. These interments
were often accompanied by grave goods consisting of ornaments, tools, and
pottery vessels (Fairbanks 1956:47). An unusual mortuary offering recovered
from one of the Funeral mound burials was a pair of sun disks made of
oval sheets of copper and decorated with a repoussé design consisting of a
semicircle with radiating lines. Objects of this type have been found at only
one other site in the Southeast, the Bessemer site in Alabama, and serve to
support the contemporaneity of these two ceremonial centers. Two
radiocarbon dates have been obtained on organic materials from Macon
sites, A.D. 1015 ± 110 from the Macon Earth Lodge and A.D. 980 ± 110 for
the early Mississippian occupation at Brown's Mount.

The Langston Phase

In Alabama, two major areas, the Guntersville Basin region and the Black
Warrior River drainage system, have produced substantial remains of early
Mississippian communities. In the Guntersville Basin of northeastern
Alabama, a number of sites that were excavated during the 1930s contained
components of one of these early Mississippian developments, the Langston
phase. The spatial distribution of Langston phase components overlaps that
of the late Woodland Flint River culture, although the later appears to have
spread downriver toward the Wheeler Basin. There are hints in the Guntersville Basin region, similar to those discovered at Martin Farm, of an
internal emergence from a late Woodland base. Heimlich (1952:16) has reported the presence at three Guntersville Basin sites of limestone-tempered
loop and narrow-strap handles, and several sites with Langston phase components have yielded large amounts of plain limestone-tempered pottery.

The Langston phase is culturally related to Hiwassee Island and shares a
number of characteristics with Macon. Langston villages were often fortified,
and substructure mounds and elaborate Mississippian mortuary ritual were

introduced into northeastern Alabama during this time. Langston pottery exhibits obvious links to Hiwassee Island. Ceramics are largely confined to plain shell-tempered bowls; globular pots, sometimes with added loop or narrow-strap handles; and fabric-impressed salt pans. Minority types, perhaps representing trade vessels, include red-filmed, red-on-buff, and complicated-stamped wares. Two major Langston phase sites are Gunter's Landing and Langston, both initially reported in the Guntersville Basin survey volume (Webb and Wilder 1951).

The Langston site, on an elevated ridge in the floodplain of the Tennessee River in Jackson County, consists of a substructure mound and an adjacent village area. Only the mound was excavated. The summit of the mound had been leveled for agricultural purposes during the 1880s and at the time of investigation was 57 feet in diameter and only 2 feet high. Ten features were recorded during excavation, including two single-post construction rectangular buildings and seven clay-lined fire basins. Five burials were discovered, of types similar to those reported at Macon. Only one complete burial was discovered, the remainder having been subjected to postmortem decapitation and reburial. The complete burial was extended, and two unidentifiable copper fragments were found in the grave. Three isolated skull burials were present. The fifth burial was that of an extended adult with only the skull removed; the mandible was found lying on its lower chest.

Seven complete pottery vessels were found in the mound area. One of these is a blank-faced effigy bottle, and the rest are plain, shell-tempered globular jars with flaring rims, some with paired-loop or narrow-strap handles. The sample of shell-tempered pottery fragments recovered from the Langston site was confined to two types, plain and fabric-impressed salt-pan ware. These shell-tempered sherds constitute 80 percent of the 1,600 sherds recovered. The remaining 20 percent of this sample are largely plain limestone-tempered sherds and a small amount of clay-tempered plain and cord-marked pottery. One thick, clay-tempered, fabric-impressed sherd was recovered that resembles the shell-tempered salt-pan ware. Other cultural material recovered at this site include a mushroom-shaped ceramic trowel; pottery and stone discoidals; greenstone celts; and small triangular projectile points.

The other major Langston phase site, Gunter's Landing, was located on high ground in the Tennessee River floodplain half a mile northwest of the present-day city of Guntersville. The Gunter's Landing site was in a triangular-shaped area of land bordered on one side by the Tennessee River and on another by a swamp and small stream. The site was thus well protected by bluffs and swamps on two approaches. However, to add to this natural defense, the inhabitants constructed a log stockade around their village. Within this stockaded area, the early Mississippian peoples constructed a temple mound.

The investigation of this site proved to be one of the most challenging salvage efforts attempted by TVA-WPA archaeologists. Questions of legal title prevented archaeological investigation until only five weeks remained before inundation of the basin. With this small amount of time left, they decided to concentrate on the village area surrounding the mound. Toward the end of this period, the TVA engineers discovered that the mound was situated in the center line of a proposed railway ferry channel. Subsequently, excavators were dispatched to the area to begin removal of the mound. This leveling work was accomplished in only a few days by employing twenty-four-hour shifts. Archaeologists were likewise on the site twenty-four hours a day in an attempt to salvage as much information as possible before total destruction of the mound. Often working under lights, archaeologists quickly checked the exposed surface as each Letourneau swept by. Utilizing this unusual technique, they found that this mound, which prior to destruction had stood 13 feet high with basal dimensions of 180 by 230 feet, was built in a series of stages, each with a truncated summit supporting a rectangular building.

Due to these circumstances, only a small portion of the village area was excavated. Two rectangular structures were exposed. One of these, almost square in shape, was a single-post construction dwelling that measured some 17 feet on each side. The second structure was a wall-trench, open-cornered dwelling with an interior, clay-lined fire basin. This house was 17 feet long and 14 feet wide. Two burials were found in the village area, but both had been disturbed and were poorly preserved.

The wooden palisade enclosed an area of 2.4 acres. The stockade line formed a circle 365 feet in diameter with its center at the highest point of the temple mound. Three rectangular bastions located during the excavation were set 80 feet apart and probably supported elevated platforms upon which defenders could stand and fire arrows upon attackers attempting to breach the fortifications. This may imply that the distance between these bastions was determined by the effective range of arrows fired from such positions.

Another type of extension built on the outside of the stockade line apparently served as a protected gateway. This gateway consisted of an enclosed line of posts paralleling the stockade, with an opening at one end. A second narrow space in the stockade at the opposite end of the passageway served as an entrance. This design would have allowed only a few people at a time entry into the interior of the stockade. This factor, and the necessity of making sharp turns before gaining access into the village, would have negated the effectiveness of a frontal assault or mass charge on the gate.

Only a small sample of cultural material was recovered during the excavation of Gunter's Landing. No whole or restorable pottery vessels were recovered. Limestone-tempered and shell-tempered plain sherds were the most common types of pottery fragments. Shell-tempered loop and narrow-strap handles, some decorated with flattened nodes, were present. Small

Langstone Phase Jar Forms, AMNH 140 Ma 48, 93 Ms 55, 109 Ms 55

Gateway and Stockade Line at the Gunter's Landing Site, AMNH 39 Ms 7

amounts of fabric-impressed salt-pan fragments and red-filmed sherds were also found. Eight incised sherds were reported in the original study, but a reexamination of these specimens indicates that the incisions were probably not intentional decorations but instead were remnant tool marks. Greenstone celts, stone and pottery discoidals, and small, triangular projectile points were also recovered from the village area.

The information obtained from Gunter's Landing indicates that early Mississippian Langston phase peoples settled this area of the Tennessee Valley, built the stockade around their village, and erected the large temple mound. This mound grew by increment as various structures were built in succession on its summit. By locating their village in this place, Gunter's Landing inhabitants could control the rich bottomlands to the north and south and could have maintained a strategic control over river traffic.

It has not yet been possible to identify an early Mississippian occupation downriver, in the Pickwick Basin area of northeastern Alabama. In an attempt to demonstrate the presence of such an occupation, Walthall reanalyzed a large sample of the pottery from the McKelvey mound (Webb and DeJarnette 1942) in Hardin County, Tennessee, just north of the

Alabama border. This site consisted of a small, truncated mound and an underlying village area containing large amounts (over 20,000 sherds) of late Woodland clay-tempered pottery. The cultural and temporal placement of this assemblage and its spatial position within 75 miles of early Mississippian settlements in west Tennessee indicated a high probability that a similar component would be present. Key traits searched for were clay-tempered handles and Mississippian rim forms. No such clay-tempered ceramic forms were found in this sample, and the Mississippian component, which included the truncated mound, was found to be a fully mature Mississippian occupation.

The negative result of this examination raises two possibilities. First, it may be that Mississippian settlement or influence did not reach this area until the mature Mississippian period. Or the absence of any emergent Mississippian traits in the Pickwick Basin may be due to sample error. This latter hypothesis is favored here for the following reasons: During the WPA-TVA salvage program, time and money allowed investigation of only shell mounds, burial mounds, and other large or impressive sites. Literally hundreds of smaller sites, including many habitation areas, were located during the survey but not excavated. This factor, coupled with the known settlement pattern of the Harmon's Creek peoples (small, dispersed hamlets), suggests that emergent Mississippian villages may yet be found in this area. Only future investigations will demonstrate which of these alternatives is valid.

The West Jefferson Phase

Another factor supporting the presence of a yet unrecognized emergent Mississippian occupation in the Pickwick Basin area is the existence of a well-documented early Mississippian sequence in the Black Warrior River drainage system less than a hundred miles to the south. Sites in this region have yielded evidence of an early Mississippian development culminating in the mature Mississippian Moundville phase (A.D. 1200–1500). Jenkins and Walthall have proposed the following cultural sequence. During the early ninth century A.D. late Woodland McKelvey peoples in the Black Warrior drainage area began to be influenced by early Mississippian diffusion probably emanating from settlements to the north, although the exact source and mechanism of this diffusion is still open to debate. The result of this cultural interaction is the emergent Mississippian West Jefferson phase, which is thought to have had its highest expression during A.D. 900–1000. Spanning the temporal gap between West Jefferson and the Moundville phases, an early Mississippian development, the Bessemer phase, can be recognized.

During the Bessemer phase (A.D. 1000–1200), Mississippian traits such as rectangular buildings, earthen temple mounds, and elaborate mortuary ritual appeared in the Black Warrior area for the first time. There also seems to have been a trend toward an increase in the use of crushed shell over clay as a tempering agent during this time.

The West Jefferson phase was initially defined by Ned Jenkins and Jerry Nielsen (1974) and has been the subject of further research by Jenkins (n.d.) and John O'Hear (1975). Three West Jefferson phase habitation sites, designated 1 Je 31, 1 Je 32, and 1 Je 33, are known, although similar components are present at the Bessemer site and at Moundville, where fragments of clay-tempered globular jars with narrow-strap handles have been found (Ned Jenkins: personal communication). The three Jefferson County sites were excavated during a University of Alabama archaeological salvage project conducted in 1973 under the direction of David L. DeJarnette in an area some twenty miles west of Birmingham near the confluence of Village Creek and the Locust Fork of the Black Warrior River.

All three village areas were found within a square-mile area along the edge of the small alluvial floodplain of Village Creek. Numerous features were recorded at each of these sites. Post holes were abundant but only a few semicircular structure patterns could be recognized. Many pits and hearths had been dug into the living areas. Charred acorns, hickory nuts, and maize were recovered from some of these features. Clay-tempered plain sherds represented the most common type of pottery at these West Jefferson phase components. Many of these sherds appear to have been fragments of globular jars with occasional loop or narrow-strap handles. Minority pottery types are represented by plain, red-filmed, black-filmed, and incised shell-tempered sherds, a few clay-tempered sherds bearing cord marking, brushing, punctations or check stamping, and by a small number of sand-tempered, check-stamped or pinched sherds resembling the Autauga series of central Alabama that may represent trade vessels. Autauga pottery has been dated in the Alabama River area at A.D. 920 ± 105 (Dickens 1971). There is some indication that the shell-tempered pottery sherds found at these West Jefferson phase sites may date to an occupation coeval with the later Bessemer phase. John O'Hear (1975) has reported that at site 1 Je 32 the weighted average for pits containing shell-tempered pottery is A.D. 1014 ± 30, and the weighted average for pits containing only clay-tempered pottery is A.D. 928 ± 43.

Other West Jefferson traits include stone and pottery discoidals; small, triangula   ; and a large number of mortars, mullers, and nutting stones. N\   uls were encountered during the excavations at these habitation areas. In general, the West Jefferson phase compares favorably with other emergent Mississippian cultures like Harmon's Creek. Both of these groups produced clay-tempered pottery and had settlement patterns composed of small, dispersed hamlets. Absent in West Jefferson are wall-trench structures and, conversely, Harmon's Creek lacks the Mississippian vessel forms typical of West Jefferson. Both of these cultures appear to have emerged from a late Woodland base, and both exhibit varying combinations of Woodland and Mississippian traits.

The Bessemer Phase

Some twenty-five miles upstream from the West Jefferson phase sites is the Bessemer site, in a small meander of Village Creek. This site, presently within the city limits of Bessemer, was a small ceremonial center consisting of three mound structures and a surrounding village area. Carl E. Guthe of the University of Michigan supervised the first controlled excavations at Bessemer in 1934. Archaeological investigations were continued in the following year and again in 1939 by Alabama Museum of Natural History research teams headed by David DeJarnette and Steve Wimberly (1941).

The three major structures at Bessemer were designated by the excavators—the ceremonial mound, the domiciliary mound, and the burial mound. The ceremonial mound was oval in shape with a relatively flat top and had a truncated knob at its smaller or western end. The mound base was 130 feet long and 102 feet wide. The summit of the mound was 10 feet high and the knob added an additional 8 feet. Excavation revealed that the ceremonial mound had a stone pavement laid over an old village area. Two flat-top earthen structures were later added in increments, and as a final effort the smaller knob was added. No structure patterns were noted on the summits of the earthen platforms. One burial was made in the mound during the construction of the final knob-like projection. This interment was that of a young adult female buried in a partially flexed position. Two pottery vessels, both plain jars, one with paired narrow-strap handles, were placed near the body.

Four structure patterns were found under and around the ceremonial mound. Three of these were wall-trench rectangular structures with open corners. One of these buildings contained a central clay-lined fire basin and a raised clay seat near the center of the west wall trench. The fourth structure was a rectangular building with individually set wall posts.

The domiciliary mound was a truncated pyramid 11 feet high and 120 feet in diameter at the base and was built in six stages. The primary mound was a low flat-topped pyramid with an eight-step clay ramp. Ten rectangular structures had been built on the summits of the successional stages. All of these were open-cornered, wall-trench buildings with separate corner posts, and some contained clay-lined fire basins. Under the mound in the old village area 17 additional structure patterns were found, 14 of which were typical wall-trench buildings. The other 3 were circular patterns of individually set posts. The rectangular structures ranged in dimensions from 20 by 23 feet to 39 by 61 feet; the circular patterns ranged from 26 to 33 feet in diameter. One structure, No. 12, is of special interest. This was a rectangular wall-trench structure that had a double curvilinear stockade or enclosing fence

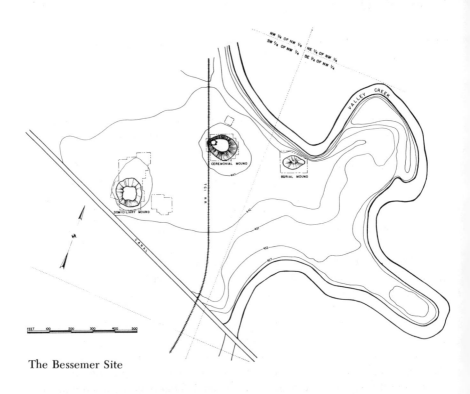

The Bessemer Site

Rectangular and Circular Structure Patterns at the Bessemer Site, AMNH 94 Je 14

extending from one side. At the opposite end of the fenced courtyard were two parallel wall trenches each 10 feet long and set 18 feet apart to form a large entranceway.

The third structure found at Bessemer was termed the burial mound, although excavations revealed that, like the Funeral mound at Macon, this structure was actually a truncated earthen pyramid with both inclusive and intrusive burials. No structure patterns were noted on top of either of the two construction stages. The primary mound was a low (3 feet high) platform that had been surrounded by a double line of posts forming a stockade. No burials were found under or within this initial stage. Later, during and after the addition of the final construction stage (which covered the old stockade), twenty-two burials were dug into the mound or around its base. Burial treatment was varied and, like the burials at Macon, extended burials, re-burials, and skull burials were present. Eleven of these were in groups of two, three, and four. Pottery vessels were the most common mortuary offering; the only other artifacts recovered in association with these burials were thirty-eight shell beads and a copper sun disk like those found at Macon.

The pottery vessels recovered from the burials in the vicinity of this third mound were the most elaborate ceramic forms recovered from Bessemer. These vessels include globular jars, bowls, and water bottles, usually with plain-surface treatments but at times decorated by black filming and simple incised patterns.

Some 2,500 pottery sherds make up the ceramic sample from Bessemer. Approximately half of these were clay tempered. Most of these sherds appear to represent globular jars with occasional narrow-strap handles; minor types include sherds with punctated, cord-marked, or brushed surfaces. The remaining half of the ceramic sample was tempered with crushed shell, most of which have a plain-surface finish; both loop and narrow-strap handles are present. Minor shell-tempered types include sherds decorated with black filming and/or incising. Many of the shell-tempered sherds were found in the area of the burial mound and may represent broken mortuary offerings. Other artifacts recovered from Bessemer include a pottery trowel, stone and pottery discoidals, triangular projectile points, and greenstone celts and hoes.

Douglas McKenzie (1964a, 1966) and Christopher Peebles (1971) have associated the Bessemer site with the Moundville phase, thus equating this ceremonial center with the mature Mississippian period. However, a review of the data recovered from Bessemer indicates that the major occupation of this settlement dates to the early Mississippian period and that this locality was abandoned before the mature Mississippian florescence at Moundville. Comparison of the material culture from these two sites further suggests that there may be a Bessemer-like early Mississippian component at Moundville.

The early Mississippian placement of the Bessemer site is supported by the presence of large amounts of West Jefferson clay-tempered pottery and by a constellation of early Mississippian traits like those previously discussed from sites in northeastern Alabama, Tennessee, and Georgia. DeJarnette and Wimberly (1941) prepared a trait list comparing Bessemer to Moundville and some of the mature Mississippian sites in the Tennessee Valley. Moundville and the Tennessee Valley sites (especially those in the Pickwick Basin) were found to share a large number of traits. Prominent among these were artifacts and motifs associated with the Southeastern Ceremonial Complex. It is important to note that, although the Bessemer site is strategically situated between Moundville and the Tennessee Valley, not one southeastern ceremonial complex artifact was recovered during its excavation. One can only conclude that Bessemer was abandoned before the appearance and spread of this manifestation. Diagnostic traits shared by Moundville and Bessemer are confined to the black-filmed and incised shell-tempered pottery forms, which are probably late Bessemer traits, inasmuch as these vessels and many of the fragments of such vessels were intrusive into the final stage of the burial mound or were found around its outer perimeter. These data indicate that the Bessemer site should be considered to represent, like Obion, Hiwassee Island, and Macon, one of the major early Mississippian settlements in the Southeast.

One of the most perplexing problems concerning the West Jefferson and Bessemer phases is the absence, or near absence, of burials. Only twenty-five burials were found at Bessemer, while sites like Moundville have yielded thousands of human burials. It is possible that during the early Mississippian period the treatment of the dead was not conducive to preservation or that cemetery areas have not yet been found. One site that may shed some light on this problem is Pinson Cave, located just north of Birmingham in Jefferson County, some twenty-five miles northeast of the West Jefferson phase sites.

The archaeological potential of Pinson Cave was first discovered by Carey Oakley (1971) of The University of Alabama, who conducted an excavation of this site in 1969 and 1970, revealing that Pinson Cave had been used as an ossuary. Half of the cave deposit was excavated, yielding the remains of more than fifty individuals. Most of these interments were apparently made in the flesh, although one occurrence of a cremated bundle burial was noted. Most of the burials had been dropped into the cave through a vertical shaft that penetrated the roof. A small number of other burials had been carried into the cave through a small entrance and were placed on a natural shelf. Only a small amount of cultural material was recovered in association with these burials. Two pottery sherds were found; one of these was a small, plain limestone-tempered sherd. The other pottery fragment was a sand-tempered, red-filmed sherd similar to both the Tennessee Valley Laws Red Filmed and central Alabama Montgomery Red Filmed types, which date to the late Woodland and early Mississippian periods. Other artifacts recovered from Pinson Cave include marine-shell ornaments; bone pins; sandstone saws; and small, triangular projectile points. Several of these projectile points were found imbedded in human bone.

Pinson Cave was investigated and reported prior to the discovery of the West Jefferson sites. At that time Oakley interpreted the Pinson Cave component as being associated with the late Woodland Hamilton complex because many of the projectile points matched the Hamilton point-type description. However, Hamilton-like points have also been reported from a number of early Mississippian sites (including West Jefferson). A radiocarbon date of A.D. 1040 ± 80 was later obtained on Pinson Cave materials. These factors, plus the increased evidence of warfare among early Mississippian communities, suggest that the burials at Pinson Cave date to this period and may provide further insight into early Mississippian mortuary customs.

The Mature Mississippian Period: A.D. 1200–1500

Moundville

The largest and best-known mature Mississippian site in the Southeast is Moundville, located on the high bluffs of the Black Warrior River in Hale County, Alabama. Moundville is situated near the northern edge of the Coastal Plain in the fall line hills physiographic region some fifteen miles south of Tuscaloosa. In sheer size and number of earthen pyramids, Moundville ranks second only to the great Mississippian town of Cahokia in Illinois. Excavations were not conducted at Moundville until the turn of this century when C. B. Moore (1905a, 1907a) made two expeditions up the Black Warrior Valley. Moore dug into most of the mound structures and the enormous amount of elaborate cultural material he found made Moundville one of the most famous archaeological sites in North America. Unfortunately, Moore's beautifully illustrated reports on his investigations at Moundville also stimulated the imagination of relic collectors and dealers. During the following twenty years portions of the site were vandalized and looted. Cultivation and subsequent erosion also took their toll. For a time it appeared that Moundville, like many other prehistoric sites, was facing slow, but total, destruction.

Thanks to a small number of concerned local citizens, Moundville has been saved from this fate. Today, the mounds and surrounding lands are a state monument, containing a museum, archaeological laboratories, reconstructions, campgrounds, and wooded paths open to the public on a year-round basis. David L. DeJarnette served as curator of the monument for over twenty years. He participated in the first scientific excavation at the site in 1929 and saw Moundville transformed over a period of forty years from a cotton field to one of the finest facilities of its nature in the world.

Beginning in 1923 local citizens, headed by Mrs. Jeff Powers of the nearby

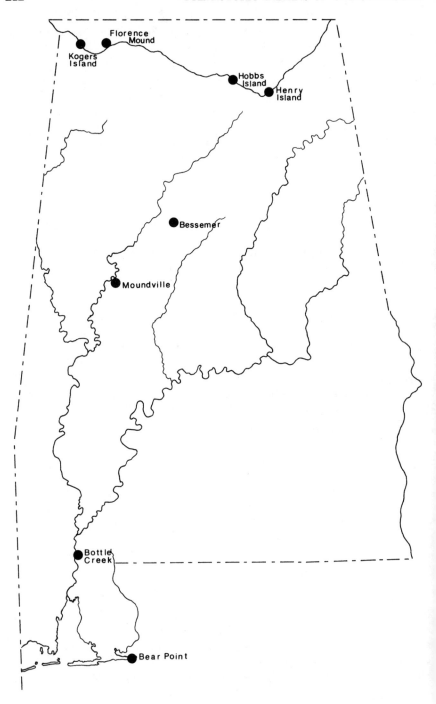

Major Mississippian and Protohistoric Sites in Alabama

Site at Moundville

community of Moundville, began a drive to preserve and protect the site and its mounds. Through the efforts of these people and Alabama Museum of Natural History personnel, the land surrounding the mounds was purchased piecemeal, beginning in 1929. In 1933 the name given the purchased property, Mound Park, was changed to its present form, Mound State Monument. The Civilian Conservation Corps, a depression-era work force, began an erosion control program that in 1938 was enlarged to include restoration of the mounds and lakes and construction of roadways and buildings, including an impressive museum (DeJarnette 1968). During this time (from 1933 to 1941) the Alabama Museum of Natural History excavated almost 500,000 square feet of the site. This project was directed at various times by Walter B. Jones, David L. DeJarnette, and other museum personnel. It produced approximately 2,200 burials and associated cultural material, 100 clay fire basins, 75 structure patterns, almost a million pottery sherds, and thousands of other artifacts. These excavations, coupled with Moore's previous investigations, provide the data base for Moundville.

However, much of this information was contained in notes, diaries, and other forms of records in the Moundville files. In the early 1960s Douglas McKenzie of Harvard University examined this large volume of raw data and produced a dissertation and several reports (McKenzie 1964a, 1965a, 1966). During this time it became increasingly apparent that too much information was available on Moundville to be properly studied by a single archaeologist utilizing traditional techniques of analysis.

Very seldom do archaeologists find themselves faced with too much data. This problem confronted archaeologists working in the Tennessee Valley during the 1930s, but they solved their dilemma by employing scores of WPA workers in assembly-line fashion. Each worker was trained to do one specific task of laboratory work and analysis. A solution to the more recent problem of analyzing the voluminous Moundville material was found when Christopher Peebles of the University of Michigan began work on a dissertation at Moundville in the late 1960s. Peebles did not have a large work force at his command, but he did have a viable alternative—his specialized skills, computer technology, and statistical analysis. The results of Peebles's research constitute the most thorough statement on Moundville today. From the countless files of data, Peebles has produced a detailed map of all excavations at Moundville, a 1,200-page summary of these excavations, and a dissertation and several published papers on the Moundville culture (Peebles 1970, 1971, 1974; DeJarnette and Peebles 1970). The following description of prehistoric Moundville, unless otherwise noted, is based upon this work.

During the mature Mississippian period Moundville was a major ceremonial center with a large resident population, perhaps as many as 3,000 individuals, including nobles, priests, artisans, and commoners. The site covers some 300 acres. Within this area are extensive habitation zones, 20 truncated earthen pyramids, and a large central plaza. The mounds range from 3 to 60

Wall Trench Structures, Moundville, AMNH MSM 3897

Burials Excavated at Moundville, AMNH MSM 3273

feet in height, though most of them are from 12 to 15 feet high. Excavations of these structures indicate that they were built in sequential construction stages. These mounds formed substructures for timber buildings that served as temples, council houses, or elite residences. They also contained burials of high-status individuals and offerings of human infants.

A wooden stockade and ditch may have surrounded a large portion of the site, probably forming an arc from the high bluffs of the Black Warrior River. Four lakes, perhaps originally borrow pits for mound construction, were also located inside the stockaded area. These small lakes were stocked with fish and served as natural storage containers. Some fishermen, however, lost their tackle; fishhooks of both bone and copper have been found in the beds of these lakes.

The principal reason that Moundville was located in the Black Warrior Valley appears to have been ecological. The sandy loam soils found in this area of the valley had a high agricultural potential and, when tilled with even the most primitive of techniques, produced substantial yields of corn, squash, and other cultigens. Hunting and gathering were also important in the Moundville economy. The ecotone zone of the fall line region surrounding the site provided rich seasonal harvests of deer, turkey, and nut foods. Fish, taken in traps or with tackle, also provided a valuable protein source, especially during the summer season.

There is evidence that Moundville was a planned community. Peebles's analysis of features and artifact distribution indicates that there were areas for domestic occupation, for public compounds, and for industrial activities such as pottery making, shell-bead manufacturing, and the weaving of cane mats and baskets. Certain areas were also used as game courts. Large public buildings were built near the northern end of the plaza. Domestic dwellings were located in the curved strip between the stockade and the plaza and in the area near the river. Specialized structures, including two charnel houses for the honored dead, bordered the plaza. A single structure, interpreted by Peebles as a sweathouse, was found inside the plaza area. This sweathouse was a double-walled building containing a central room with a hard-packed, clay floor. Two clay fire basins, one round and one square in shape, were sunk into the floor. This structure, like most other dwellings at Moundville, was of the rectangular, wall-trench construction type.

At its height, Moundville was a major Southeastern Ceremonial Complex center. The abundance of cult objects and paraphernalia found there suggests that Moundville both imported and produced these highly stylized luxury goods. Moundville artisans excelled in working such natural raw materials as stone, bone, and shell into a variety of forms. Their pottery is the finest ever manufactured in prehistoric Alabama. Utilitarian jars, bowls, and bottles were made of plain, shell-tempered pottery. On the other hand, their ceremonial and mortuary vessels were elaborate, decorated by modeling, incising, and engraving and often covered with a black paint or film. Black-filmed pottery was fired before the application of the paint. An organic wash was then applied and, finally, the vessel was refired to make the color permanent. This technique of double firing is unusual, if not unique, in North America. Over 80 percent of the mortuary vessels recovered from the burials at Moundville were black-filmed ware—commonly bowls, at times in effigy forms, and bottles, often with elaborate Southeastern Ceremonial Complex motifs engraved on their surface.

There are abundant indications that Moundville was also a major trade center. Raw materials and some finished products were imported and, in turn, the highly valued finished products of the Moundville artisans were exported. Exotic pottery vessels from the central Mississippi Valley, Tennessee, and Georgia have been found at Moundville, while Moundville pottery and design elements have been recovered throughout the Gulf Coast region. Copper axes and ornaments found by C. B. Moore in some of the mounds were derived from Great Lakes sources; shell was imported from the coast; and galena, flint, and other minerals were imported from a variety of highland quarries.

Many of these exotic artifacts have been recovered from Moundville burials. Over 3,000 burials have been found in the 14 percent of the sites investigated so far. Burials were made in cemetery areas, in charnel houses, and at times in the village areas and in the mounds. Most were primary inhumations, although minor numbers of bundle and isolated skull burials have been reported. Of the primary inhumations, 90 percent were extended and the remainder were partially flexed. The mounds were found to contain significantly greater proportions of secondary, isolated-skull, and bundle burials than the cemeteries. Grave goods were associated with about 40 percent of these burials in both mounds and cemetery areas.

Items placed into graves as mortuary offerings can be divided into two classes, sociotechnic artifacts and technomic artifacts (Binford 1962). Sociotechnic artifacts are not strictly utilitarian nor merely ornamental but function to differentiate social rank or status in society. Common examples of sociotechnic artifacts in other societies are a king's crown, a warrior's baton, or a gentleman's walking cane. On the other hand, technomic artifacts are utilitarian in nature, such as stone projectile points, bone tools, and wooden implements. Peebles has recognized two major sets of sociotechnic artifacts associated with the Moundville burials. The first set, composed of supralocal symbols, contains Southeastern Ceremonial Complex items of dress and office, including copper axes, celts, earspools, gorgets, hair ornaments, and symbol badges; stone ceremonial celts, disks, blades, and palettes; various minerals and shell beads and gorgets; and some specialized pottery vessels. Artifacts of this type are widely distributed throughout the Southeast and their distribution must have cut across the boundaries of many distinct ethnic groups. Peebles has called the second set of sociotechnic artifacts "local symbols." These served to differentiate individuals within a single community,

Pottery Vessel Forms from Moundville

Walnut Bark Plaque with Spider Motif, Moundville (Courtesy Chicago Natural History Museum, 50639)

Stone Palettes from Moundville

Stone Bird Effigy Bowls, Moundville (Courtesy Museum of the American Indian, Heye Foundation, 17-20 and 16-5232)

Monolithic Axe, Moundville, 11¼ inches long (Courtesy Museum of the American Indian, Heye Foundation, 17-891)

Stone Pipes, Moundville (Courtesy Museum of the American Indian, Heye Foundation, 17-2810 and 17-893)

and they probably had culture-wide significance. Local symbols have a much more restricted distribution than supralocal symbols. At Moundville and other mature Mississippian settlements these local symbols usually take the form of animal effigy vessels or parts of animals such as canines, claws, and shells. Peebles's analysis of the associations of these two sets of sociotechnic artifacts in the Moundville burials has demonstrated that their distribution is not random but reflects a pattern characteristic of a ranked society. His study of the mortuary activities at Moundville thus corroborates other supporting data suggesting that Moundville was once the center of a powerful prehistoric chiefdom.

The Moundville Phase

Douglas McKenzie (1966) first formally defined the Moundville phase on the basis of certain pottery types, including shell-tempered plain, incised, and black-filmed wares. The most diagnostic series of Moundville pottery is black filmed: Moundville Black Filmed, Moundville Filmed Engraved, Moundville Engraved Indented, and Moundville Filmed Incised. The core of the Moundville phase is a fifty-mile stretch of the Black Warrior River Valley between the fall line at Tuscaloosa and the swamps just north of Demopolis. Within this area some seventeen Moundville phase sites have been located (Nielsen, O'Hear, and Moorehead 1973). Only two of these sites have been excavated, Moundville itself and Snow's Bend (DeJarnette and Peebles 1970). The size of these sites varies from small farmsteads with no associated mounds, less than an acre in extent, to Moundville, which covers some three hundred acres. An analysis of the soils in catchments of a half-mile radius around these sites shows that they were not only located on the best, most easily worked self-renewing soils, but also that the size of these sites was correlated with soil productivity (Peebles 1974).

Four small truncated mounds, three of which have associated village areas, and a cluster of four hamlets are located within a two-mile radius of Moundville. The nearest of these sites to Moundville is 1Tu50, a small isolated mound half a mile to the north. A University of Alabama archaeological field school under the direction of Richard A. Krause has recently investigated this structure.

Moundville influence, via trade and at times perhaps involving actual colonization, was widespread. During the mature Mississippian period, Mississippian cultural material began appearing in the Chattahoochee Valley (Caldwell 1955; DeJarnette 1975) and in the Alabama and Tombigbee river systems south to Mobile Bay. Truncated earthen mounds and mature Mississippian habitation sites have been reported in the Alabama River area (Cottier 1968). One of these habitation areas, the Liddell site in Wilcox County, contained a burned structure associated with Moundville Black Filmed and Moundville Filmed Incised pottery. Charcoal taken from this structure was tested and produced a radiocarbon date of A.D. 1365 ± 60 years (Shelton 1974:169). Later, during protohistoric times, these areas of central and southern Alabama witnessed rapid demographic growth and cultural florescence. In the Tombigbee River Valley to the west of Moundville, Ned Jenkins and Jerry Nielsen have reported the presence of both truncated mounds and Mississippian habitation sites. Small amounts of black-filmed pottery have been reported from some of these sites (Nielsen and Jenkins 1973). The Mississippian settlement pattern in the central Tombigbee Valley was largely confined to scattered farmsteads. It appears that population density was consistently low in this region during late prehistoric times.

Middle Tennessee Valley Settlements

During the mature Mississippian period the middle Tennessee Valley of northern Alabama supported a large resident population. Three archaeological phases can be identified in this area, each possibly representing an autonomous, yet related, ethnic group. There is sufficient documentation in the archaeological record to suggest that each of these riverine territories supported chiefdoms that collectively had a higher population density than even the Black Warrior Valley chiefdom centered at Moundville.

In the Pickwick Basin in northwestern Alabama, several sites, including truncated mounds, can be assigned to the Kogers Island phase. Kogers Island peoples were responsible for the construction of the great mound at Florence, which in Alabama is second in size only to Mound B at Moundville. Kogers Island peoples buried their dead in cemeteries and occasionally in substructure mounds. The presence of exotic pottery in some of these graves, including a few black-filmed bowls and bottles, suggests trade with Moundville to the south and with Tennessee-Cumberland peoples to the north. The Pickwick Basin area is strategically situated between the Black Warrior and the central Mississippi valleys, and the Kogers Island population appears to have profited from exchange between these two regions. Moundville's influence in the Tennessee Valley is more in evidence in this area than in any other. Moving upstream, Moundville influence declines and is replaced by a concomitant increase in evidence of contact with populations in Tennessee and northern Georgia.

In the Wheeler Basin east of the Kogers Island territory, three sites, including two villages, can be assigned to the Hobbs Island phase. Hobbs Island peoples built temple mounds and burial mounds for their dead. These mortuary structures, unlike the truncated funeral mounds at Macon and Bessemer, were true conical burial mounds like those built by the earlier Copena peoples. Burials in these mounds were often accompanied by pottery vessels, shell gorgets, and large numbers of beads. Further upriver, in the Guntersville Basin region of northeastern Alabama, a third mature Mississippian phase, the Henry Island phase, can be recognized. Henry Island peoples had strong cultural ties with Tennessee-Cumberland populations to the northwest, with early Dallas peoples to the north, and with the Etowah chiefdom to the east. Numerous, and often large, settlements were occupied in the valley lands during this time and well over a dozen earthen pyramids have been located that date to this period. Burials were made in cemetery areas and in mounds. Stone-box graves were at times made by Henry Island peoples for their honored dead. Mortuary offerings included copper plates with repoussé designs, copper-covered wooden earspools, shell gorgets and beads, pottery vessels, and other elaborate goods.

The Kogers Island Phase

In the Pickwick Basin area three types of Kogers Island phase sites have been reported—cemetery areas such as the Kogers Island, Perry and Little Bear Creek Sites (Webb and DeJarnette 1942, 1948); substructure mounds, some with associated villages like the McKelvey, Seven Mile Island (Webb and DeJarnette 1942) and Florence sites; and upland hunting camps like the Stanfield-Worley and Buzzard Roost Creek bluff shelters (DeJarnette, Kurjack, and Cambron 1962; Jolly 1974). Douglas McKenzie (1966:38) originally assigned the majority of these sites to the Moundville phase primarily on the basis of ceramic types. However, even a cursory examination and comparison of these Pickwick Basin sites to Moundville reveal differences of sufficient magnitude to clearly warrant separate phase designations. First, of the twenty-two complete Moundville structure patterns studied by McKenzie, twenty-one are of the wall-trench type while only one is of single-post construction. Conversely, all of the structure patterns from the one site where they are reported in the Pickwick Basin, Seven Mile Island, are of the single-post construction type.

Mortuary customs also differ. Of the 250 primary inhumations studied by McKenzie, 85 percent were extended and 15 percent were partially flexed. Peebles, who studied a sample of 2,053 Moundville burials, reports that 90 percent of these were extended and 10 percent partially flexed. In the Pickwick Basin, significantly more primary inhumations were partially flexed: Seven Mile Island 25 percent partially flexed (N=16), Kogers Island 53 percent partially flexed (N=102), Perry (Unit 2) 63 percent partially flexed (N=41), and Little Bear Creek 92 percent partially flexed (N=26). Of the total 185 primary inhumations in the Pickwick Basin sample, over 55 percent were partially flexed. Also, Peebles reports that 80 percent of the burials at Moundville were single interments. However, in the Pickwick Basin sample multiple interments are much more common. For example, at the Kogers Island cemetery 33 percent of the forty-one burials were placed into graves containing from two to six individuals.

Comparison of Moundville and Pickwick Basin pottery demonstrates even more divergence. Of a sample of 390 vessels recovered in burial association at Moundville, 315 (80 percent) were black-filmed bowls and bottles. The remaining 20 percent of this sample contained 25 plain jars (7 percent), incised vessels, 11 types of effigy forms, and vessels of several unusual forms. A sample of 144 mortuary vessels from Pickwick Basin sites (Kogers Island; Seven Mile Island; and Perry, Units 2, 3 and 4) contains 109 plain vessels (including 85 jars), 4 effigy vessels (3 ducks, 1 owl) and only 8 black-filmed bowls and bottles. Plain ware constitutes 76 percent of this sample while black-filmed ware comprises some 6 percent. The inverse proportions of plain and black-filmed wares in these two samples do not support strong affiliations between these cultures. More significantly, the numbers of ceramic traits present in the Pickwick Basin sample suggest strong ties not with Moundville but with the geographically closer Tennessee-Cumberland cultures. In summary, the evidence now at hand indicates that Moundville and the Pickwick Basin area were populated by distinct ethnic groups, each with its own political and economic systems. The presence of some types of Moundville black-filmed ware in the Pickwick Basin can be attributed to trade relations between these populations over the more than 125 miles of rugged terrain that separated the two cultures.

One of the major islands containing Kogers Island phase sites is Seven

Kogers Island Phase Burials, Perry Site, AMNH 275 Lu 25

Mile Island, which was investigated by C. B. Moore in 1914 and again in the
1930s by TVA archaeologists as part of the Pickwick Basin project. Two sites
were found on the island that contained Kogers Island phase components. It
is no accident that all three of the mature Mississippian phases in the middle
Tennessee Valley are named for islands; every island of any size in the
Tennessee River was heavily occupied by Mississippian peoples. This was
the result of two major factors. First, these islands provided natural fortification and, second, most were covered by deep deposits of arable silt loam
soils. Like most of these islands, Seven Mile Island was annually flooded—an
event that renewed the rich soils every spring before planting.

One of the Mississippian sites on Seven Mile Island is Lu°21, which shares
the island's name. This site consists of a substructure mound and what
appears to have been a large village. The mound stood 11 feet high and
excavation revealed that it had been built in four stages. The primary mound
was a low black-sand structure made by scraping up the surrounding village
midden. Two areas containing structure patterns were encountered in the
vicinity of this low mound. Under the center of the mound four superimposed rectangular, single-post construction buildings were uncovered.
Three of these had central clay-lined fire basins. An infant, associated with a
small pottery jar, was buried in this area. On the outer edge of the mound, in
the village area, two other superimposed buildings were found. Both were
constructed of single posts; one was rectangular and the other circular in
shape. Eight burials were discovered in and around these building
patterns—four extended adults, three infants, and an isolated skull. Pottery
vessels, a greenstone celt, and shell beads were found in association with
these interments.

Above the black-sand mound, two clay-capped truncated mounds were
successively constructed. Mound 2, the first of these clay pyramids, was 3
feet thick and 70 feet square at its base. Two rectangular single-post construction buildings were erected on its summit. Two burials were associated
with this building phase, one flexed and one extended. Grave goods were
more elaborate than the ones found with the primary burials: a decorated
water bottle, a shell gorget, a celt, a pair of copper earspools, a copper
pendant, and a stone discoidal. The second clay pyramid, Mound 3, contained scattered post holes, indicating that one or more structures had been
built on its summit. Three burials were associated with this construction
stage, all accompanied by pottery vessels. This second clay cap was covered
with 4 feet of dark sandy loam that was later disturbed by erosion and
cultivation. In the surrounding village area, which was not extensively excavated, some 6,700 shell-tempered sherds were recovered. A single sherd of a
grit-tempered Georgia trade vessel, Savannah Complicated Stamped, and
one fragment of a Moundville Filmed Engraved water bottle were found in
this ceramic sample. The thirty complete vessels recovered from the mound
include predominantly plain ware. Some composite forms; a negative-

Pottery Vessels from Seven Mile Island, Kogers Island Phase, AMNH 115, 130, 136, and 138 Lu 21

painted raccoon water bottle; owl, frog, and duck effigy vessels; and two black-filmed vessels were also found.

At the upper end of Seven Mile Island, some two miles to the east, is the Perry site, which contained a small Kogers Island phase cemetery. Forty-one mature Mississippian burials were found in Unit 2 of the excavated area. Thirty-four (83 percent) of these were multiple burials ranging from two to six individuals per grave. The primary inhumations consisted of 63 percent partially flexed and 37 percent extended. Three bundle burials and three isolated skulls were also found. In one grave, a group of four burials was discovered, each decapitated. Thirty-one pottery vessels were recovered from the Unit 2 burials, including eighteen plain jars, five bowls, twenty-one plain bottles, and two black-filmed bottles. Shell beads, ear plugs, arrow points, and celts were also found in burial association.

The largest Mississippian cemetery found in the Pickwick Basin was discovered on Kogers Island. Moore (1915:242) reported a large village site on the upper end of the island. The nearby cemetery area yielded 102 burials in association with fifty-three vessels. Forty of these were plain (thirty-five jars, one bowl, four bottles), two were duck effigy bowls, and three were black-filmed water bottles (two engraved with southeastern ceremonial complex motifs). One of the Kogers Island burials, the most elaborate reported in Alabama outside of Moundville, merits special description. According to Webb and DeJarnette, Burial 23 was an extended adult male laid into a pit 6.8 feet long and 3.5 feet wide.

At the head was a conch-shell cup, ceremonially "killed" by having a large hole drilled through it. On each side of the skull were copper ear disk ornaments with bone pins, stained by copper. Under the chin was a string of 958 shell columella beads and another copper ear ornament. Over the left arm and side were the following artifacts:

One ungrooved greenstone celt;
One dog-effigy pipe;
One greenstone spatulate, ceremonial form;
One beaver incisor;
Two perforated bear teeth;
Eight marine columella shell beads on left hand, lying directly under 14 bird sterna;
Fourteen bird sterna covering left hand. These were cut and drilled as pendants.

On the left side at the foot of the grave and covering the left foot were 10 well-made needle awls, covered by fragments of bird-sternum pendants. The right foot was partially covered with seven bird-sternum pendants and a fragment of weathered hematite. On the right side and covering the right arm were the following:

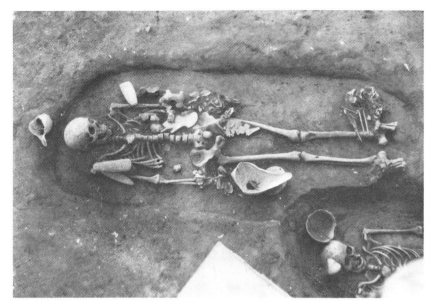

Burial 23 with Some Sixty-three Field Specimens, Kogers Island Site, AMNH
72 Lu 92

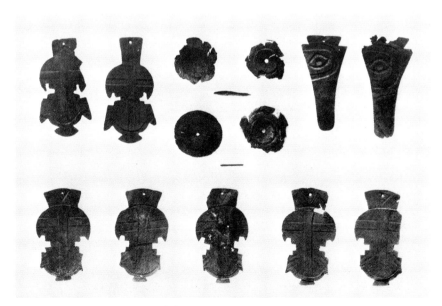

Copper Ornaments Recovered from Burial 23, Kogers Island

One ungrooved greenstone celt;
One well-finished flint knife, 7 inches long;
Two copper-covered wood-dish ear ornaments;
Seven columella shell beads on right hand under 7 bird sterna;
Seven bird sterna covering right hand.

Below the right hand, opposite the right thigh, there was a large marine shell cup, ceremonially "killed," and in it 4 needle awls. Under the shell cup was a stone disk. Between the legs, almost on top of the left femur, were 8 copper pendants and a small copper pin. About the pelvic girdle were 75 shell columella beads and a cube of galena about 1.5 inches on the edge. . . . In this grave was a fragmentary pot with one strap handle mounted on an incised collar. [1942:219]

The regional ceremonial center of the Kogers Island phase was located near the present city of Florence where a great mound and earthwork were raised. This mound is now the site of an archaeological museum built and operated by the citizens of Florence. The museum houses well-coordinated displays of cultural material from local sites representing all stages of prehistoric development. The Florence mound is the highest such structure in the entire Tennessee Valley. E. G. Squier and E. H. Davis (1848:109–10) reported that in the early nineteenth century this mound stood 45 feet high and measured some 440 feet in circumference. In 1914, C. B. Moore visited this site and reported that at that time the mound rose 42 feet above the floodplain and its base measured 310 by 230 feet. Moore excavated some thirty-four trial pits in the mound without result. He did, however, report the presence of village debris in an adjacent field, suggesting that a habitation area was associated with the mound. Moore also reported that a portion of what had once been an earthwork, now totally destroyed by erosion and industrial development, was present near the mound structure. This earthwork was still intact during the early nineteenth century and Squier and Davis described it as follows.

Partly surrounding the mound is a wall two hundred and seventy feet distant from its base, which extends from the main river below to a branch formed by Cane island above, constituting a segment of a circle, the center of which would be the Tennessee River. The wall is forty feet across the top, and, making allowances for the ravages of time, must have been originally from twelve to fifteen feet high; it is now eight feet in height . . . the wall has what appears to be a ditch on the outside.

Kogers Island peoples appear to have lived in settlements in the valley near areas of arable soil during at least the spring and summer seasons. In the fall and winter, small work parties made forays, at times for extended periods, into the fall line hills to the south, where they collected nut foods and hunted deer, turkey, and other game. Fletcher Jolly (1974) recently

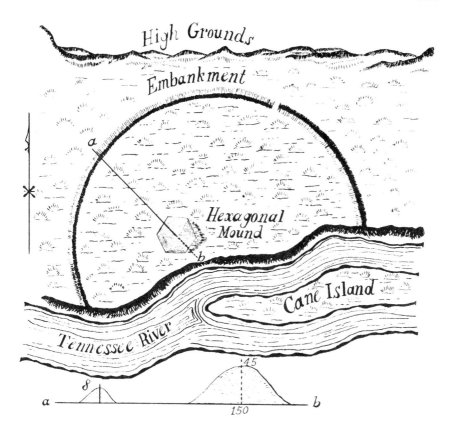

Florence Mound and Earthwork (After Squier and Davis 1848)

outlined this settlement system and reported one of these upland limited activity camps, Buzzard Roost Creek bluff shelter in Colbert County, which appears to have been occupied by only small groups during the Mississippian period. Some 137 shell-tempered sherds and 125 small, triangular arrow-points were recovered from the upper zones at this site. This high ratio (1:1) of points to sherds, combined with seasonality data based upon fauna analysis, suggests a fall and winter hunting camp. A similar situation was reported from the upper stratum at the nearby Stanfield-Worley bluff shelter some three miles to the northeast. DeJarnette reported that 242 triangular arrowpoints were recovered there, while only 163 shell-tempered sherds were found. The utilization of the uplands bordering the Tennessee Valley as collecting and hunting territories seems to have been widespread during the Mississippian development. The valley and uplands form an ecological edge area, or ecotone, like that described by Lewis Larson. The high economic potential of this zone, combined with Mississippian technology, allowed the establishment of large, often permanent communities throughout the bottomlands and on the islands of the Tennessee River.

The Hobbs Island Phase

Upriver in the Wheeler Basin are sites that have been assigned to the Hobbs Island phase. The spatial distribution of Hobbs Island sites is confined to that portion of the valley between Tick Island in western Lawrence County and the Flint River in eastern Madison County. Three major mature Mississippian sites have been investigated within this area—burial mounds on Tick Island (Moore 1915:254–56; Webb 1939:61–67), mounds and a village on Hobbs Island (Webb 1939:83–91), and mounds and a village near Whitesburg Bridge in Madison County.

Tick Island is an almost perfectly level expanse of land, having once been part of the river floodplain before it was cut off by a meander channel. The river flooded the island almost every spring before the construction of Wheeler Dam. C. B. Moore excavated a small mound on this island during his 1914 expedition and discovered three burials associated with pottery vessels and an unassociated cache of three vessels, all shell-tempered. These Mississippian burials were apparently intrusive; subsequent investigations of this mound, La⁰14, in 1934 by David L. DeJarnette revealed that it also contained Copena burials. Nearby, on the upper end of Tick Island, TVA archaeologists discovered another small conical burial mound, La⁰13, which proved to have been completely constructed during Mississippian times. This structure was only three feet high and was found to contain six primary inhumations, three bundle burials, and eighteen isolated skull burials. The first burial encountered in this mound was an extended adult associated with a cache of three vessels and four skulls. Only one other primary inhumation was extended; the others were flexed or partially flexed. With the separate skulls was usually deposited one or more open pottery bowls and sometimes a large sherd. All of the mortuary vessels were shell-tempered plain ware. Most were jars with wide-strap handles, shallow bowls, and water bottles. One vessel decorated with nodes had rim elevations at opposite sides, each point terminating in a strap handle. Two duck effigy bowls were also found.

Hobbs Island, a long, narrow stretch of land (2.5 miles long and .5 miles wide) upriver from Tick Island, was also explored during the 1930s. Four Mississippian sites were found on its lower end—two burial mounds (Ma°1 and Ma°3) similar to the one on Tick Island, a substructure mound (Ma°2), and a village area on a low ridge between the mounds (Ma°4 and Ma°5). The southern portion of the village area was designated Ma°4. Burned clay floors and clay-lined hearths were uncovered in this area. Ten burials were also discovered. The northern portion of the habitation zone, Ma°5, had been disturbed by erosion; however, a good sample of cultural material was recovered. Pottery types included a majority of plain and incised wares, and one fragment of a Moundville Filmed Engraved water bottle was found. Pottery trowels, ceramic and stone discoidals, and stone celts and hoes were also recovered. Ma°2 was a truncated mound 20 feet high. Test excavations were limited in this mound and all that is known is that it was built in three construction stages.

The two burial mounds were completely excavated. Ma°1 was circular in shape and had a basal diameter of 80 feet and a height of 3 feet. The forty-nine burials recovered from this structure included sixteen fully flexed, five partially flexed, and thirteen extended inhumations. Thirty-one pottery vessels were found in association with these burials (fifteen jars, eight bowls, and eight water bottles), including a duck effigy bowl. Two water bottles had annular bases, and one had been painted with black and red stripes. Greenstone celts, stone discoidals, elbow pipes, and large numbers of marine-shell artifacts were also recovered. One burial was associated with 2,000 shell beads and another with 1,100. Three shell gorgets found with these burials were decorated with sun symbol, spider, and turkey cock designs.

The second burial mound, Ma°3, was oval in shape and two feet high at the time of investigation. Twenty-four burials were discovered in this structure; ten of these were extended, ten were fully flexed, one was partially flexed, and three were disturbed. Six plain shell-tempered jars and six water bottles were found. One of the water bottles was a hooded form with three circular knoblike podal supports. Two other water bottles were decorated by negative painting depicting sun symbol designs. These painted vessels represent trade ware and are typically found in small numbers at sites of other mature Mississippian cultures in the Middle South (early Dallas, Tennessee-Cumberland, Etowah, and the Henry Island phase in the Guntersville Basin).

Madeline Kneberg (1959) has studied a sample of Southeastern Ceremonial

Complex shell gorgets recovered from sites in the upper Tennessee River area. She has recognized eight major designs and by plotting their associations has constructed a relative chronology of gorget motifs. The earliest group of designs includes the square cross, circular cross (sun symbol), eagle dancer, spider, and turkey cocks. These motifs are associated with the most elaborate ceremonial expression of the Mississippian stage and are dated between circa A.D. 1200–1400. The second group is composed of the circular cross design in cruder form, the conventionalized dancer, and the scalloped triskele. It is dated circa A.D. 1350–1450. The third and latest group of gorget motifs is confined to only two designs, the mask gorget and the rattlesnake, and is dated circa A.D. 1450–1700. Douglas McKenzie (1966:46) has noted the following designs at Moundville: circular cross or sun symbol, eagle dancer, turkey cock or woodpecker, and spider (wooden tray). Motifs of this type, like those recovered from Ma⁰1, fall into the earliest group of design elements. These associations, combined with the recovery of a fragment of a Moundville Filmed Engraved water bottle in the village area, support the contemporaneity of the Moundville and Hobbs Island phases.

The final Hobbs Island phase site to be discussed is the Walling II site in Madison County .4 mile north of the Tennessee River and 1 mile northwest of Whitesburg Bridge. Within the four-acre site are two mounds and a village. A third mound, a truncated pyramid, was located some 2,000 feet to the west. The Walling II site was excavated from May 1940 to January 1941 by a crew under the direction of H. Summerfield Day. Only the isolated mound structure has been reported (Walthall 1973a:394–95); all other information concerning this site is contained in the files at Moundville. Mound A, designated Ma⁰31, was a small burial mound that stood 4 feet high and measured 40 feet in diameter at the time of investigation. Four burials were found within this structure, one flexed, one extended, and two isolated skulls. A human effigy pipe and three pottery vessels were recovered. One of these vessels was a water bottle with an annular base like those found at Hobbs Island. One feature was encountered during the excavation of Ma⁰31: Under the mound the investigators found a small, circular structure pattern of the single-post construction type. Excavations in the village area (Maᵛ31) revealed twenty-one rectangular structure patterns of both the single-post and wall-trench types. Only fifteen of these structures could have been occupied at one time; considerable overlapping was noted. Fourteen of these dwellings had central clay-lined fire basins. Four partially flexed burials were also found in the village area.

Mound B, designated Ma⁰32, was a truncated earthen pyramid 10 feet high and 75 by 105 feet at the base. This mound had been built in increments and was found to contain thirteen structure patterns (twelve rectangular and one circular in shape). The largest of these structures was found at the base of the mound, a rectangular building measuring 28 by 39 feet. The surface of the clay-lined floor was found to have been 18 inches below the original ground

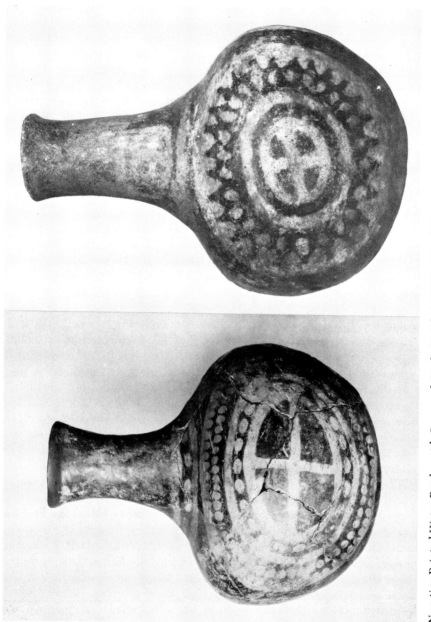

Negative Painted Water Bottles with Cross and Circle Motif. A, Hobbs Island Phase; B, Henry Island Phase. AMNH 10 Ma 3 and 42 Ja 180A

surface, thus creating a semisubterranean structure. Interior posts forming partitions, a large central roof support post, and a raised, clay rectangular hearth were found within this primary structure. Some 2,000 feet west of this mound was another truncated pyramid, Maᵖ50. This mound was found to have been built in four stages. Two single-post construction structure patterns, one rectangular and one circular, were found on the surface of the second building stage. Two partially flexed burials were discovered in Maᵖ32, and one partially flexed burial was found in Maᵖ50.

The Henry Island Phase

In the Guntersville Basin area of northeastern Alabama a third mature Mississippian phase can be recognized, the Henry Island phase. Settlements of this phase were located between a number of large neighboring populations, including the Tennessee-Cumberland cultures of the Nashville Basin area with their unusual stone-box graves, early Dallas peoples to the north in eastern Tennessee, and the Etowah chiefdom and related cultures of northern Georgia. The large number of both settlements and mounds that have been identified in this area suggests that the Guntersville Basin supported a large population during the mature Mississippian period. Among the sites assigned to the Henry Island phase (all reported in Webb and Wilder 1951) are two cemeteries—Hardin and Sublet Ferry—and several mound groups, some with associated villages—Snodgrass, Henry Island, and Rudder.

Two Henry Island phase cemeteries were excavated during the Guntersville Basin salvage project of the 1930s. The Hardin cemetery, Jaᵛ27, contained twelve burials: seven partially flexed, one extended, and four disturbed. Two of these burials deserve special mention. Burial 2, a partially flexed interment, was associated with a conch-shell cup and two trade vessels. One of these vessels was a negative-painted water bottle decorated with sun symbols, and the other, a sand-tempered jar, was a vessel of the Savannah Complicated Stamped type of the northern Georgia area. The grave of Burial 3 also contained two pottery vessels, a plain bowl and a raccoon effigy water bottle similar to the one recovered at the Seven Mile Island mound (where a trade vessel of the Savannah Complicated Stamped type was also found). The second cemetery site, Sublet Ferry, Jaᵛ102, yielded twenty-four burials, seventeen partially flexed and seven fully flexed. One stone-box grave was also discovered at this site. Burial goods recovered include a plain shell-tempered jar, a turtle effigy bowl, a noded rim bowl, a water bottle, greenstone celts, stone discoidals, a large flint blade, shell beads and gorgets, and a large sheet of copper with a repoussé design of a hawk. Three other large copper plates have been reported from this region. C. B. Moore recovered a copper plate from a stone-box grave at the Henry Island site in 1914. This ornament was decorated with a repoussé design depicting the head of a hawk dancer. Two other plates from sites in Jackson County are in

Copper Ornaments from Burials, Guntersville Basin, Henry Island Phase.

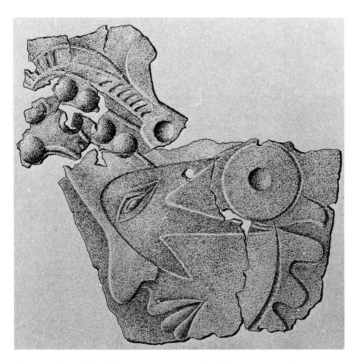

From a Stone Box Grave on Henry Island (Moore 1915)

Kilted Warrior Ornament, Jackson County (Courtesy Museum of the American Indian, Heye Foundation, 23517)

Hair Ornament, 10 inches long, Jackson County (Courtesy Museum of the American Indian, Heye Foundation, 28285)

the Museum of the American Indian collections. One of these is a kilted dancer plate 17.5 inches long (Hamilton 1974:Figure 96) and the other is a hair ornament 10 inches long, decorated with a snake design, with a fragment of a bone pin still attached at the base. The three shell gorgets recovered at the Sublet Ferry cemetery had designs depicting a pair of turkey cocks, an excised design of a single bird, and an endless scroll and pileated woodpecker. All of these design elements can be placed into Kneberg's early motif group.

One-quarter mile downstream from Sublet Ferry is the Snodgrass site. Two truncated mounds were raised at this site, but only the larger mound was excavated. At the time of investigation it stood 22 feet high and measured 130 by 160 feet at the base. Ten structure patterns were found on old surface levels in the mound. Six rectangular, single-post construction buildings, and two circular structures, each containing a central fire basin, were encountered in the upper levels of the mound. Two earlier rectangular structures, both of the wall-trench construction type, were found in the lower portion of the mound. Charred corncobs, a pottery trowel, shell hoes, and stone discoidals were recovered from the mound fill. Pottery sherds

Structure Patterns and Stone Box Graves, Rudder Site, Henry Island Phase, AMNH 36 Ja 180A

were also found in the fill, with plain shell-tempered sherds the dominant type and incised sherds second in frequency. Minor types included fabric-impressed salt-pan ware, sand-tempered and shell-tempered complicated-stamped sherds, and sherds decorated with red-film, red-on-buff, and black-film paints. The nature of this ceramic sample suggests that the lower stages of the Snodgrass mound with the wall-trench structures were built during the late Langston phase and that subsequent stages and single-post construction buildings were added during the Henry Island phase.

Perhaps the most interesting Henry Island phase site excavated in the Guntersville Basin was the Rudder settlement, which consisted of a village and a pair of mounds. This site is in Jackson County some four miles south of the town of Stevenson on a low rise in the floodplain paralleling the river. The larger of the two mounds, Mound A, was a truncated pyramid 14 feet high and 110 feet in diameter at the base. Webb and Wilder (1951) reconstructed ten major events in the history of this mound. From the bottom of the mound to the final construction stage these are:

1. Post holes in the old humus under the mound, indicating precedent structures, probably an old village area.

2. Construction of a large rectangular building with a clay seat. This structure was of the joined-corner wall-trench type and was 33 feet wide and 55 feet long. In the center against the southwest wall was a clay seat or altar, 4 feet by 3 feet in dimension and 1 foot high. Three large interior posts were found in this structure.

3. This building was torn down and fill material was added over the old floor area, creating a low mound.

4. Five burials were made in this level.

5. A cap of gray clay was then added, forming a level summit.

6. A rectangular building, 27 feet wide and 40 feet long, was raised on this surface. This structure had four wall trenches with joined corners and a doorway in the eastern side.

7. This building was torn down and a second rectangular building was constructed in the same area. This new structure was circular in shape and was 45 feet in diameter. A square fire hearth, bounded by four burned logs (representing the four world quarters?), was found in the center of this building.

8. Another rectangular structure was then raised in the northwestern corner of the mound summit, the last structure to be built on the mound. It was a small wall-trench construction building with joined corners.

9. Fill material was then brought in to cover the entire mound, including the area where the final structure had stood. Evidently this last building had burned or had been torn down prior to this final construction stage.

10. After this final layer of earth was added to the mound, nineteen individuals were buried in graves dug into the mound. These and the five burials associated with the first construction stage consisted of eighteen partially

flexed burials, four extended burials, one fetus, and one isolated skull burial. Pottery vessels, greenstone celts, and shell beads were placed into the graves of these individuals.

Mound B was a low earthen structure located some 100 feet west of Mound A. Four rectangular wall-trench building patterns were found under this mound. The largest of these was 41 feet wide and 55 feet long. Fifty-seven burials were discovered in the mound area—ten extended, thirty-four partially flexed, and four reburials. Four stone-box graves had been made in the mound; other graves were lined with stone or bark. Grave goods found in association with the Mound B burials include fifty-eight pottery vessels, shell beads and gorgets, galena nodules, mica sheets, graphite, ground hematite and limonite, a large flint blade, greenstone celts, copper-covered wooden earspools, pearl beads, pottery and stone elbow pipes, and a sandstone palette five inches in diameter with hematite stains on one side. Nine shell gorgets were included as mortuary offerings. One was decorated with a design of an eagle dancer, one with a spider, three with a sun symbol, and three with an endless scroll and pileated woodpecker. All of these fall into Kneberg's early shell-gorget category.

The ceramics recovered with these burials include both shell-tempered and sand-tempered vessels. The form of some of these vessels suggests contact with both the Tennessee-Cumberland cultures (especially the jars with four-cornered, peaked rims and high necks with flanges) and northern Georgia (complicated-stamped jars). Eight sand-tempered vessels were found with these burials, including two plain jars, one cord-marked jar with four horizontal legs and four peaked corners, an incised jar with six arches paralleled by punctations on the shoulder and paired-strap handles, a combed-incised jar with a peaked rim and marked with incised lines that appear to have been made by a six-toothed comb, a negative-painted water bottle with sun-symbol designs, a brushed jar, and a complicated-stamped jar with flaring rim and conical base. The shell-tempered ceramics include plain jars with strap handles, plain bowls and bottles, a cord-marked bowl, complicated-stamped jars, a black-filmed water bottle, an opossum effigy bottle, and a duck effigy bowl.

Literally thousands of stone-box graves have been found at Tennessee-Cumberland culture sites in the Nashville Basin area. Burials of this type are most commonly found in a corridor zone extending from the lower Tennessee Valley through the core area in the Nashville Basin, southeastward through the Guntersville Basin, and across northern Georgia to the Atlantic coast region, where they have been reported at the Nachoochee mound near Augusta. Negative-painted water bottles with the sun symbol design and repoussé copper plates have been reported from several mature Mississippian sites in this zone (including sites of the Gray, Duck River, and early Dallas cultures of Tennessee, and of Etowah, Nachoochee, and the nearby Hollywood mound in Georgia). These two traits should serve as horizon markers for these geographically distant cultures and probably date to A.D. 1200–1400.

Cyrus Thomas (1894:301–09) has reported the excavation of a mound, Mound C, at Etowah in Georgia that is similar in a number of ways to Mound B at the Rudder site. Mound C was 15 feet high and 375 feet in diameter. Three construction stages were delineated, but no structure patterns were reported. Eleven burials were found within this mound, eight of which had been placed into stone-box graves. Burial goods placed with these individuals include two shell gorgets with eagle dancer motifs, shell beads, conch-shell cups, pottery vessels (one water bottle and one jar) and copper plates with cut-out and repoussé designs. The designs on the copper plates consisted of hawk dancer and hawk motifs. Hair ornaments of sheet copper were also noted.

The Henry Island settlement pattern in the Guntersville Basin appears to parallel that of the Kogers Island phase. Large settlements with mounds and scattered small farmsteads were occupied in the valley near fertile bottomlands. Upland rock shelters like Russell Cave (J. W. Griffin 1974) and those on Sand Mountain (Clayton 1965, 1967) served as specialized fall and winter hunting camps. The intensity of occupation in the Guntersville Basin area can be attributed to its high ecological potential. The narrow valley was bordered by highland mesophytic forests that provided abundant mast for game animals and man alike. This ecotone habitat allowed substantial population growth once the Mississippian exploitative strategy was established in this region.

8: The Twilight of Prehistory

The mature Mississippian florescence in the Southeast appears to have been on the wane by the latter part of the fifteenth century. The reason for this decline, and in some instances total abandonment of old territories, is unknown at the present time. The next two centuries, comprising the protohistoric period, witnessed the emergence of the last totally aboriginal cultures in the Southeast. The protohistoric period is marked by four major events. In the Alabama area there was a major demographic shift as population density rose in the south and east. Moundville and much of the Tennessee Valley were abandoned. Vigorous new cultures, whose heritage appears in some cases to be directly linked to the old Moundville culture, developed along the coast and in the major river valleys of the Coastal Plain. To the north in the highland valleys only the Guntersville Basin communities continued to thrive.

During protohistoric times many traits of the Southeastern Ceremonial Complex disappeared, and there seems to have been a major reformation in ritual and ceremony. Some of the basic concepts of the Southeastern Ceremonial Complex continued to be practiced in modified form without the exotic trappings of the earlier, more flamboyant cult. Temple mounds continued to be constructed but on a much smaller scale than before. New technological and stylistic traits also replaced old ones. The ceramic arts were now largely confined to two major vessel forms, carinated bowls and globular jars. Shallow-plate forms also appear in the ceramic assemblages in some areas. Small lanceolate arrowpoints became popular and largely replaced the traditional triangular forms. Marine shell continued to be utilized to make ornaments. The most common protohistoric shell forms are pins with knobbed heads, and gorgets, at times plain or with a scalloped design.

Another major event of the protohistoric period is the first contact between aboriginal society and European culture. This initial meeting of these diverse peoples was confined to brief encounters with Spanish explorers and would-be colonists. Acculturation was minimal during this period; not until the beginning of the eighteenth century with the start of sustained contact with British and French colonists did aboriginal life give way to the dominant European culture. Thus the temporal parameters of the protohistoric period are marked by the first encounter with Europeans during the early sixteenth century and by the beginning of the full historic period and the establishment of the deerskin trade in the early eighteenth century. This latter development signaled a brief period of rapid acculturation and almost total loss of traditional aboriginal culture in the Southeast.

The Spanish came to the lands of the northern Gulf of Mexico in search of riches and religious converts. Although their search was vigorous, and in the end costly, they found little of value to them, and although they fought, befriended, and at times subjugated the indigenous populations, they made few conversions and even fewer friends.

The earliest Spanish explorer to reach Alabama was Alonzo Alverez de Pineda, who was sent on an expedition to find a westward passage around Florida, which at that time was thought to be an island. Pineda's command consisted of four ships that worked their way along the Gulf coast from Florida to Mexico (Summersell 1961). In 1519 this small expedition entered Mobile Bay, which Pineda named the "Bahia Espiritu Santo," the Bay of the Holy Ghost. He also sailed a short distance up the Mobile River (Rio del Espiritu Santo) and reportedly sighted some forty Indian villages along the shoreline. Pineda remained in Mobile Bay for over a month repairing his vessels and trading with the natives of a large coastal village. Little else is known of this first brief encounter. Pineda apparently did not find these indigenous peoples particularly remarkable, and inasmuch as the Indians themselves left no written account, we know nothing of what they thought about these strange visitors.

Less than a decade later another Spanish expedition blundered its way into Alabama history. This was the ill-fated expedition of Panfilo de Narvaez, who set a standard of incompetence matched only by the three Spanish explorers who were to follow him into Alabama during the remainder of the sixteenth century. (Perhaps this evaluation is overcritical. However, even when viewed in light of historical perspective, the accounts of these early Spanish explorations of the Gulf Coast states still read like something drawn out of Cervantes's Don Quixote.)

In 1528 Narvaez landed his expedition of 400 soldiers and horses at Tampa Bay. Once organized, Narvaez marched north and then westward until his force reached the present-day area of Tallahassee, where they began to run short of supplies and resorted to eating their horses. Once this emergency food supply was depleted, Narvaez decided to abandon his plans of conquest and colonization and head for Mexico, which he calculated (fatally) to lie only some eighty to ninety miles away. The Spaniards, accordingly, built five small vessels and on 22 September 1528 left the site of Saint Marks on Apalachee Bay and sailed westward along the coast. After a month of coasting the northern Gulf, Narvaez's expedition entered Mobile Bay. Soon after entering the bay the small fleet of boats was approached by a party of Indians in a dugout canoe. Narvaez asked them for water, and two members of the expedition went ashore with the Indians to supervise the victualing. They never returned. With this impolite reception, Narvaez decided to sail for more hospitable waters. As a footnote to this brief episode in Alabama history it should be noted that shortly afterwards Narvaez was drowned when his boat was swept out into the Gulf by the current of a large river. In the end only a handful of his men, led by Cabeza de Vaca, eventually reached Mexico—and then only after following a circuitous overland route that included wandering all the way to the Pacific coast.

Another decade passed before the Indians of Alabama were to again encounter a Spanish expedition. In 1539 Hernando DeSoto, governor of Cuba, landed at Tampa Bay after sailing from Havana with a fleet of nine vessels and an expedition composed of six hundred soldiers; a hundred or so camp followers, servants, and slaves; some two hundred horses; a herd of hogs; some mules; a pack of bloodhounds; and a large quantity of provisions for equipping the army and founding a colony (Swanton 1946:40). His troops were provided with "helmets, breastplates, shields, and coats of steel to repel arrows of the Indians; and with swords, Biscayan lances, crude guns called arquebuses, crossbows, and one piece of artillery" (Pickett 1851:19). On 15 July 1539 DeSoto began the march northward over a route that would lead him through portions of present-day Florida, Georgia, South Carolina, North Carolina, and Tennessee before entering Alabama. The route followed by the expedition has been extensively researched by John Swanton, who chaired the DeSoto Commission that produced a detailed study (Swanton 1939) commemorating the 400th anniversary of DeSoto's *entrada*.

According to Swanton, DeSoto marched into Alabama on or around 1 July 1540 in what is now Jackson County in the extreme northeastern portion of the state. In late December of the same year DeSoto crossed through Pickens County in western Alabama into what is now Mississippi. In the intervening five months the Spaniards visited village after village, requiring food and guides and taking hostages as well as slaves. Each village greeted them politely and at times even cordially, but each was eager to be rid of them and hurried them on their way with stories of gold farther on.

Swanton (1946:39–59) gives the following account of the DeSoto expedition in the Alabama country. Shortly before entering Alabama DeSoto reached the settlement of Chiaha on an island in the Tennessee River just above the present Alabama state line. There he spent three weeks recuperating and resting the horses and hogs. On 28 June he marched southward down the Tennessee Valley to the town of Coste, or Costehe, which Swanton believed to have been situated on Pine Island. All that is known about the week the Spaniards spent at Coste comes from Ranjel, one of the chroniclers of the DeSoto expedition, who wrote of trouble over the barbacoas (corn cribs). DeSoto then continued down the Tennessee to the village of Tali, which Swanton places on McKee Island near Guntersville. Tarrying only a day at Tali, the expedition headed for Coca, about which they had heard glowing accounts when they were in central Georgia. They reached the great town on the Coosa River on 16 July. The chief of that town came out to meet them in great state, borne on a litter carried upon the shoulders of his principal warriors. The Spaniards remained for more than a month at Coca and, after taking the cordial chief hostage, left on 20 August, heading south.

They passed through Ulibahali, a fortified village on the north side of the Tallapoosa River, and through Tuasi, a town believed to have been situated near present Montgomery, before coming to Talisi, near Durant's Bend on the Alabama River.

At Talisi, DeSoto received a message from Tascalusa, a powerful chief living on the lower portion of the Alabama River. On 5 October the expedition left Talisi to accept Tascalusa's offer to visit his lands; they entered the territory of the Mobile Indians on 6 October. The Spaniards continued their journey through the Mobile territory, stopping at night at a number of villages, until they reached Athahachi where Tascalusa had taken up residence. Tascalusa met the Spaniards in state and "impressed them profoundly on account of his gigantic stature and imperial bearing" (Swanton 1946:50). Nevertheless, they took him hostage. DeSoto and his prisoner then marched to Piachi, Tascalusa's capital town. During their stay there two of the men guarding the chief were killed by his followers. Continuing on, they reached the fortified town of Mabila where Tascalusa had promised to give them carriers and supplies and to turn over to them the murderers of the Spanish guards. While at Mabila, which is thought to have been in present Clarke County, Tascalusa's warriors mounted an attack and twenty Spanish soldiers and a number of horses were killed, and a large amount of the expedition's provisions were burned. According to Swanton (1946:50), "This battle had a decisive influence upon the entire course of the expedition. Coming as it did just before DeSoto planned to meet Maldonado at the port of Achusi, it discouraged his followers so completely that many of them fully intended to desert as soon as they reached the ships." To avoid the loss of many of his followers through desertion and to continue his explorations, DeSoto marched northward away from the waiting Spanish fleet at Mobile. Before leaving Alabama the expedition crossed the Black Warrior River just south of the site of Moundville. Archaeologists believe that, inasmuch as the Spanish chroniclers did not mention so large a town even though they passed nearby, Moundville must have been abandoned by 1540. Once across the Black Warrior the Spaniards trekked westward out of Alabama toward their respective destinies. Some, including DeSoto himself, met death before they could escape the wilderness.

Shortly after DeSoto's *entrada*, the Spanish king, Philip II, conceived a plan to protect his galleons loaded with treasure from Peru and Mexico on their voyage through the pirate-infested Gulf of Mexico. Philip's plan was simple. All that was required to accomplish this goal was to found a colony at Mobile to serve as a port where the treasure fleets could find safety and where ships of war could be based to protect Spanish interests. For the first time the Spanish were making plans for a settlement on the northern shores of the Gulf of Mexico.

The king passed his plan down the bureaucratic line to the viceroy of Mexico, Don Luis Velasco, who immediately appointed Tristan de Luna to head the colony. This seemed a wise decision because Luna was a veteran of nearly thirty years in the New World with Cortez and Coronado. Luna embarked on 11 June 1559, commanding thirteen ships. According to Herbert Priestly (1936:102–03), with him "were five hundred cavalry, arquebusiers, shield-bearers and cross-bowmen, one thousand colonists and servants—men, women, and children, Negro men and women, friendly Indians—and two hundred and forty horses. . . . A full hundred of the faithful beasts were destined to be thrown overboard during the voyage. . . . Ample supplies of corn, biscuit, bacon, dried beef, cheese, oil, vinegar, wine, and cattle for breeding were on board. There were tools for building and digging, so as to plant crops; axes and mattocks for the farmers, and everything else necessary, all of which was provided by command of the viceroy entirely."

Luna's colonists settled first on the shores of Pensacola Bay but also established an outpost near the head of Mobile Bay. An expedition composed of 200 soldiers was soon sent to explore inland. They traveled a short distance up the Alabama River and found an abandoned town, Nanipacana (Choctaw for "Hilltop"). This was a village of the Mobile Indians and here the soldiers found cached corn and beans. Soon afterwards, Luna moved the entire colony to this location. By the following spring, however, the colonists' provisions were almost depleted and a detachment of 50 horse soldiers and 150 foot soldiers was sent north in search of DeSoto's Coca (Swanton 1946:60–61). Backtracking on the trail DeSoto had taken twenty years earlier, the Spaniards arrived at the village of Ulibahali on the Tallapoosa River in early June. There they were treated well by the inhabitants, but their voracious appetites soon proved them to be an intolerable burden. The Ulibahalis turned to chicanery to induce their guests to go on toward Coca where there were supposedly greater stores of food. After a few days' march, the hungry Spaniards reached Coca where, instead of the large town represented in the glowing accounts of both Indians and former DeSoto expedition members, they found a small village of only thirty houses with seven small satellite hamlets. Nevertheless, food was plentiful enough to support the Spaniards for three months. While at Coca they learned that two of DeSoto's men who had been left behind at Coca had lived a dozen years among the inhabitants. The Cocas were at war with a Choctaw-related group, the Napochies, who lived west of them on the Black Warrior River. The Cocas persuaded the Spanish soldiers to take part in a raid on the Napochies. The multiethnic raiding party burned a Napochie village and compelled the tribe to make peace again and pay tribute to the Cocas. The expedition soon afterwards left Coca and returned to the main Spanish camp, where they found that growing dissensions among the colonists were at the point of open conflict. When a supply fleet arrived in April 1561, Luna was forced to abandon his colony and the Spaniards departed the Alabama shores en masse.

Thus the Spanish gave up plans to found a colony on the northern Gulf coast. Instead, they founded Saint Augustine on the Atlantic coast of Florida in 1565, the first permanent settlement in the United States (Summersell 1961). Within a year after the founding of Saint Augustine, a Spanish expedition (the last exploration of the sixteenth century) again set out for the Alabama country. The 1566 expedition of Jaun Pardo and Sergeant Boyano departed from present-day Beaufort (Santa Elena), South Carolina, searching for a land passage to Mexico that would circumvent the dangerous sea voyage around Florida. Pardo and his small band of 125 soldiers were destined to get no farther than northeastern Alabama before they turned back. Traveling through the interior, the Spaniards noted many fortified towns. Upon reaching Chiaha on the Tennessee River, Pardo received word that the chiefs of four nearby tribes, the Carrosa, Chisca, Costehe, and Coca, had united against him. Pardo decided to continue his explorations in spite of these threats but soon turned back, though some of his soldiers reportedly reached Coca and found friendly reception. After Juan Pardo and his ragged band of Spanish explorers retraced their steps eastward out of Alabama country, the Indians of this region were to live for over a century before Europeans once again entered their lands and disrupted their prehistoric world.

Protohistoric Cultures

The routes taken through Alabama country by the sixteenth-century Spanish explorers were not the haphazard wanderings that they may appear to be. Rather, they purposely sought out major population centers or areas with potential for furnishing them with food, slaves, and information. Retracing their steps through Alabama reveals the locations of important protohistoric chiefdoms. We have briefly described what history tells us about these societies; now we turn to what the archaeologist has learned.

Before describing these findings, it should be noted that ethnohistorians and archaeologists alike have been frustrated in their search for the towns visited by DeSoto and other early Spanish explorers. Not one of these sites has yet been located, but not due to a lack of effort. Some of the problems that have hindered this search are the intervening changes in the courses of streams, the inconsistences among contemporary accounts and maps, and the mobility of the settlements themselves. This last factor has proved especially critical in preventing identification of settlement locations and confirmation of ethnic affiliation. For example, the location of Coca in 1540 may be far removed from the site of Coca in 1700, or even 1560. Indian towns were frequently moved to new locations for a variety of reasons, ranging from depletion of easily procured firewood, to decreasing yields on nearby fields, to flooding, and political turmoil. Three sites identified by Swanton (1939) as the locations of towns visited by DeSoto in Alabama have been excavated. In each case they proved to be historic villages, but all dated to over 150 years after the DeSoto expedition. Coste on the upper end of Pine Island and Tali on McKee Island have been sought, but the locations excavated yielded English and French trade goods dating to circa 1700. David DeJarnette (1958) excavated the location pinpointed by Swanton as being that of Coca, but again the European trade items recovered dated to the eighteenth century. These findings do not mean that these towns did not exist or that Swanton was completely wrong in his calculations.

The sites in the Guntersville Basin are a good example. On the islands and in the floodplains of this area are long natural ridges elevated from 2 to 4 feet above the surrounding bottoms. Archaeologists surveying these ridges often found a continuous scatter of cultural debris all along these ridges, at times for over a mile. Thus there are sites in the basin that have dimensions of 150 feet in width and 6,000 feet in length, but this entire elevation was not necessarily occupied at the same time; when campsites and villages were relocated, they were often shifted up and down the same ridge. Thus the Tali of DeSoto may lie only a few hundred yards from the Tali of early eighteenth-century English traders. The enormous amount of time and expense required for testing an entire ridge area of this nature has so far proved impractical; perhaps archaeologists of future generations, armed with new survey equipment and techniques, will succeed where others have so far failed.

The Crow Creek Phase

While the exact settlements visited by DeSoto have not been located, archaeologists have conducted extensive investigations in the areas he passed through and have reconstructed a fair picture of the lifestyles of these peoples. In the Guntersville Basin region of the Tennessee Valley the mature Mississippian Henry Island phase developed into the protohistoric Crow Creek phase, a contemporary of late Dallas culture of east Tennessee and of the Barnett phase in northern Georgia with its blending of Dallas and Lamar traits (Hally 1970). The material culture recovered from Crow Creek sites exhibits characteristics indicative of especially strong relations with Dallas culture, which during protohistoric times expanded to the east and south.

Crow Creek peoples continued to practice floodplain horticulture and constructed the last earthen pyramids in the Guntersville Basin. Burials were commonly partially flexed and usually were not accompanied by grave goods. When they were, the grave goods were generally confined to only pottery vessels and shell ornaments, such as knobbed pins and gorgets. Large bowls were at times inverted over the crania of some burials, a trait much more common to the south. Elbow pipes of stone or clay, at times plain but also in the form of human and monolithic axe effigies, became increasingly popular, as did the small, lanceolate Guntersville arrowpoints.

Crow Creek Phase Burial with Pottery Cache, AMNH 16 Ja 176a

A major development during the Crow Creek phase was the introduction of new pottery forms and techniques of decoration and finish treatment. These new ceramics are the McKee Island series, which continued to be produced in early historic times (Heimlich 1952:26–28). McKee Island plain ware, which is shell tempered, was made into three major vessel forms— globular jars, bottles, and carinated bowls. The globular-jar forms include a flattened type with paired-strap handles; large, shallow wide-mouthed jars; and smaller, flattened jars with high necks and narrow mouths. Rims are at times plain but are more commonly decorated with an incised, beaded, or notched flange that encircles the exterior rim at or below the lip, or by four to six horizontal flanges or lugs per vessel.

Three decorative or finish treatments are found on McKee Island series ceramics—cord marking, incising, and brushing. McKee Island Cord Marked vessels have impressions of a cord-wrapped paddle from the shoulder to the base on jars and bowls. Cord marking frequently occurs on vessels with incised rim decorations. The rise in popularity of cord marking reflects the strong influence of late Dallas culture, for this trait is much more common in that area.

McKee Island Incised decorations occur most often on carinated bowls and occasionally on jars. On both forms the area between the vessel lip and shoulder is decorated. These incised decorations take on four basic design motifs: (1) two- to four-line guilloche, commonly a false guilloche, (2) two-line interlocking scroll, (3) parallel straight lines alternating with concentric or half circles, and (4) obliquely opposed groups of parallel lines. These incised motifs are similar to those found on Lamar Bold Incised vessels and may be derived from this Georgia-country type. Like Lamar vessels, McKee Island Incised jars and bowls frequently are also decorated with rows of punctations, commonly bordering the vessel shoulder. Complicated stamped motifs similar to those of the Lamar Complicated Stamped varieties have also been noted on sherds in Crow Creek ceramic samples, though this finish treatment is rare in the basin area.

The third Crow Creek ceramic treatment is McKee Island Brushed, which appears during the final years of the Crow Creek phase and marks the inception of the early historic McKee Island phase. Carinated bowls and jars of this type bear fine-brush roughening or twig marking on the vessel body below the shoulder. The ancestral form of this type appears to be Walnut Roughened, which is found in association with some Lamar assemblages to the southeast. Brushing became increasingly popular during the historic period and is a common finish treatment on vessels from Creek villages to the south along the Coosa, Tallapoosa, and Chattahoochee rivers. In connection with this it should be mentioned that Swanton (1922) believed that the Creek-related Koasati tribe inhabited the Guntersville Basin before being driven south to the Coosa by Cherokee war parties during the early eighteenth century. Thus the Crow Creek phase may, and probably does, represent the material remains of protohistoric Muskogee populations.

Three sites with major Crow Creek phase components were excavated during the Guntersville Basin survey (Webb and Wilder 1951). The Sauty site, at the juncture of North Sauty Creek and the Tennessee River, contained a Crow Creek cemetery. Partially flexed burials and a small number of fully flexed and extended inhumations were found in association with shell beads, pearl beads, and McKee Island series vessels. European trade goods were not found with these burials; nor have they been reported from any Crow Creek site. One of these Sauty site burials is of particular interest. Burial 8, an extended adult, was accompanied by three pottery vessels—a small bowl and a jar, both of plain ware, found on each side of the head and a large, plain carinated bowl found inverted over the skull.

On Crow Creek Island a protohistoric village was discovered and investigated. This island is a mile long and a quarter of a mile wide and has a low ridge running its length. Cultural debris was noted along the entire length of the ridge top. In one of the investigated areas numerous post holes, clay-lined fire basins, midden pits, and burials were found, indicating the former presence of a large village. Fourteen partially flexed burials were found, some of which were accompanied by pottery vessels, greenstone celts, bone

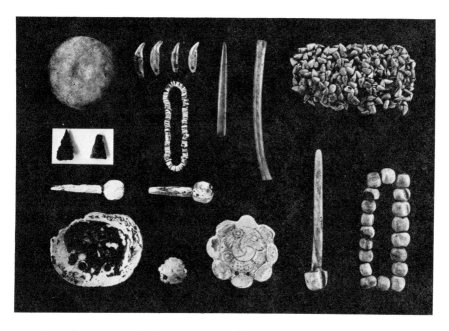

Burial Goods Associated with Crow Creek Phase Interments, AMNH 42 Ja 176a

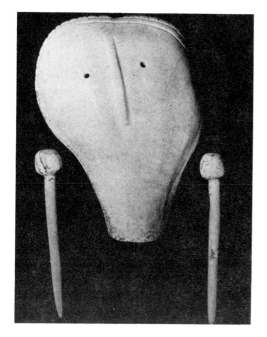

Shell "Death Mask" Gorget and Pins Associated with Crow Creek Phase (Courtesy Victor K. Fleming)

Protohistoric Arrow Points (Courtesy Victor K. Fleming)

awls, shell beads, knobbed pins, and antler flakers. The large collection of complete vessels recovered in burial association at this site is particularly revealing because the vessels display a fusion of modes of Henry Island phase domestic ware with traits of the McKee Island series. Vessels in this sample are characteristically small, globular-bodied, relatively narrow-mouthed, high-rimmed jars with four to six horizontal flanges. Bowls with sharply incurving rims were also present.

A major Crow Creek phase village was discovered at the Cox site, located on the left bank of the Tennessee River some four miles north of Crow Creek Island. The Cox site was found to contain an extensive protohistoric habitation area and an associated truncated mound, one of the last (perhaps even the last) earthen pyramid to have been built in this region.

The Cox mound stood 8 feet high and measured 100 feet in diameter at the base. When visited by C. B. Moore in 1915, a barn and other recent structures stood on its summit. The mound had been constructed in three major phases over an old village area containing the remains of Woodland and earlier Mississippian occupations. McKee Island series ceramics were found inclusive in the fill of the primary building stage, thus confirming the full protohistoric placement of this mound. Five structure patterns were found on prepared clay floors within the mound. Four of these were rectangular buildings of the closed wall-trench construction type. One of these buildings had dimensions of 17 by 25 feet. On the outside of its line of trenches, on all sides, was a wall of hard-packed clay nearly two feet high. Lying on this clay wall to the northwest were several horizontal charred logs and on the south-east, outside the building and on a sloping shelf of the clay wall, was a well-formed fire basin. Inside the building were three fired areas on the hardpacked clay floor. Lying some ten feet out from this structure were lines of single-post construction walls forming an enclosing screen. The fifth structure discovered was an unusual semicircular wall-trench building 19 feet wide, built during the early stages of mound construction. A straight line of posts enclosed the large opening, leaving a narrow doorway. Five partially flexed burials were found under the hard-packed sand floor of this structure.

The Cox site village covered a two-acre area. Large numbers of scattered post holes and a large amount of structure debris indicate the former presence of wattle and daub construction buildings. Some 93 burials were found within the habitation area, twenty of which were associated with typical Crow Creek phase burials goods—shell beads, knobbed pins, plain or scalloped gorgets, and pottery vessels.

Burial Urn Culture

To the south of the Crow Creek settlements, protohistoric peoples of the interior Coastal Plain valleys practiced an unusual mortuary custom. While they continued to bury many of their dead in the traditional manner (extended or partially flexed), large numbers of infants and children, as well as adults, were placed into large pottery vessels prior to burial. According to Peter Brannon (1938:230), fully three-fourths of the burial urns found in this region contain the remains of children or infants. These were usually primary burials; the urns were large enough to contain the entire body. Adult inhumations in such urns represent secondary burials. Brannon believes that prior to urn interment the remains of adults were first picked and cleaned in the custom of the historic Choctaw.

The urns used for such burial were not specially made receptacles but were simply large pots that were taken out of domestic use as cooking vessels or storage jars. The most common type of burial urn is a globular jar ranging in size from ten to twenty inches in orifice diameter. Before the urns were placed into the grave, they were usually covered with another vessel, commonly a shallow bowl that may have been specially made for such a purpose. Burial urns were placed into small pits apparently dug only large enough to receive them. They occur singly or in groups, sometimes in rows or clusters.

Craig Sheldon, who has recently completed a dissertation on the Burial Urn culture, has provided an excellent summary of the archaeological background of this complex (1974:13–20). In 1899 Clarence B. Moore conducted an expedition up the Alabama River to its headwaters at Montgomery. He located and excavated twenty-six sites during his survey, the first organized investigation of prehistoric sites in this area. At the Little River and Matthew's Landing sites on the lower Alabama, Moore discovered single burial urns, but it was not until he reached Durant's Bend, ten miles east of Selma, that a major burial urn site was discovered. At the Durant's Bend site Moore found forty-three burials, sixteen of which were infants or dismembered adults placed into large shell-tempered jars, covered by inverted bowls, and buried in shallow pits. Late in 1904, Moore compiled a nationwide summary of burial urn occurrences. He noted that, while this custom was widely practiced in eastern North America, it was apparent that urn burial occurred more frequently in the Gulf Coastal Plain of Alabama and Georgia than in any other region.

Moore also observed that ceramic vessels stylistically similar to those recovered at Durant's Bend had been found during his excavations at the Bear Creek mound on the Alabama coast, where they had been inverted over the crania of extended burials or over bundle burials. Moore summarily added the trait of vessel inversion to the general burial urn complex. He further noted that inasmuch as European trade goods had been discovered with the Bear Creek mound burials, the practice of urn burial must have continued into the historic period.

In 1905 Moore made a second foray into the Alabama Coastal Plain, this time surveying the lower Tombigbee River from its junction with the Alabama River to just below Demopolis. He located four sites with urn burials and extended or secondary burials with bowls inverted over them. At the Hook's Plantation and Three Rivers sites such burials were found in association with glass beads, fragments of iron, and brass religious medallions, adding further documentation for the continuation of burial urn interment into historic times.

Study of the Burial Urn culture intensified with the founding in 1909 of the Alabama Anthropological Society at Montgomery. The amateur members of this organization concentrated on the excavation of local burial urn sites, often with remarkable results. They dug large portions of the sites of Pintlalla and Taskigi, both major towns during protohistoric times. By 1933 they had recovered over two hundred urns from Taskigi alone. The results of the society's investigations were reported in various issues of its publication, *Arrowpoints*, from 1920 through 1937.

Peter A. Brannon, president of the society and its most prolific writer, was the first to use the term "Urn-Burial Culture" (1935:22), which he recognized as a distinct cultural complex of burial practices and ceramic forms and designs along the Alabama River. Noting that European trade materials were associated with the urns, Brannon agreed with Moore that this custom extended into historic times but further specified that it had probably ceased by circa 1700. His calculation of this terminal date for burial urn interment was based upon the fact that the paucity of European objects found with them argued against any extended contact with the French at Fort Toulouse, erected at the fork of the Coosa and Tallapoosa rivers in 1715. Brannon also believed that the Burial Urn culture represented the material remains of the Alabama tribe, an ethnic group related to the Choctaw, known to have inhabited the Alabama River area during the historic period.

Only a few field investigations of Burial Urn sites have been conducted since the heyday of the Alabama Anthropological Society, but in 1952 and again in 1960 David DeJarnette set aside a special subdivision of his Alabama chronology to encompass the Burial Urn culture. DeJarnette divided the late Mississippian into two temporal units, the Climax Mississippian represented by the florescence at Moundville, and the Decline Mississippian characterized by the Burial Urn materials. In his definition of the Decline Mississippian, DeJarnette was the first to propose a stylistic connection between the urns and the earlier Moundville ceramics. He interpreted the Burial Urn ceramics "as a dilute Moundville ceremonial ware, with degeneration in care of execution and a loss of 'cult' designs, except for an occasional occurrence of the hand-eye and cross designs" (1952:284). This degeneration of ceramic styles, concurrent with the decline of temple mound construction and the disappearance of many southeastern ceremonial complex traits, began toward the end of the Moundville era (circa 1500) and continued through the Decline Mississippian or protohistoric period to culminate in the Ocmulgee Fields ceramics of the historic Creek settlements of the eighteenth century (DeJarnette 1958:20). DeJarnette also correctly predicted that the sites of the aboriginal settlements visited by DeSoto would ultimately be identified as belonging to the Fort Walton, Lamar, and Burial Urn archaeological manifestations.

In recent years, limited excavations have been conducted by DeJarnette at Fosters Ferry, one of three Burial Urn sites discovered on the Black Warrior River near Moundville, and under his direction in the Jones Bluff, Millers Ferry, and Claiborne reservoirs (1964–1966) along the Alabama River. The field investigations associated with these latter projects were supervised by Joseph Benthall, John Cottier (1968), Roy Dickens (1971), Jerry Nielsen, Edward Prince, and Craig Sheldon.

Based upon these salvage investigations, John Cottier (1970b) has defined a subdivision of the Burial Urn culture, the Alabama River phase, and has recognized two series of Alabama River phase ceramics, the shell-tempered Alabama River series and the grit-tempered Wilcox series. Both assemblages are characterized by plain or decorated globular jars, at times with strap handles and notched rims, and carinated bowls. Four types of decoration are found on vessels of both series—incised, applique (added strips of clay, or nodes), pinched (bands of pinched lines), and filmed-incised. Red-filmed and

Burial Urn Exposed at Site WX-1, Wilcox County, AMNH 194 WX 1

Burial Urn and Cover in Place (After Fundaburk and Foreman 1957)

red-on-buff wares have also been recognized but are rare. The incised decorations, often combined with punctations, include designs composed of
parallel lines, spirals, stepped frets, fuilloches, cross hatching, and cult symbols (hands, skull, and cross motifs). Bird-head adornos have been reported
on open-bowl forms and represent one of several ceramic traits derived from
Fort Walton period cultures to the south.

The Alabama River phase settlement pattern is presently known only from
river or creek-bank sites. Several of the village sites investigated exhibited
an extended linear pattern, perhaps indicative of a loose village arrangement
with cultivated fields and house sites intermingled (Cottier 1970b). Two of
the Millers Ferry sites reported by Cottier (1968), the Liddell and Goat
Pasture sites, can be considered to represent towns or important villages,
while several nearby smaller sites may represent satellite hamlets or
farmsteads. Houses were rectangular in shape, with packed-clay floors,
single-post walls, and wattle and daub construction. Ethnohistorical and
archaeological evidence indicates that the Alabama River phase economy
centered around floodplain horticulture, hunting, and the utilization of
riverine flora and fauna.

From Sheldon's dissertation on the Burial Urn culture the following conclusions have been drawn (1974:66–67, 119–21): The Burial Urn culture
represents a uniform archaeological manifestation characterized by urn inhumation, shell- and grit-tempered ceramics, specific design motifs, floodplain horticulture and settlement orientation, and a material culture clearly
recognizable as a variant of the Mississippian culture type. Known Burial
Urn sites are geographically restricted to localities on the major rivers of the
north and central Coastal Plain of Alabama. Three major clusters of Burial
Urn sites have been recognized within these regions. The largest number of
sites are found in the core area of the Alabama River from Montgomery to
the Tombigbee junction. Smaller concentrations of Burial Urn sites are on
the lower Tombigbee and on the Black Warrior River between Moundville
and the fall line at Tuscaloosa.

Temporally, the Burial Urn culture falls within the protohistoric period of
A.D. 1500 to 1700. Similarities in certain pottery types and designs—as well
as other aspects of a more general nature such as lithic and shell assemblages, burial practices, and subsistence and settlement—strongly
suggest a genetic cultural relationship between the preceding Moundville
phase and the Burial Urn culture. Sheldon characterizes the cultural changes
within the late mature Mississippian and protohistoric periods as those of a
"reducing" area tradition.

   The central core of the Burial Urn assemblage appears to be derived from
the "domestic" and technomic artifacts and activities of the Moundville phase,
and there is considerable evidence that the basic Mississippian techno environmental adaptation in subsistence and settlement systems continued

Burial Urn Covers from the Lower Tallapoosa. Drawings by Dr. R. P. Burke, Montgomery (After Fundaburk and Foreman 1957)

throughout the Proto-historic period. The elaborate Southeastern Ceremonial Complex, ceremonial mound construction, and pronounced differences in burial associations, all appear to follow a different course of change, and either disappear or become greatly reduced during the Mississippian Decline. Their extinction and the abandonment of the actual site of Moundville tends to indicate a substantial decline in the scale and level of socio-political organization during the subsequent Proto-historic era. [1974:120]

Allowing for the problems surrounding attempts at ethnic identification, Sheldon's research suggests that there is good ethnohistorical and archaeological evidence that the Burial Urn culture may be associated in varying ways with historic Muskogean groups such as the Alabama, Mobile, and Tohome, and perhaps even the Napochi of Luna's time. Following the initiation of sustained contact with European colonists, burial urn interment, as well as many other technological and social aspects of protohistoric aboriginal culture, ceased to be practiced as the process of acculturation accelerated.

Fort Walton Period Cultures

The protohistoric cultures of the Alabama and northwest Florida coastal regions have been assigned to what Gordon Willey (1949:452–58) has termed the Fort Walton period. During his survey of this region Willey recorded some thirty-nine Fort Walton period sites, including shell middens, temple mounds, cemetery areas, and burial mounds. Large amounts of pottery fragments were recovered from these locations and were divided by Willey into two series on the basis of tempering. These ceramic assemblages—the shell-tempered Pensacola series and the sand-tempered Fort Walton series—contain high frequencies of plain ware and vessels decorated with incised designs, often combined with punctations. Red-filmed, red-on-buff, black-filmed, and engraved decorations are present but constitute only minor types. Sherds roughened by brushing have also been noted at late Fort Walton period middens. Modeled zoomorphic effigy adornos are common on bowl rims. Vessels frequently took the form of flattened globular jars, casuela bowls, carinated bowls, shallow plates, and bottles. Rims are often pinched or fluted and decorated with appliqué nodes or with punctations.

Willey also noted that the shell-tempered Pensacola types occur more frequently at the western end of the northwest coast of Florida. Fort Walton period sites on Mobile Bay contain almost pure assemblages of Pensacola ware, while contemporary sites east of the Apalachicola River yield almost pure assemblages of the sand-tempered Fort Walton series. Sites in the intervening area display mixed assemblages of the two tempering groups. William Lazarus, a noted authority on the Fort Walton period, has further documented this distribution. Lazarus (1961) compiled data from eighty-eight Fort Walton period sites and noted that, "Around Perdido and Pensacola bays the shell tempered percentage ranges from 100% downward to about 60%. The Choctawhatchee Bay area has no known site that exceeds 72% and the average is slightly less than 50%. On the eastern side of the region under discussion (St. Johns Bay and the west side of the Apalachicola River) the highest recorded percentage is 35% with an average of less than 20%."

Based upon these spatial shifts in ceramic tempering, some researchers have recognized two geographically distinct, yet contemporary, Fort Walton period cultures along the northeastern Gulf coast. According to William Sears, a specialist on Gulf Coast prehistory:

> In southern Alabama the Pensacola culture . . . , which is one with great emphasis on carinated bowls with the characteristic scroll and guilloche designs— became prominent. The culture, derived from the Moundville variant of Middle Mississippi, suddenly expanded down to and along the coast. The

huge shell-midden sites are found all the way to the Mississippi Delta and
eastward to Pensacola. In the same period Fort Walton culture, with a ceramic
complex very similar to that of Pensacola, quickly materialized through the
area from the valley of the Chattahoochee and Apalachicola westward to the
Pensacola area. There are many large coastal and inland Fort Walton sites,
with multiple temple mounds and the other appurtenances of ceremonial
centers. Coastal sites are shell middens although I am sure that some agriculture was practiced. Inland sites represent almost fully agricultural economies. I
am not at all sure where Fort Walton comes from, although Moundville pottery
(and copies of it) which appears in the earliest sites of the Chattahoochie, are
suggestive. . . .

Pensacola and Fort Walton completely and abruptly replaced the old
Weeden Island culture and certain of its close Gulf-tradition relatives in the
coastal plain between peninsular Florida and the Mississippi. This is, I am
convinced, a clear case of invasion and complete expulsion of an old population
by Middle Mississippian peoples. I would date the appearance of both as late
sixteenth century, with continued existence through the seventeenth century.
This is based on the continued association in graves and mounds of artifacts of
both complexes with odds and ends of European materials dating from the
earliest European contacts along the coasts. [1964:283–84]

Large Pensacola populations settled in the Mobile Bay region and were
well established by the time of Pineda's visit. At almost every point along the
shoreline where streams and springs empty into Pensacola Bay and the Gulf
of Mexico major shell-midden sites are found. In sheer size and number,
these collecting stations and villages document the importance of littoral
resources in the Pensacola economy. Oysters comprise the major inverte-
brate species on the middens near the mouth of the bay and along the sand
spits running out into the gulf. Farther up the bay and into the swamps at its
head, brackish-water clams become the major form of food debris littering
the old camp sites. Cailup Curren (1975a) has studied the food remains from
some of these middens and has suggested that they represent seasonally
occupied villages and collecting stations that formed components of an annual economic cycle like that followed by the historic Choctaw. According to
Campbell:

The Lincecum manuscript indicates that the Choctaw had an annual economic cycle that involved hunting, fishing, food collecting, and horticulture. In
mid-winter, the fields were prepared for spring planting. After the crops had
been planted in the spring and were growing well, the Choctaw dispersed to
various streams and lakes, living on fish, turtles, and fruits until time for the
Green Corn Dance in early summer. This ceremony completed, they returned
to the streams and lakes and remained until time for harvesting corn in the fall.
When the corn had been harvested and stored, the men went off on their
regular fall and early winter hunt, and the women, children, and old people
searched the woods for nuts and autumnal fruits. By mid-winter all had re-

turned and the cycle was begun again with the preparation of the fields for spring planting. [1959]

In 1940, as part of an extensive archaeological program in southwestern Alabama sponsored by the WPA and the Alabama Museum of Natural History, David DeJarnette, Harold Andersen, and Steve Wimberly investigated one of the large shell middens in Gulf State Parkway. The site was on a narrow sand spit bordered by the Gulf on the south and Bon Secour Bay on the north. The midden deposit was located on the bay side of the spit and was, at the time of investigation, 13 feet high, 250 feet wide, and 500 feet long. Tons of oyster shell were scattered about in the midden, at times concentrated in lenses near old roasting pits. Of the 15,837 pottery sherds recovered during the investigation, over 99 percent were shell-tempered types of the Pensacola series, indicating that this enormous amount of shell and other food debris were deposited over a span of just a few generations.

Farther up the eastern shore of Mobile Bay, another Pensacola collecting station has recently been investigated by University of Alabama personnel. This shell midden, which contained thick lenses of clam shell, was located at the mouth of D'Olive Creek just north of Daphne. Excavation of the site was deemed necessary because it lay in the path of a proposed highway. Salvage operations were conducted first in 1973 by a crew under the direction of Jerry J. Nielsen and John Walthall and later in 1974 by Ned Jenkins and Carlos Solis. A sample of faunal remains recovered during floatation screening operations at the D'Olive Creek site has been studied (Curren n.d.), and its composition suggests economic concentration on estuarine vertebrates such as fishes and reptiles, as well as shellfish. Botanical remains from this site have also been studied under the supervision of C. Earle Smith, University of Alabama ethnobotanist. Acorns, hickory nuts, persimmons, and corn were identified in the study sample. The presence of corn at this site represents the first documented occurrence of this cultigen at a Pensacola site.

Steve Wimberly (1960) has reported the results of other Alabama Museum of Natural History–WPA excavations at Pensacola sites in Clarke and Mobile counties during 1940–41. Two inland habitation sites were investigated in Clarke County along the Tombigbee River floodplains. The Wilson site was a small habitation midden situated on a narrow point extending into the Tombigbee swampland. Occupational debris was found over an area 40 by 60 feet in extent. A single partially flexed burial was the only feature encountered during the investigation. A sample of 2,100 pottery sherds was collected from the site, all representing Pensacola types. The second Pensacola site investigated in Clarke County, the Beckum village, was located near a major salt spring in the Tombigbee swamps. The habitation zone covered an area of 100 by 200 feet. Excavations revealed a partially flexed burial and twelve circular midden pits, 2 to 3 feet in diameter and 1 to 2.5 feet deep. The Pensacola ceramic sample recovered from the Beckum village contained 528 plain sherds, 8 incised sherds, 1,337 Langston Fabric Impressed, and 387 plain salt-pan sherds. The high frequency of fragments of these large, shallow bowls used in salt production suggests that the major activity conducted during the Pensacola occupation of this site was the procurement of salt, perhaps for both domestic consumption and barter with interior ethnic groups.

Five sites with major Pensacola components were discovered and investigated in the coastal salt marshes west of Mobile Bay in lower Mobile County. All of these sites were littoral middens containing large amounts of oyster shell, fish bone, and aquatic vertebrate remains—evidence of the high economic potential of the salt marsh ecosystem. Partially flexed, extended, and bundle burials were encountered in some of the midden deposits; none were accompanied by grave goods. Large quantities of Pensacola ceramics were encountered in the shell lenses comprising these sites. Only on rare occasion were any lithic tools found. The largest of these middens was the Andrew's Place site in the grassy marsh on the shore of Portersville Bay. This midden covered an area 400 feet wide and 1,000 feet long and was reported to have stood 10 to 12 feet high prior to the removal of tons of shell by commercial operators.

A major Pensacola ceremonial center, the Bottle Creek site, was located in the swamps north of Mobile Bay. The first published description of this important site was contained in a brief account by A. Bigelow (1853) of the Wesleyan Institute of Newark, New Jersey. Bigelow twice visited Bottle Creek during a two-year period of residence near Hall's Landing on the Tensaw River. Major passages in his account are given below.

> About twenty miles north of Mobile, the Tensaw separates from the Mobile river, running to the east by a very tortuous course as far as Stockton, then to the south, emptying into the east side of Mobile bay. Between these two rivers is enclosed a tract of land, twenty miles long and about seven wide, consisting of marsh and swamp land. Much of it is impassable; some of it quakes and sinks beneath the tread, and is covered with tall grass and aquatic plants; the larger portion supports heavy forests, and is called swamp land. Only small portions of the whole tract are dry even in dry weather, or elevated above spring floods. North of the Tensaw, land of a similar character extends for ten miles. The tract between the two rivers is intersected by several creeks and rivers; Middle river, which is wide and deep, flows out of the Tensaw soon after the latter leaves the Mobile, and running southeast, empties again into the Tensaw; thus cutting off a triangular portion of land from the northeast corner of the tract. Again, Bottle Creek leaves the Tensaw not far to the east of Middle river, and running south or west of south, empties into Middle river. In this latter triangular piece, are the mounds. This area is also intersected by the Dominique creek, which runs near to the west side of the mound field, and with which the mounds are connected by a series of small mounds now concealed by the forest . . .

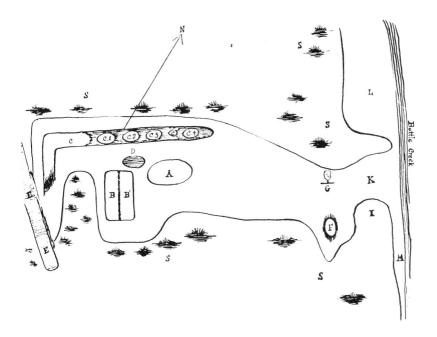

The Bottle Creek Site by Bigelow (1853)

On the west side of Bottle Creek, where it leaves the Tensaw, is probably the most elevated portion of the land above described. Here the first inhabitants found sufficient room and material to construct these mounds; and the French a plantation ready for seed...

The plantation before spoken of, lies on the Tensaw and Bottle creeks, and has a crescent shape; at its southern extremity the eye is attracted through an opening in the forest, by an elevated mound nearly in the center of a large field. . . . This mound is now oval, but has the appearance of having been somewhat rectangular when built. . . . It has a wide base and gradually tapers to the summit, which is 104 feet long by 46 feet wide and elevated about 49 feet above the river at mean tide. The mound stands on ground a little below the surface of the river banks; its sides are covered with trees 40 feet high and with scrubs and a few palmetto bushes. It has frequently been cultivated in corn, and its sides have been worked with the plough and hoe, as well as furrowed and washed with rains, we may suppose, that it has been thereby changed in figure and elevation. Near to this is a large rectangular mound of small elevation, one-half its breadth about five feet higher than the other, and about six feet above high water. On the north and west side of these is a series of low mounds, so connected as to form a ridge of raised earth, extending along one side of a rectangle and part of another till it ends near the swamp. The diameters of the high mound lie in the same directions with the sides of the other mounds; and the whole arrangement is so regular and nearly rectangular, as to induce one to suppose it was laid out by a compass. But I think it to have been done by the eye, according to the position of the ground and river. Its position as respects the compass on the north side is E. by N.E., but it is parallel with the river and general direction of the sides of the field. The entrance looks directly upon the large mound and fronts the whole arrangement. A swamp covered with forests surrounds the whole except the entrance from the river.

For a more particular description the reader is referred to fig. 2. Bottle Creek is represented on the east side; L is a part of the plantation extending to the Tensaw; SS, the swamp which surrounds the whole; K, the entrance to the mound field. On the west is a small mound F, in which the bones of an Indian, together with a large collection of beads and other articles usually attending an Indian interment. The beads are globular, three-quarters of an inch in diameter, having a large hole for the string; they are of glass translucent, and of a bluish color. C, C1, C2, and C3, form the portion of a rectangle outside of the larger mounds: C3, and the next one to it are much used now for stacking hay to prevent injury by the floods; the others are not quite so huge. On C1 and C2 many images, beads, and pieces of copper have been found, having been turned up by the plough. Upon C2 I found an old fire-hearth a short distance below the surface, and beside it the bones of various animals now existing there. Those of the alligator were most abundant. BB' is the large rectangular mound; B is about five feet higher than the part B'; it is 344 feet long by 250 wide. . . . Upon this are found great quantities of broken crockery, which evince considerable skill in modeling and finishing . . .

D, in fig. 2, is an excavation of some depth, containing water in which some trees are now growing. It appears by its position, to have been designed as a water hole, or well. It is also an excavation from which material was probably taken for the mound B. A is the large mound occupying the center and over-looking all. EE is a ditch beginning a little south of the mound BB' and extending northwest nearly to Dominique creek. It contains water and trees, being in the edge of the swamp, and has the appearance of an ancient canal. It is sufficiently long to have afforded nearly all the material for the mounds, and may have been used as a way of approach from the northwest. As before remarked, this system of mounds continues across this ditch towards Middle river... [1853:186–92]

Half a century later C. B. Moore (1905c) visited the Bottle Creek site and published a brief description of the major earthen pyramid and ridged earthworks noted by Bigelow. Moore did not conduct an excavation during his exploration of the site but did observe considerable village debris sur-rounding the earthen tumuli. It was not until some twenty-five years later that a systematic excavation was conducted at Bottle Creek. David DeJar-nette, directing a crew of Alabama Museum of Natural History personnel, dug a large test trench (15 feet by 30 feet) and several five-foot squares around the base of the principal mound. In the main excavation unit DeJar-nette encountered lines of intersecting post holes, probably representing portions of a rectangular structure. The sample of cultural materials recov-ered during this investigation was later the subject of a study by Nicholas Holmes (1963), who noted that the lithic tools contained in the Bottle Creek sample were interesting only because of their paucity; only a single projectile point and nine chipped fragments were recovered. Bone awls, an eyed needle, and a number of faunal fragments (deer, alligator, catfish, turtle, water fowl, etc.) were noted. Pottery sherds were abundantly represented; of the 1,400 sherds studied, all but 63 were Pensacola types. The remaining 63 ceramic fragments were sand- or grit-tempered types representing a wide range of forms of unknown cultural provenance.

These investigations and accounts of the Bottle Creek site indicate that this ceremonial center, in size and magnitude of construction, ranks second only to the great center at Moundville and represents one of the major protohistoric sites in Alabama and the Southeast. In the intervening years since its discovery, Bottle Creek has suffered large-scale vandalism and loot-ing. Recently, Read Stowe, archaeologist at the University of South Alabama, and the Alabama Historical Commission, have managed to have the Bottle Creek site, which is on private property, added to the National Register of Historic Sites in hopes of preserving it for posterity.

Another important Pensacola culture site in Alabama is the Bear Creek site, a mound and large village on the western shore of Perdido Bay in Baldwin County (Willey 1949:197–200). C. B. Moore (1901) visited the site around the turn of the century and excavated a large portion of the mound, a truncated pyramid, 80 feet in diameter and 7 feet high. Moore found that the mound had been constructed in two stages. In the upper layer and in pits extending from the upper into the lower stage he discovered forty-four burials, all of which were secondary burials; frequently the remains of more than one individual were placed into a common grave. Bunched or bundle burials were common, as were single isolated skulls. In several cases skulls, accompanied by both aboriginal and European grave goods, had been placed beneath inverted pottery bowls. Aboriginal grave goods include numerous pottery vessels of the Pensacola series, projectile points, celts, pebble hammers, stone discoidals, hematite and limonite, and shell beads and pins. European grave goods found include iron nails, metal tools, sword fragments, glass beads, silver buttons, copper or brass objects, and coins. One of these coins was "an undated silver coin of Spanish Mexico, which we were informed at the United States Mint, was struck by Charles and Joanna between 1531 and 1550 A.D." (Moore 1901:426). William Lazarus (1965) has more recently reported the recovery of another coin at a Fort Walton period site, a cemetery near Alaqua Bayou, where a small copper coin was found that proved to represent a coin struck in the name of Charles I at Santo Domingo between 1532 and 1557.

To the east, one of the largest Fort Walton sites is located within the limits of present Fort Walton on Santa Rosa Sound. The Fort Walton site consists of an extensive shell midden and an associated truncated mound twelve feet high with a ramp on one side. Investigations of the mound and village area have been reported by Walker (1885), Moore (1901), Willey (1949), Fairbanks (1965), and Y. W. Lazarus (1970). Moore recovered some sixty-six burials from the summit and sides of the mound. Secondary (single-skull and bunched) and primary burials were noted. Pottery vessels and other aboriginal grave goods were found with many of these interments. European artifacts have not been reported. In some instances bowls were found inverted over the skulls of burials. Ceremonially destroyed caches of pottery were also found in the mound apart from burial associations.

The Fort Walton mound has been preserved by concerned local citizens and is now the site of the impressive Temple Mound Museum, directed by the indefatigable Yulee Lazarus, wife of the late William Lazarus. The Temple Mound Museum is open to the public six days a week (closed on Mondays) and houses large collections of cultural material from all periods of Gulf Coast prehistory arranged in chronological displays.

Inland sites of the Fort Walton culture extend northward into Alabama. A large Fort Walton mound was investigated in the summer of 1959 by a Smithsonian research team on the right bank of the Chattahoochee in Houston County. This site, the Seaborn mound, first reported by C. B. Moore (1907b:444) was a truncated pyramid 8 feet high and 120 feet long. The Smithsonian excavations were conducted along the west side and the south end of the mound (Neuman 1961). The exposed profile revealed that the mound had been built in four stages over a low natural levee. The primary structure had been a low truncated mound, constructed of fill taken from the surrounding village area and capped with a mantle of bright orange clay. A line of five post holes, representing a portion of a rectangular structure, was found under the fill of the last two stages and to the side of the first two superimposed, smaller mounds. One of the post holes contained charred corn fragments identified by Hugh Cutler as eight-row northern flint. Corn has been reported at three other inland Fort Walton sites, strengthening the prediction of some researchers that these interior sites represent agricultural villages.

Ninety percent of the large ceramic sample recovered from the Seaborn mound were types of the sand-tempered Fort Walton series. Shell-tempered sherds were rare. The absence of European artifacts at this site suggests that the mound was constructed during early protohistoric times.

The Middle Chattahoochee Sequence

Farther north, in the middle Chattahoochee region, archaeologists have located and investigated a number of protohistoric and historic lower Creek villages. These investigations have led to the establishment of a local sequence of three late archaeological phases (Schnell 1971). The earliest recognized protohistoric phase of the middle Chattahoochee is the Bull Creek phase, which is characterized by a Lamar cultural assemblage exhibiting strong Fort Walton influence. Bull Creek settlements were inhabited by lower Creek groups when DeSoto's expedition passed through southern Georgia, and certain neighboring villages were actually visited by the Spaniards. The succeeding Abercrombie phase, which is thought to date from circa 1600–1690, represents the material remains of settlements occupied by the Creek populations visited by Antonio de Matheos between 1683 and 1685, during his several trips made from Spanish Florida up the Chattahoochee in an effort to expel English traders from Apalachicola villages on Alabama's eastern border. Matheos failed to capture the Carolina fur merchants led by Doctor Henry Woodward, but, in retribution for protecting the English, he burned four aboriginal villages (Pearson 1964). Shortly afterwards, in 1689, the Spanish built a small fortress near present-day Phenix City to keep the English out of lower Creek country. This outpost, Fort Apalachicola, was located and excavated during The University of Alabama's Walter F. George Reservoir Survey (DeJarnette 1975).

Since the presence of the Spanish garrison prohibited contact with the English, whose trade items were of superior quality and in greater supply than those available through the Spanish, the Lower Creeks abandoned the Chattahoochee and moved eastward to the Ocmulgee, where the English had established a trading post. The Spanish fort was abandoned in 1691, for it then served no purpose. For over thirty years the middle Chattahoochee was depopulated, until 1729 when the Creeks began to return and again establish villages. These later sites, occupied between 1730 and 1830, when

the removal of the Creeks to the west began, have been placed into a third
and final archaeological phase, the Lawson Field phase. Lawson Field components are characterized by large amounts of grit-tempered Chattahoochee
series ceramics, (plain, brushed, and red-filmed) and quantities of European
trade materials.

The earliest ethnohistoric account of a Creek village, that of the Gentleman of Elvas (one of the DeSoto chroniclers), describes Toalli, probably a
Hitchiti (Lamar) settlement to the east of Chattahoochee:

> The houses of this town were different from those behind [in the march from
> Florida]. [These] were covered with dry grass; then upward they are roofed
> with cane after the fashion of tiles. They are kept clean; some have their sides
> so made of clay as to look like tapia. . . . Throughout the cold country every
> Indian has a winter house, plastered inside and out, with a very small opening,
> which is closed at dark and a fire being made within, it remains heated like an
> oven, so that clothing is not needed at night. He has likewise a house for
> summer and near it a kitchen, where fire is made and bread baked. Maize is
> kept in barbacoas, which is a house with wooden sides like a room or raised
> aloft on four posts and has a floor of canes. The difference between the houses
> of the masters of principal men and those of the common people is beside being
> larger than the others, they have deep balconies on the front side, with cane
> seats like benches; and about are many barbacoas in which they bring
> together the tribute their people give them of maize, skins of deer, and
> blankets of the country. [Bourne 1904:53]

The contemporary Bull Creek phase settlements along the Chattahoochee, which were probably very similar to neighboring Toalli, are
characterized by large amounts of grit-tempered Lamar pottery and smaller
percentages of Fort Walton ceramics. Complicated-stamped vessels are
marked with curvilinear designs such as the filfot cross and concentric circles. Incising, common on carinated bowls, takes the form of scrolls, guil-
loches, semicircles, and designs of parallel lines. Notches, bosses, or punctations are applied below the lip on jars or bowls, or at the point of the
shoulder on carinated-bowl forms. Jars are deep with slightly flaring rims.
Charles Fairbanks (1952) has noted that, compared to central Georgia
Lamar, there is less stamping and more plain and incised ware in the western Lamar area of the middle Chattahoochee.

In the core area of central Georgia, Lamar sites typically have two mounds
facing each other across an open plaza. The Lamar village at Macon, the type
site, was fortified with an encircling palisade of vertical posts. Lamar burials
were usually made in the village area and were commonly partially flexed
with few or no grave goods. When burial offerings are present, they usually
take the form of pottery vessels, pipes, stone celts, shell gorgets (plain or
scalloped), knobbed shell pins, and shell beads. Few urn burials have been
noted. The pipes found with Lamar burials take on a variety of forms includ-

ing grotesque men's faces, monolithic axe effigys, bird heads, boat shapes, and animal heads (Fairbanks 1952:294).

During University of Alabama surveys of the portion of the Chattahoochee to be inundated by the construction of the Walter F. George Reservoir, major Bull Creek phase components were excavated. One of the more important of these was found at the Shorter site, which consisted of a mound and associated village just north of Eufaula in Barbour County. David De-Jarnette directed field operations at the Shorter site in the summers of 1960 and 1961. The mound was a rectangular pyramid that stood 15 feet above the surrounding floodplain. Excavation revealed that it had been constructed in three stages. Beneath the primary mound, on the old ground surface, De-Jarnette found post holes and a fire basin, indicating the existence of a precedent timber structure. Large refuse pits were found in the village area, and, like the mound fill, they contained large amounts of Bull Creek phase pottery sherds. One feature in the habitation area contained charred corn. (DeJarnette 1975).

Bull Creek phase sites were also discovered farther upstream in the Oliver Reservoir immediately north of the Columbus–Phenix City area (McMichael

Typical Creek Storage Jar with Incised Design (After Fundaburk and Foreman 1957)

and Kellar 1959). The Oliver Reservoir, which inundated a 10-mile stretch of the Chattahoochee, lies just north of the fall line (the major falls were at Columbus). McMichael and Kellar divided the basin into two physiographic sections: an upper section comprising two-thirds of the basin, where there were few shoals and rapids but large bottomlands; and a lower section with many islands, shoals, and rapids but no bottomlands. Several small, compact Bull Creek phase settlements were found in the floodplain of the upper section of the basin. Rectangular, wattle and daub houses were found at some of these sites, suggesting small villages. However, in the lower basin only small, scattered campsites were found, often in narrow rock shelters. These Oliver Basin sites appear to represent components of a seasonal round during which time the population fanned out from their villages, dividing into small family groups to fish, hunt, and gather plant foods. The smaller lower basin sites may represent summer fishing camps.

Further evidence of the exploitation of the Alabama Piedmont by Lamar-related groups has been provided by recent University of Alabama excavations in the proposed Crooked Creek Reservoir in Randolph County.

One of the sites found during the survey, a small rock shelter on the north bank of the Tallapoosa River, was excavated by John O'Hear. This shelter, designated 1 Ra 28, was 9 feet high, 23 feet wide, and 24 feet deep, forming only a small living area. Excavations within this area and on the narrow slope outside the shelter revealed four stratified zones dating back to the Archaic. Beneath the uppermost stratum, O'Hear discovered a deep zone containing an enormous amount of Lamar pottery. Although the cultural material from 1 Ra 28 and the other sites located during the survey has not yet been completely analyzed, the large quantity of Lamar pottery and lithic artifacts identified so far suggests an intensive utilization of the Piedmont uplands by protohistoric populations. Because agriculture is not feasible in the narrow stream valleys of this region, it appears likely that sites such as 1 Ra 28 represent seasonally occupied hunting and foraging stations.

The following Abercrombie phase of the middle Chattahoochee sequence is characterized by three pottery types—Abercrombie Plain, Ocmulgee Fields Incised, and Walnut Roughened. Although much of this ware was tempered with crushed shell, fine grit particles were also at times added to the paste. Two major Abercrombie phase sites were excavated during the Walter F. George survey. One of these was the type site, the Aber-crombie mound and village, situated on the second terrace of the Chatta-hoochee six miles south of Phenix City (Fairbanks 1955b; DeJarnette 1975). Excavations at this site, conducted in 1962 under the direction of Edward Kurjack, revealed three major components, major Bull Creek and Aber-crombie occupations, and a less extensive historic Lawson Field occupation. The mound, which C. B. Moore (1907b) reported to have stood 14 feet high and to measure 85 to 95 feet in basal dimensions, was associated with the Bull Creek phase remains. The Abercrombie component represented a compact village with rectangular houses containing shallow central fire basins.

Excavations at Fort Apalachicola revealed a second major Abercrombie phase component, representing the town of Apalachicola, which was chosen as the site of the Spanish *presido*. Historical documents indicate that the aboriginal occupation of this site was terminated in 1691 by the eastward withdrawal of the Lower Creeks. The small fortress built at this location was a timber stockade with an encircling moat and four corner bastions. Only small amounts of Spanish material were discovered during the excavation of this site, reflecting its short occupation by the Spanish garrison. Kurjack and Pearson (1975) gave the following account of the history of the fort.

Governor Diego de Quiroga y Losada of Saint Augustine, after visiting the Apalachee province in 1687, ordered Captain Primo de Rivera to construct a *Casa fuerte* on the Chattahoochee to protect Spanish Florida's northern flank from English encroachment. Governor Quiroga sent one hundred Indians, many of whom were carpenters, with Rivera, so that the fortress could be completed in two months' time. In the spring of 1690 Lieutenant Favian de Angulo traveled up the Chattahoochee to assume command of the garrison. Two of his reports to Governor Quiroga have survived. He wrote on 14 April 1690 that the garrison consisted of a corporal, two *reformados* (officers deprived of former commands), seventeen regular soldiers, and twenty Apalachee Indians. Angulo's letters described the fort itself and also negotiations with the Indians in which he warned them not to attempt to trade with the English. Little heed was paid to his words because the lure of English trade goods was stronger, and soon the village around the fort was abandoned. The threat of French pirate raids on Saint Augustine in 1691 forced Governor Quiroga to recall many interior garrisons to bolster his defenses. Before leaving, Angulo demolished the fortification, filled the moat, and removed arms, food, and other supplies in order to make the site useless to Carolina merchants.

Angulo's retreat and the Spanish abandonment of the Chattahoochee left the Middle South open to French and English trade and colonization. Carolina traders soon reached the Tennessee River, and the French established Fort Toulouse on the Alabama some two decades later. The following century was a period of rapid acculturation, incessant warfare, and political intrigue. These processes resulted in the almost total subjugation of regional aboriginal societies and eventually led to the forced movement of entire communities westward to Oklahoma. In this manner over ten thousand years of indigenous cultural development was brought to an abrupt end. All that remains of this remarkable prehistoric human experience are the scraps and pieces of tangible evidence found at the abandoned sites that present-day archaeologists are attempting to preserve for posterity.

Glossary

antler flaker   A tool made from an antler tip used in pressure-flaking stone.

artifact   An object made by human hands.

atlatl   A spear thrower consisting of a stick or board, approximately two feet long, with a handle at one end and a hook at the other.

biface   A stone tool, such as a knife or scraper, with flaking on both faces. A biface blank is an unfinished stone tool partially worked to the size and shape of the intended implement.

bodkin   A pin or awl made of bone, or rarely, copper. It is used to make holes in fabric or hide.

burial, bundle   A reburial, or secondary burial, of defleshed and disarticulated bones tied together in a bundle.

burial, extended   A form of primary burial in which the body is placed into a grave in a prone position with legs extended and arms positioned straight against the side.

burial, flexed   A form of burial in the fetal position with arms and legs bent up against the body.

check-stamping   A grid pattern of small squares used in decorating pottery vessels. The grid was usually carved onto the face of a wooden paddle and was stamped into the wet clay surface.

culture   Archaeologically, a culture may be defined as a single group of technologies or assemblages reflecting a similar economic adjustment shared by multiple social groups; a group of specific, named units (i.e., phases) about whose temporal and spatial existence definite data exists.

debitage   An assemblage of by-products or waste materials produced during flint-working activities such as flakes, cores, and other stone shatter.

ecotone   An edge zone at the contact area of divergent environment units such as forest/prairie or valley/uplands.

galena   Lead ore, gray with a metallic luster. Cubes and nodules were ground to form a white or sparkling paint.

gorget   An ornament, usually made of stone, shell, or copper, which was worn over the chest. Gorgets are commonly perforated for attaching to clothing or suspending from a cord.

graver   A sharp-pointed cutting tool used for working bone or wood.

hammerstone   A hard, rounded stone implement used as a hammer.

horizon   A spatial continuity of culture traits or complexes that have a wide geographical distribution and are believed to have diffused rapidly and persisted for a relatively brief duration.

jasper   An opaque, uncrystalline form of quartz often occurring in red or tan hues.

mano   The hand-held stone used on a metate to grind corn or other foods.

midden   The accumulated organic refuse near a habitation site.

mortar   A stone or wooden trough, with a deep concavity used as the lower part of a hand grinding mill. Usually used to grind seed foods.

muller   A club-shaped, ground, stone tool, also called a pestle, used to crush or mill various materials in a mortar.

percussion flaking   A stone-tool manufacturing technique used to shape tools. A hammerstone or antler baton is struck against a core to chip off flakes.

pressure flaking   A finishing technique used in the manufacture of stone tools. Flakes are removed from a stone by pressing a blunt, pointed implement of antler or bone against the edge being worked. This technique permits greater control than percussion flaking.

rocker stamping   A motif consisting of connecting zigzag lines used to decorate pottery. The lines are produced by rocking a sharp-edged tool back and forth over a wet clay surface.

seriation   A method of determining a relative chronology commonly utilizing variations in ceramic decorative or stylistic variables through time. Usually consists of calculating increases or decreases in the popularity of styles.

sherd   A broken fragment of a pottery vessel.

stage   A broad developmental unit implying widespread cultural unity, and a sequence and ranking of cultures by level of complexity toward some terminal level.

steatite   A type of talc, or soapstone, which can be carved and ground into pots and other utilitarian objects.

trait   A diagnostic artifact or characteristic element of a culture.

Bibliography

Ahler, S. A.
    1971   Projectile point form and function at Rodgers shelter, Missouri. *Missouri Archaeological Society Research Series*, no. 8.

Asche, N. B.; Ford, R. I.; and Asch, D. L.
    1972   Paleoethnobotany of the Koster site. *Illinois State Museum Reports of Investigations*, no. 24.

Atkeson, T.
    1959   A burial by the river. *Journal of Alabama Archaeology* 5:13–15.

Baldwin, E. E.
    1966   The Obion site: An early Mississippian center in western Tennessee. Doctoral dissertation, Harvard University.

Barksdale, J.
    1929   Possible salt deposits in the vicinity of the Jackson Fault, Alabama. *Alabama Geological Survey, Circular* 10.
    1930   Ochers of Alabama. *Geological Survey of Alabama, Bulletin* 41.

Barlow, J. A.
    1971   Recent geological history of the St. Albans site. In the St. Albans site, Kanawha County, West Virginia, by B. J. Broyles. *West Virginia Geological and Economic Survey, Report of Archaeological Investigations*, no. 3.

Beardsley, R. K.
    1955   Functional and evolutionary implications of community patterning. In Seminars in archaeology, 1955, edited by R. Wancope. *Memoirs of the Society for American Archaeology*, no. 11.

Benthall, J. L.
    1965   A study of flint and ceramic relationships at four selected Alabama aboriginal sites. Master's thesis, The University of Alabama.

Bigelow, A.
    1953   Observations on some mounds on the Tensaw River. *The American Journal of Science and Arts* 65:186–92.

Binford, L. R.
    1962   Archaeology as anthropology. *American Antiquity* 28:217–25.

Birdsell, J. B.
    1968   Some predictions for the Pleistocene based on equilibrium systems among recent hunters and gatherers. In *Man the Hunter*, edited by R. B. Lee and I. DeVore. Chicago: Aldine.

Bohannon, C. F.
    1972   *Excavations at the Pharr mounds*. Washington, D.C.: National Park Service.

Bourne, E. G. (editor)
    1904   *Narratives of the career of Hernando de Soto*. New York: Trail Makers.

Brannon, P. A.
    1935   The archaeology of Taskigi. *Arrowpoints* 20: 1–26.
    1938   Urn burial in central Alabama. *American Antiquity* 3:228–35.

Brock, O. W.
    1969   The transition from the Paleo-Indian to the Archaic in the Tennessee
              Valley. Master's thesis, The University of Alabama.

Brock, O. W., and Clayton, M. V.
    1966   Archaeological investigations in the Mud Creek–Town Creek drain-
              age area of northwest Alabama. *Journal of Alabama Archaeology*
              12:79–137.

Brown, J. A.
    1971   The dimensions of status in the burials at Spiro. In Approaches to the
              social dimensions of mortuary practices, edited by J. A. Brown.
              Memoirs of the Society for American Archaeology, no. 25.

Brown, P. H.
    1954   A cave shelter. *Tennessee Archaeologist* 10:68–74.

Broyles, B. J.
    1958   Russell Cave in northern Alabama. *Tennessee Archaeological Society,
              Miscellaneous Paper*, no. 4.
    1971   The St. Albans site, Kanawha County, West Virginia. *West Virginia
              Geological and Economic Survey, Report of Archaeological Investiga-
              tions*, no. 3.

Bullen, R. P.
    1950   An archaeological survey of the Chattahoochee River Valley in
              Florida. *Journal of the Washington Academy of Sciences* 40:101–25.
    1958   Six sites near the Chattahoochee River in the Jim Woodruff Reservoir
              area. *Bureau of American Ethnology, Bulletin* 169:317–58.
    1970   The Transitional period of southern southeastern United States as
              viewed from Florida, or the roots of the Gulf Tradition. *Southeastern
              Archaeological Conference, Bulletin* 13.
    1972   The Orange period of Peninsular Florida. In Fiber-tempered pottery
              in southeastern United States and northern Colombia, edited by R. P.
              Bullen and J. B. Stoltman. *Florida Anthropologist* 25.

Bullen, R. P., and Stoltman, J. B. (editors)
    1972   Fiber-tempered pottery in the Southeastern United States and north-
              ern Colombia: Its origins, context, and significance. *Florida An-
              thropologist* 25:1–72.

Burke, R. P.
    1933   Orange-red pottery people. Montgomery: *Arrowpoints* 20:17–36.

Butler, B. M.
    1968   The Brickyard site (40 Fr 13). In Archaeological investigations in the
              Tims Ford Reservoir, Tennessee, 1966, edited by C. H. Faulkner,
              Department of Anthropology, University of Tennessee.

Byers, D. S.
    1959   An introduction to five papers on the Archaic stage. *American An-
              tiquity* 24:229–32.

Caldwell, J. R.
    1954   The Old Quartz Industry of Piedmont Georgia and South Carolina.
                Chapel Hill: *Southern Indian Studies* 5:37–39.
    1955   Investigations at Rood's Landing, Stewart County, Georgia. *Early
                Georgia* 2:1–28.
    1958   Trend and tradition in the prehistory of the eastern United States.
                American Anthropological Association, memoir 88.
Cambron, J. W.
    1955   Preliminary report on the Stone Pipe site in north Alabama. *Tennes-
                see Archaeologist* 11:54–62.
    1956   The Pine Tree site—A Paleo-Indian habitation locality. *Tennessee
                Archaeologist* 12:1–10.
    1958   Paleo points from the Pine Tree site. *Tennessee Archaeologist* 14:80–
                84.
Cambron, J. W., and Hulse, D. C.
    1960   The Transitional Paleo-Indian. *Journal of Alabama Archaeology* 6:7–
                33.
    1964   *Handbook of Alabama archaeology, Part I*, point types. University:
                Archaeological Research Association of Alabama, Inc.
Cambron, J. W., and Mitchell, J.
    1958   In search of the blademen. *Journal of Alabama Archaeology* 4:2–8.
Cambron, J. W., and Waters, S. A.
    1959   Flint Creek rock shelter (Part I). *Tennessee Archaeologist* 15:73–87.
    1961   Flint Creek rock shelter (Part II). *Journal of Alabama Archaeology*
                7:1–46.
Campbell, T. N.
    1959   Choctaw subsistence: Ethnographic notes from the Lincecum manu-
                script. *Florida Anthropologist* 12:9–24.
Chapman, J.
    1973   The Icehouse bottom site—40MR23. *Report of Investigations*, no.
                13. Department of Anthropology, University of Tennessee, Knox-
                ville.
    1975   The Rose Island site and the bifurcate point tradition. *Report of
                Investigations*, no. 14. Department of Anthropology, University of
                Tennessee, Knoxville.
    1976   The Archaic period in the lower Little Tennessee River Valley: The
                radiocarbon dates. *Tennessee Anthropologist* 1.
Chard, C. S.
    1961   Invention versus diffusion: The burial mound complex of the eastern
                United States. *Southwestern Journal of Anthropology* 17:21–25.
Chase, D. W.
    1965   A ceramic sequence in central Alabama as seen to date. *Journal of the
                Alabama Academy of Science* 36:179.
    1966   A stratified Archaic site in Lowndes County, Alabama. *Florida An-
                thropologist* 19:91–101.
    1967a   Weeden Island period sites in central Alabama. *Journal of Alabama
                Archaeology* 13:61–63.

1967b   New pottery types from central Alabama. *Southeastern Archaeological Conference, Bulletin* 5:41–49.

1968a   The Hope Hull complex. *Journal of Alabama Archaeology* 14:17–29.

1968b   Pottery typology, committee for Alabama. *Southeastern Archaeological Conference, Bulletin* 8:11–22.

1968c   New pottery types from Alabama. *Southeastern Archaeological Conference, Bulletin* 10:17–25.

1972   Evidence of Bayou La Batre—Archaic contact. *Journal of Alabama Archaeology* 18:152-61.

Clafin, W. H.

1931   The Stallings Island mound, Columbia County, Georgia. Harvard University: *Papers of the Peabody Museum* 14.

Clayton, M. V.

1965   Bluff shelter excavations on Sand Mountain. *Journal of Alabama Archaeology* 11:1–98.

1967   Boydston Creek bluff shelter excavations. *Journal of Alabama Archaeology* 13:1–41.

Coe, J. L.

1964   The formative cultures of the Carolina Piedmont. *Transactions of the American Philosophical Society* 54 (new series).

Corkron, D. H.

1967   *The Creek Frontier.* Norman: University of Oklahoma Press.

Cotter, J. L., and Corbett, J. M.

1951   Archaeology of the Bynum mounds, Mississippi. Washington, D.C.: *National Park Service, Archaeological Research Series,* no. 1.

Cottier, J. W.

1968   Archaeological salvage investigations in the Millers Ferry Lock and Dam Reservoir (Alabama). National Park Service Report.

1970a   A ceramic figurine from Tallapoosa County, Alabama. *Journal of Alabama Archaeology* 16:126-28.

1970b   The Alabama River phase: A brief description of a late phase in the prehistory of south-central Alabama. Manuscript on file at Mound State Monument.

Craig, A. B.

1958   A dwarf burial from Limestone County, Alabama. *Journal of Alabama Archaeology* 4:15–17.

Curren, C. B.

1974   An ethnozoological analysis of the vertebrate remains, Little Bear Creek site (CTº8). *Journal of Alabama Archaeology* 20:1–18.

1975a   Prehistoric occupation of Mobile Delta and Mobile Bay area of Alabama. Paper read at the 40th annual meeting of the Society for American Archaeology, Dallas.

1975b   Preliminary analysis of the faunal remains. In Archaeological investigations in the Gainesville Lock and Dam Reservoir: 1974, by N. J. Jenkins. Department of Anthropology, The University of Alabama.

DeJarnette, D. L.

1952   Alabama archaeology: A summary. In *Archeology of Eastern United States,* edited by J. B. Griffin, Chicago: University of Chicago Press.

1958	An archaeological study of a site suggested as the location of the Upper Creek Indian community of Coosa visited by Hernando De-Soto in 1540. Master's thesis, The University of Alabama.
1967	Alabama pebble tools: The Lively complex. *Eastern States Archaeological Federation Bulletin* 26:11–12.
1968	History and prehistory of the mounds. Moundville, Alabama. Paper read at the 11th annual pilgrimage of the Alabama Historical Association, Moundville.
1975	*Archaeological salvage in the Walter F. George Basin of the Chattahoochee River in Alabama.* University: The University of Alabama Press.

DeJarnette, D. L.; Andersen, H. V.; and Wimberly, S. B.
n.d.   Report on a Gulf State Park shell bank, Ba^v 81, in Baldwin County, Alabama. Manuscript on file at Mound State Monument.

DeJarnette, D. L.; Kurjack, E. B.; and Cambron, J. W.
1962   Stanfield-Worley bluff shelter excavations. *Journal of Alabama Archaeology* 8:1–11.

DeJarnette, D. L.; Kurjack, E. B.; and Keel, B. C.
1973   Archaeological investigations of the Weiss Reservoir of the Coosa River in Alabama. *Journal of Alabama Archaeology* 19:1–201.

DeJarnette, D. L., and Peebles, C. S.
1970   The development of Alabama archaeology—the Snow's Bend site. *Journal of Alabama Archaeology* 16:77–119.

DeJarnette, D. L.; Walthall, J. A.; and Wimberly, S. B.
1975a   Archaeological investigations in the Buttahatchee River Valley, Lamar County, Alabama. *Journal of Alabama Archaeology* 21:1–37.
1975b   Archaeological investigations in the Buttahatchee River Valley II; Excavations at Stucks Bluff rock shelter. *Journal of Alabama Archaeology* 21:99–119.

DeJarnette, D. L., and Wimberly, S. B.
1941   The Bessemer site: Excavation of three mounds and surrounding village areas near Bessemer, Alabama. University: *Geological Survey of Alabama Museum Paper,* no. 17.

Dickens, R. S.
1971   Archaeology in the Jones Bluff Reservoir of central Alabama. *Journal of Alabama Archaeology* 17:1–107.

Dickens, R. S.; Prince, E. L.; and Benthall, J.
1968   Archaeological investigations in the Jones Bluff Reservoir of the Alabama River. Department of Anthropology, University of Alabama.

Dragoo, D. W.
1973   Wells Creek—An Early Man site in Stewart County, Tennessee. *Archaeology of Eastern North America* 1:1–55.

Driver, H. E.
1965   *Indians of North America.* Chicago: University of Chicago Press.

Dunning, A. B.
1964   The Tallahatta formation in Clarke County, Alabama. *Journal of Alabama Archaeology* 10:50–60.

Dye, D.
   1973   The Alexander culture in the Tennessee Valley. Paper read at the
             30th annual meeting of the Southeastern Archaeological Conference,
             Memphis.
Fairbanks, C. H.
   1952   Creek and pre-Creek. In *Archeology of Eastern United States*, edited
             by J. B. Griffin. Chicago: University of Chicago Press.
   1955a   1953 excavations at site 9 Hr 64, Buford Reservoir, Georgia. *Florida
             State Studies* 16:1–25.
   1955b   The Abercrombie mound, Russell County, Alabama. *Early Georgia*
             2:13–16.
   1956   Archaeology of the Funeral mound, Ocmulgee National Monument,
             Georgia. Washington, D.C.: *National Park Service, Archaeological
             Research Series*, no. 3.
   1965   Excavations at the Fort Walton Temple mound, 1960. *Florida An-
             thropologist* 18:239–44.
Faulkner, C. H.
   1968   *The Old Stone Fort.* Knoxville: University of Tennessee Press.
   1970   Adena and Copena: A case of mistaken identity. In *Adena: The seek-
             ing of an identity,* edited by B. K. Swartz. Muncie: Ball State Univer-
             sity Press.
   1971   The Mississippian-Woodland transition in the Middle South. Paper
             read at the 29th Southeastern Archaeological Conference, Macon.
Faulkner, C. H., and Graham, J. B.
   1966   The Westmoreland-Barber site (40 Mi 11), Nickajack Reservoir: Sea-
             son II. Department of Anthropology, University of Tennessee.
Fernald, M. L., and Kinsey, A. C.
   1943   Edible wild plants of eastern North America. Cornwall-on-Hudson:
             Idlewild Press.
Fitting, J. E.
   1964   Bifurcate-stemmed projectile points in the eastern United States.
             American Antiquity 30:92–94.
   1970   *The Archaeology of Michigan.* Garden City: Natural History Press.
Flannery, K. V.
   1968a   Archaeological systems theory and early Mesoamerica. In *An-
             thropological archaeology in the Americas,* edited by B. J. Meggers.
             Washington, D.C.: Anthropological Society of Washington.
   1968b   The Olmec and the Valley of Oaxaca: A model for interregional in-
             teraction in Formative times. In *Dumbarton Oaks conference on the
             Olmec,* edited by E. Benson. Washington, D.C.: Dumbarton Re-
             search Library and Collection.
Ford, J. A.
   1969   A comparison of Formative cultures in the Americas. *Smithsonian
             Contributions to Anthropology* 2.
Ford, J. A., and Quimby, G. I.
   1945   The Tchefunte culture, an early occupation of the lower Mississippi
             Valley. *Memoirs of the Society for American Archaeology*, no. 2.

Ford, J. A., and Willey, G. R.
   1941   An interpretation of the prehistory of the eastern United States.
             American Anthropologist 43:325–63.
Fowke, G.
   1928   Archaeological investigations-II. Washington, D.C.: *Bureau of
             American Ethnology, Forty-fourth Annual Report:* 399–540.
Fried, M. H.
   1960   On the evolution of social stratification and the state. In *Culture in
             history: Essays in honor of Paul Radin,* edited by S. Diamond. New
             York: Columbia University Press.
Fundaburke, E. L., and Foreman, M. D.
   1957   Sun circles and human hands: The southeastern Indian's art and in-
             dustry. Luverne, Alabama.
Futato, E. M.
   1973   I-65 highway salvage: The position of twelve archaeological sites
             in central Alabama prehistory. Master's thesis, The University of
             Alabama.
Gibson, J. B.
   1967   Salvage archaeology in the Claiborne Lock and Dam Reservoir,
             Alabama. Department of Anthropology, The University of Alabama.
Griffin, J. B.
   1939   Report on the ceramics of the Wheeler Basin. In An archaeological
             survey of Wheeler Basin on the Tennessee River in northern
             Alabama, by W. S. Webb. Washington, D.C.: *Bureau of American
             Ethnology, Bulletin* 122.
   1946   Culture change and continuity in eastern United States archaeology.
             In Man in northeastern North America, edited by F. Johnson. An-
             dover: *Papers of the Robert S. Peabody Foundation for Archaeology*
             3:37–95.
   1967   Eastern North American archaeology: A summary. *Science* 156:175–
             91.
Griffin, J. B. (editor)
   1952   *Archaeology of eastern United States.* Chicago: University of Chi-
             cago Press.
Griffin, J. W.
   1974   Investigations in Russell Cave. Washington, D.C.: *National Park
             Service Publications in Archaeology,* no. 13.
Haag, W. G.
   1939   Type descriptions. *Southeastern Archaeological Conference Newslet-
             ter,* vol. 1.
   1942   Pickwick Basin pottery. In An archaeological study of the Pickwick
             Basin, by W. S. Webb and D. L. DeJarnette. Washington, D. C.:
             Bureau of American Ethnology, Bulletin 129.
   1962   The Bering Strait land bridge. *Scientific American* 206:112–23.
Hally, D. J.
   1970   Archaeological investigation of the Pott's Tract site, Carter's Dam,
             Murray County, Georgia. Athens: *University of Georgia Laboratory
             of Archaeology Series, Report,* no. 6.

Hamilton, H. W.; Hamilton, J. T.; and Chapman, E. F.
    1974   Spiro mound copper. *Missouri Archaeological Society,* memoir 11.
Harper, R. M.
    1942   Natural resources of the Tennessee Valley region in Alabama. *Geolog-
                ical Survey of Alabama, Special Report,* no. 17.
Hay, O. P.
    1923   The Pleistocene of North America and its vertebrated animals from
                the states east of the Mississippi River and from Canadian provinces
                east of longitude 95°. Washington, D.C.: *Carnegie Institution of
                Washington,* no. 322.
Haynes, C. V.
    1966   Elephant hunting in North America. *Scientific American* 214:104–12.
    1973   The Calico site: Artifacts or geofacts. *Science* 181:305–09.
Hays, H. D.
    1973   Weather and climate. In *Atlas of Alabama,* edited by N. G.
                Lineback. University: The University of Alabama Press.
Heimlich, M. D.
    1952   Guntersville Basin pottery. University: *Geological Survey of
                Alabama, Museum Paper* 32.
Hemmings, T.
    1970   The emergence of Formative life on the Atlanta coast of the South-
                east. *Southeastern Archaeological Conference, Bulletin* 13.
Hill, M. C., and Smith, C. S.
    1975   A study of the skeletal remains. In Archaeological investigations in the
                Gainesville Lock and Dam Reservoir: 1974, by N. J. Jenkins. De-
                partment of Anthropology, The University of Alabama.
Holmes, N. H.
    1963   The site on Bottle Creek. *Journal of Alabama Archaeology* 9:16–27.
Holmes, N. H., and Trickey, E. B.
    1974   Late Holocene sea-level oscillations in Mobile Bay. *American An-
                tiquity* 39:122–24.
Holmes, W. H.
    1897   Stone implements of the Potomac-Chesapeake Tidewater province.
                Washington, D.C.: *Bureau of American Ethnology Fifteenth Annual
                Report:* 13–150.
Hooks, W. G.
    1973   Physiography and topography. In *Altas of Alabama,* edited by N. G.
                Lineback. University: The University of Alabama Press.
Howard, J. H.
    1968   The Southeastern Ceremonial Complex and its interpretation. *Mis-
                souri Archaeological Society,* Memoir 6.
Hubbert, C. M.
    1961   A LeCroy bifurcated site. *Journal of Alabama Archaeology* 7:47–49.
    n.d.   Paleo-Indian settlement patterns in Colbert and Lauderdale counties,
                Alabama. Master's thesis in preparation, The University of Alabama.
Jenkins, N. J.
    1972   A fiber-tempered vessel from the central Tombigbee Basin. *Journal
                of Alabama Archaeology* 18:162–66.

1973   The position of the Wheeler series in southeastern prehistory. Paper
          read at the 30th Southeastern Archaeological Conference, Memphis.
1974   Subsistence and settlement patterns in the western middle Tennessee
          Valley during the transitional Archaic-Woodland period. *Journal of
          Alabama Archaeology* 20:183-93.
1975a   The Wheeler series and southeastern prehistory. *Florida An-
          thropologist* 28:17-26.
1975b   Archaeological investigations in the Gainesville Lock and Dam Reser-
          voir: 1974. Department of Anthropology, The University of Alabama.
1976   An inventory and evaluation of archaeological resources in and around
          the proposed Alabama enrichment plant site in Houston County,
          Alabama. Department of Anthropology, The University of Alabama.
n.d.   Terminal Woodland-Mississippian in northern Alabama: The West
          Jefferson phase. Master's thesis in preparation, The University of
          Alabama.
Jenkins, N. J.; Curren, C. B.; and DeLeon, M. F.
1975   Archaeological site survey of the Demopolis and Gainesville Lake
          navigation channels and additional construction areas. Department of
          Anthropology, The University of Alabama.
Jenkins, N. J., and Nielsen, J. J.
1974   Archaeological salvage investigations at the West Jefferson steam
          plant site, Jefferson County, Alabama. Department of Anthropology,
          The University of Alabama.
Jennings, J. D.
1941   Chickasaw and earlier Indian cultures of northeast Mississippi. *Jour-
          nal of Mississippi History* 3:155-226.
1946   Hopewell-Copena sites near Nashville. *American Antiquity* 12:126.
1947   *Prehistory of North America.* New York: McGraw-Hill.
Jeter, M. D.
1973   An archaeological survey in the area east of Selma, Alabama, 1971-
          1972. Montgomery: Alabama Historical Commission.
Jolly, F.
1969   A single component Alexander assemblage from the Mingo mound
          site in the Bear Creek watershed of N.E. Mississippi. *Tennessee
          Archaeologist* 27:1-38.
1971   Poverty Point zoomorphic beads from the Pickwick Basin in N.W.
          Alabama. *Journal of Alabama Archaeology* 17:134-39.
1974   The Buzzard Roost Creek bluff shelter: A late Woodland-
          Mississippian hunting station in N.W. Alabama. *Tennessee Ar-
          chaeologist* 30:1-67.
Jones, W. B.
1939   Geology of the Tennessee Valley region of Alabama. In An ar-
          chaeological survey of Wheeler Basin, by W. S. Webb. Washington,
          D.C.: *Bureau of American Ethnology, Bulletin* 122.
Josselyn, D. W.
1960   The lithic material. In Indian pottery from Clarke County and Mobile
          County, southern Alabama, by S. B. Wimberly. University: *Geologi-
          cal Survey of Alabama, Museum Paper* 36.

1965   The Lively complex, discussion of some of the ABCs of their technology. Birmingham: Alabama Archæological Society.

Kaye, J. M.
1974   Pleistocene sediment and vertebrate fossil associations in the Mississippi Blackbelt: A genetic approach. Doctoral dissertation, Louisiana State University.

Keel, B. C.
1960   The Money's Bend site, Ce^{v}3. *Florida Anthropologist* 8:1–16.

Kellar, J. H.; Kelly, A. R.; and McMichael, E. V.
1962   The Mandeville site in southwest Georgia. *American Antiquity* 28:338–55.

Kneberg, M.
1952   The Tennessee area. In *Archeology of eastern United States*, edited by J. B. Griffin. Chicago: University of Chicago Press.
1959   Engraved shell gorgets and their associations. *Tennessee Archaeologist* 15:1–39.
1961   Four southeastern limestone-tempered pottery complexes. *Southeastern Archaeological Conference Newsletter* 7:3–15.

Knight, V. J.
1975   Some observations concerning plant materials and aboriginal smoking in eastern North America. *Journal of Alabama Archaeology* 21:120–44.

Krieger, A. D.
1964   Early Man in the New World. In *Prehistoric man in the New World*, edited by J. D. Jennings and E. Norbeck. Chicago: University of Chicago Press.

Kurjack, E. B., and Pearson, F. L.
1975   Special investigations of 1 Ru 101, the Spanish Fort site. In *Archaeological salvage in the Walter F. George Basin of the Chattahoochee River in Alabama*, by D. L. DeJarnette. University: The University of Alabama Press.

Lanning, E. P., and Patterson, T. C.
1967   Early Man in South America. *Scientific American* 217:44–50.

Larson, L. H.
1970   Settlement distribution during the Mississippi period. *Southeastern Archaeological Conference, Bulletin*, no. 13.
1971   Archaeological implications of social stratification at the Etowah site, Georgia. In Approaches to the social dimensions of mortuary practices, edited by J. A. Brown. *Memoirs of the Society for American Archaeology*, no. 25.
1972   Functional considerations of warfare in the Southeast during the Mississippi period. *American Antiquity* 37:383–92.

Lazarus, W. C.
1961   Fort Walton culture—west of the Apalachicola. *Proceedings of the 18th Southeastern Archaeological Conference*.
1965   Coin dating in the Fort Walton period. *Florida Anthropologist* 18:221–24.

Lazarus, Y. W.
    1970   Salvage archaeology at Fort Walton Beach, Florida. *Florida An-
                thropologist* 23:29–42.
Lenser, G. W.
    1959   New Garden, a Big Sandy Archaic site. *Journal of Alabama Archae-
                ology* 5:71–74.
Lewis, T. M. N., and Kneberg, M.
    1946   *Hiwassee Island.* Knoxville: University of Tennessee Press.
    1947   The Archaic horizon in western Tennessee. *Tennessee Anthropology
                Papers*, no. 2.
    1958   The Nuckolls site. *Tennessee Archaeologist* 14:60–79.
    1959   The Archaic culture in the Middle South. *American Antiquity*
                25:161–83.
Lewis, T. M. N., and Lewis, M. K.
    1961   *Eva, an Archaic site.* Knoxville: University of Tennessee Press.
Lively, M.
    1965   The Lively complex: Announcing a pebble tool industry in Alabama.
                Journal of Alabama Archaeology 11:103–22.
Long, A. G., and Josselyn, D. W.
    1965   The Eva family. *Journal of Alabama Archaeology* 11:152–55.
McCollough, M. C. R., and Faulkner, C. H.
    1973   Excavation of the Higgs and Doughty sites, I-75 salvage archaeology.
                Tennessee Archaeological Society Miscellaneous Paper, no. 12.
McKenzie, D. H.
    1964a   The Moundville phase and its position in southeastern prehistory.
                Doctoral dissertation, Harvard University.
    1964b   Houses of the Moundville phase. *Tennessee Archaeologist* 20:49–58.
    1965a   The burial complex of the Moundville phase, Alabama. *Florida An-
                thropologist* 18:161–74.
    1965b   Pottery types of the Moundville phase. *Bulletin of the Southeastern
                Archaeological Conference* 2:55–64.
    1966   A summary of the Moundville phase. *Journal of Alabama Archae-
                ology* 12:1–58.
McKern, W. C.
    1939   The Midwestern Taxonomic method as an aid to archaeological cul-
                ture study. *American Antiquity* 4:301–13.
McMichael, E. V., and Kellar, J. H.
    1959   Archaeological salvage in the Oliver Basin. National Park Service
                Report.
MacNeish, R. S.
    1971   Early man in the Andes. *Scientific American* 224:13–46.
Mason, R. J.
    1962   The Paleo-Indian tradition in eastern North America. *Current An-
                thropology* 3:227–46.
Milanich, J. T.
    1974   Life in a 9th-century Indian household: A Weeden Island fall-winter
                site on the upper Apalachicola River, Florida. Tallahassee: *Bureau of
                Historic Sites and Properties, Bulletin*, no. 4.

Miller, C. F.
1956   Life 8000 years ago uncovered in an Alabama cave. *National Geographic* 110:542–58.
1958   Russell Cave: New light on Stone Age life. *National Geographic* 113:427–38.
1960   The use of *Chenopodium* seeds as a source of food by the early peoples in Russell Cave, Alabama. *Southern Indian Studies* 12:31–32.

Moebes, T. F.
1974   Cave Springs site (Mg^{c}65). *Journal of Alabama Archaeology* 20: 63–84.

Moore, C. B.
1899   Certain aboriginal remains of the Alabama River. *Journal of the Academy of Natural Sciences of Philadelphia* 11:289–337.
1901   Certain aboriginal remains of the northwest Florida coast. *Journal of the Academy of Natural Sciences of Philadelphia* 11:421–97.
1904   Aboriginal urn burial in the United States. *American Anthropologist* 6:660–69.
1905a   Certain aboriginal remains of the Black Warrior River. *Journal of the Academy of Natural Sciences of Philadelphia.* 13:245–78.
1905b   Certain aboriginal remains of the lower Tombigbee River. *Journal of the Academy of Natural Sciences of Philadelphia* 13:245–78.
1905c   Certain aboriginal remains on Mobile Bay and on Mississippi Sound. *Journal of the Academy of Natural Sciences of Philadelphia* 13:279–97.
1907a   Moundville revisited. *Journal of the Academy of Natural Sciences of Philadelphia* 13:337–405.
1907b   Mounds of the lower Chattahoochee and lower Flint River. *Journal of the Academy of Natural Sciences of Philadelphia* 13:427–56.
1915   Aboriginal sites on the Tennessee River. *Journal of the Academy of Natural Sciences of Philadelphia* 16:171–422.

Morrison, J. P. E.
1942   Preliminary report on the mollusks found in the shell mounds of the Pickwick Landing Basin in the Tennessee River Valley. In An archaeological survey of Pickwick Basin, by W. S. Webb and D. L. DeJarnette. Washington, D.C.: *Bureau of American Ethnology, Bulletin* 129.

Mosley, S. A.
1958   The occurrence of soapstone in Alabama and its use by the Indians. *Journal of Alabama Archaeology* 4:9–13.

Myer, W. E.
1928   Indian Trails of the Southeast. *Bureau of American Ethnology, Forty-second Annual Report.*

Nance, C. R.
1975   Archaeological survey of the Montgomery levee project area, Montgomery, Alabama. National Park Service Report.
n.d.   The archaeological sequence at Durant Bend, Dallas County, Alabama. Unpublished manuscript. Anthropology Laboratory. The University of Alabama, Birmingham.

Neuman, R. W.
    1961   Domesticated corn from a Fort Walton mound site in Houston
                County, Alabama. *Florida Anthropologist* 14:75–76.
Nielsen, J. J.
    1970   Archaeological investigations at Site 1 Au 28 in the Jones Bluff Reser-
                voir on the Alabama River. Department of Anthropology, The Uni-
                versity of Alabama.
    1972   Archaeological salvage investigations on right of way Interstate 65,
                Morgan County, Alabama, Site 1 Mg 74. *Journal of Alabama Archae-
                ology* 18:67–136.
Nielsen, J. J., and Jenkins, N. J.
    1973   Archaeological investigations in the Gainesville Lock and Dam Reser-
                voir. Department of Anthropology, The University of Alabama.
Nielsen, J. J., and Moorehead, C.
    1972   Archaeological salvage in the Gainesville Reservoir on the Tombigbee
                River. Department of Anthropology, The University of Alabama.
Nielsen, J. J.; O'Hear, J. W.; and Moorehead, C. W.
    1973   An archaeological survey of Hale and Green counties, Alabama. Final
                report to the Alabama Historical Commission. University: Alabama
                Museum of Natural History.
Oakley, C. B.
    1971   An archaeological investigation of Pinson Cave (1 Je 20). Master's
                thesis, The University of Alabama.
Oakley, C. B., and Futato, E. M.
    1975   Archaeological investigations in the Little Bear Creek Reservoir. *Of-
                fice of Archaeological Research, Research Series* 1, The University
                of Alabama.
O'Hear, J. W.
    1975   Site 1 Je 32: Community organization in the West Jefferson phase.
                Master's thesis, The University of Alabama.
Olafson, S.
    1971   Late Pleistocene climate and the St. Albans site. In The St. Albans
                Site, Kanawha County, West Virginia, by B. J. Broyles. *West Virginia
                Geological and Economic Survey, Report of Archaeological Investiga-
                tions*, no. 3.
Parmalee, P. W.
    1962   Faunal remains from the Stanfield-Worley bluff shelter, Colbert
                County, Alabama. *Journal of Alabama Archaeology* 8:112–14.
Parmalee, P. W., and Klippel, W. E.
    1974   Freshwater mussels as a prehistoric food resource. *American An-
                tiquity* 39:421–34.
Patterson, T. C.
    1973   *America's past: A New World archaeology*. Glenview, Illinois: Scott,
                Foresman, and Company.
Pearson, F. L.
    1964   Alabama archaeology in Spanish records. *Journal of Alabama Archae-
                ology* 10:636–39.

Peebles, C. S.
    1970   Moundville and beyond: Some observations on the changing social
                organization in the southeastern United States. Paper read at the 69th
                annual meeting of the American Anthropological Association.
    1971   Moundville and surrounding sites: Some structural considerations of
                mortuary practices II. In Approaches to the social dimensions of
                mortuary practices, edited by J. A. Brown. *Memoirs of the Society for
                American Archaeology*, no. 25.
    1974   Moundville: The social organization of a prehistoric community and
                culture. Doctoral dissertation, University of California, Santa Bar-
                bara.
Peterson, D.
    1970   The Refuge phase in the Savannah River region. *Southeastern Ar-
                chaeological Conference, Bulletin* 13.
    1971   Time and settlement in the archaeology of Groton Plantation, South
                Carolina. Doctoral dissertation, Harvard University.
Phelps, D. S.
    1965   The Norwood series of fiber-tempered ceramics. *Proceedings of the
                20th Southeastern Archaeological Conference, Bulletin* 2:65–69.
    1966   Early and late components of the Tucker site. *Florida Anthropologist*
                19:11–38.
Phillips, P.
    1970   Archaeological survey in the lower Yazoo Basin, Mississippi, 1949–
                1955. *Papers of the Peabody Museum of Archaeology and Eth-
                nology* 60.
Pickett, A. J.
    1851   *History of Alabama, and incidentally of Georgia and Mississippi,
                from the earliest period.* Charleston: Walker and James.
Priestley, H. I.
    1936   *Tristan de Luna: Conquistador of the Old South.* Glendale, California.
Quimby, G. I.
    1960   *Indian life in the Upper Great Lakes.* Chicago: University of Chicago
                Press.
Reichel-Dolmatoff, G.
    1972   The cultural context of early fiber-tempered pottery in northern Co-
                lombia. *Florida Anthropologist* 25:1–8.
Ritchie, W. A.
    1932   The Lamoka Lake site, the type station of the Archaic Algonkian
                Period in New York. *Researches and Transactions, New York State
                Archaeological Association* 7.
    1965   *The archaeology of New York State.* Garden City: Natural History
                Press.
Ritzenthaler, R. E., and Quimby, G. I.
    1962   The Red Ocher culture of the Upper Great Lakes and adjacent areas.
                Fieldiana: Anthropology 36:243–75.
Roberts, R. G.
    1949   Ancient stone fortifications at DeSoto Falls, Little River, Alabama.
                Tennessee Archaeologist 5:18–21.

Sahlins, M. D.
  1968   *Tribesmen.* Englewood Cliffs: Prentice-Hall.
Salo, L. W. (editor)
  1969   *Archaeological investigation in the Tellico Reservoir, Tennessee,
              1967–1968.* Knoxville: University of Tennessee Department of An-
              thropology.
Schnell, F. T.
  1971   A comparative study of some lower Creek sites. *Southeastern Ar-
              chaeological Conference, Bulletin* 13.
Sears, W. H.
  1958   Burial mounds on the Gulf Coastal Plain. *American Antiquity*
              23:274–84.
  1962   Hopewellian affiliation of certain sites on the Gulf coast of Florida.
              American Antiquity 28:5–18.
  1964   The southeastern United States. In *Prehistoric Man in the New
              World*, edited by J. D. Jennings and E. Norbeck. Chicago: University
              of Chicago Press.
  1971   Food production and village life in prehistoric southeastern United
              States. *Archaeology* 24:322–29.
Sears, W. H., and Griffin, J. B.
  1950   Fiber-tempered pottery of the southeast. In *Prehistoric pottery of
              eastern United States*, edited by J. B. Griffin. Ann Arbor: Museum of
              Anthropology.
Service, E. R.
  1962   *Primitive social organization: An evolutionary perspective.* New York:
              Random House.
  1966   *The hunters.* Englewood Cliffs: Prentice-Hall.
Sheldon, C. T.
  1974   The Mississippian-historic transition in central Alabama. Doctoral
              dissertation, University of Oregon.
Smith, B. A.
  1975   The relationship between Deptford and Swift Creek ceramics as evi-
              denced at the Mandeville site, 9 Cla 1. *Southeastern Archaeological
              Conference, Bulletin* 18:195–200.
Smith, B. D.
  1975   Middle Mississippi exploitation of animal populations. *Museum of
              Anthropology, University of Michigan Anthropological Papers*, no. 57.
Smith, C. E.
  1975   A study of the floral remains. In Archaeological investigations in the
              Gainesville Lock and Dam Reservoir: 1974, by N. J. Jenkins. De-
              partment of Anthropology, The University of Alabama.
Smith, P. E.
  1962   Aboriginal stone constructions in the southern Piedmont. Athens:
              University of Georgia Laboratory of Archaeology Series Report, no. 4.
Soday, F. J.
  1952   A new Paleo-Indian site. *Dallas Archaeological Society Record* 11.
  1954   The Quad site: A Paleo-Indian village in northern Alabama. *Tennes-
              see Archaeologist* 10:1–20.

Squier, E. G., and Davis, E. H.
    1848   Ancient monuments of the Mississippi Valley. Washington, D.C.:
                Smithsonian Contributions to Knowledge, volume 1.

Stoltman, J. B.
    1966   New radiocarbon dates for southeastern fiber-tempered pottery.
                American Antiquity 31:872–74.

    1972a   The late Archaic in the Savannah River region. *Florida An-
                thropologist* 25:37–62.

    1972b   Preface. In Fiber-tempered pottery in the southeastern United
                States, edited by R. P. Bullen and J. B. Stoltman. *Florida An-
                thropologist* 25:i–iv.

Stowe, N. R.
    1970   Prehistoric cultural ecology in northwest Alabama. Master's thesis,
                The University of Alabama.

Struever, S.
    1965   Middle Woodland culture history in the Great Lakes riverine area.
                American Antiquity 31:211–23.

Struever, S., and Vickery, K. D.
    1973   The beginnings of cultivation in the Midwest-riverine area of the
                United States. *American Anthropologist* 75:1197–220.

Summersell, C. G.
    1961   *Alabama history.* Northport, Alabama: Colonial Press.

Swanton, J. R.
    1922   Early history of the Creek Indians and their neighbors. Washington,
                D.C.: *Bureau of American Ethnology, Bulletin* 73.

    1939   Final report of the United States DeSoto Expedition Commission.
                Washington, D.C.: *House Document 71.* 76th Congress, 1st Session.

    1946   The Indians of the southeastern United States. Washington, D.C.:
                Bureau of American Ethnology, Bulletin 137.

Thomas, C.
    1894   Report on the mound explorations of the Bureau of Ethnology.
                Washington, D.C.: *Bureau of American Ethnology, Twelfth Annual
                Report.*

Thomas, J.
    1973   Vegetation. In *Atlas of Alabama,* edited by N. G. Lineback. Univer-
                sity: The University of Alabama Press.

Thurston, G. P.
    1897   *The antiquities of Tennessee.* Cincinnati: Robert Clark Company.

Toth, Alan
    1966   Hopewell influence in the southeastern United States. Honors thesis,
                Harvard University.

Trickey, E. B.
    1958   A chronological framework for the Mobile Bay region. *American An-
                tiquity* 23:388–96.

Trickey, E. B., and Holmes, N. J.
    1971   A chronological framework for the Mobile Bay region. *Journal of
                Alabama Archaeology* 17:115–28.

Tuck, J. A.
    1974   Early Archaic horizons in eastern North America. *Archaeology of Eastern North America* 2:72–80.
Varner, J. G., and Varner, J. J.
    1951   *The Florida of the Inca.* Austin: University of Texas Press.
Walker, S. T.
    1885   Mounds and shell heaps on the west coast of Florida. Washington, D.C.: *Annual Report of the Smithsonian Institution for 1883.*
Walthall, J. A.
    1972   The chronological position of Copena in eastern states archaeology. *Journal of Alabama Archaeology* 18:137–51.
    1973a   Copena: A Tennessee Valley middle Woodland culture. Doctoral dissertation, University of North Carolina.
    1973b   A restudy of the Wright village (Lu^{v}65), a middle Woodland habitation site in Lauderdale County, Alabama. *Tennessee Archaeologist* 24:69–108.
    1974   A possible Copena burial cave in Blount County, Alabama. *Journal of Alabama Archaeology* 20:60–62.
    1975   Ceramic figurines, Porter Hopewell, and middle Woodland interaction. *Florida Anthropologist* 28:125–40.
Walthall, J. A., and DeJarnette, D. L.
    1974   Copena burial caves. *Journal of Alabama Archaeology* 20:1–59.
Walthall, J. A., and Jenkins, N. J.
    1976   The Gulf Formational stage in southeastern prehistory. *Southeastern Archaeological Conference, Bulletin* 19.
Waters, S. A.
    1959   Red Hill, A Dalton site. *Journal of Alabama Archaeology* 5:77–82.
Webb, C. H.
    1968   The extent and content of Poverty Point culture. *American Antiquity* 33:297–321.
    1971   Archaic and Poverty Point zoomorphic locust beads. *American Antiquity* 36:105–14.
Webb, W. S.
    1939   An archaeological survey of Wheeler Basin on the Tennessee River in northern Alabama. Washington, D.C.: *Bureau of American Ethnology, Bulletin* 122.
Webb, W. S., and DeJarnette, D. L.
    1942   An archaeological survey of Pickwick Basin in the adjacent portions of the states of Alabama, Mississippi, and Tennessee. Washington, D.C.: *Bureau of American Ethnology, Bulletin* 129.
    1948a   The Flint River site, Ma^{v}48. University: *Alabama Museum of Natural History, Museum Paper* 23.
    1948b   The Whitesburg Bridge site, Ma^{v}10. University: *Alabama Museum of Natural History, Museum Paper* 24.
    1948c   The Perry site, Lu^{v}25. University: *Alabama Museum of Natural History, Museum Paper* 25.
    1948d   Little Bear Creek site, Ct^{v}8. University: *Alabama Museum of Natural History, Museum Paper* 26.

Webb, W. S., and Wilder, C. G.
  1951   *An archaeological survey of the Guntersville Basin on the Tennessee River in northern Alabama.* Lexington: University of Kentucky Press.
Weigel, R. D.; Holman, J. A.; and Paloumpis, A. A.
  1974   Vertebrates from Russell Cave. In Investigations in Russell Cave, by J. W. Griffin. Washington, D.C.: *National Park Service Publications in Archaeology,* no. 13.
Wentowski, G. J.
  1970   Salt as an ecological factor in the prehistory of the southeastern United States. Master's thesis, University of North Carolina.
Wicke, C. R.
  1965   Pyramids and temple mounds: Mesoamerican ceremonial architecture in eastern North America. *American Antiquity* 30:409–20.
Willey, G. R.
  1945   The Weeden Island culture: A preliminary definition. *American Antiquity* 10:225–54.
  1949   Archaeology of the Florida Gulf Coast. Washington, D.C.: *Smithsonian Miscellaneous Collections* 113.
  1966   *An introduction to American archaeology: Vol. I, North and Middle America.* Englewood Cliffs: Prentice-Hall.
  1971   *An introduction to American archaeology, Vol. II, South America.* Englewood Cliffs: Prentice-Hall.
Willey, G. R., and Phillips, P.
  1958   *Method and theory in American archaeology.* Chicago: University of Chicago Press.
Williams, S. (editor)
  1968   The Waring papers: The collected works of Antonio J. Waring, Jr. *Papers of the Peabody Museum of Archaeology and Ethnology* 58.
Williams, S., and Stoltman, J. B.
  1965   An outline of southeastern United States prehistory with particular emphasis on the Paleo-Indian era. In *The Quarternary of the United States,* edited by H. E. Wright, Jr., and D. C. Frey. Princeton: Princeton University Press.
Wilmsen, E. N.
  1968   Paleo-Indian site utilization. In *Anthropological Archaeology in the Americas,* edited by B. J. Meggars. Washington, D.C.: The Anthropological Society of Washington.
Wimberly, C.
  1960   The geographic and historic background. In Indian pottery from Clarke County and Mobile County, southern Alabama, by S. B. Wimberly. University: *Geological Survey of Alabama, Museum Paper* 36.
Wimberly, S. B.
  1953a   Bayou La Batre Tchefuncte series. In *Prehistoric pottery of eastern United States,* edited by J. B. Griffin. Ann Arbor: Museum of Anthropology.
  1953b   McLeod Deptford series. In *Prehistoric pottery of eastern United States,* edited by J. B. Griffin. Ann Arbor: Museum of Anthropology.

1956   A review of Moundville pottery. *Southeastern Archaeological Conference Newsletter* 5:17–20.
1960   Indian pottery from Clarke County and Mobile County, southern Alabama. University: *Geological Survey of Alabama, Museum Paper* 36.

Wimberly, S. B., and Tourtelot, H. A.
1941   The McQuorquodale mound: A manifestation of the Hopewellian phase in south Alabama. University: *Geological Survey of Alabama, Museum Paper* 19.

Winters, H. D.
1968   Value systems and trade cycles of the late Archaic in the Midwest. In *New perspectives in archaeology*, edited by S. R. Binford and L. R. Binford. Chicago: Aldine.
1969   The Riverton Culture. *Illinois Archaeological Survey, Monograph* 1.
1974   Introduction to the new edition. In *Indian Knoll*, by W. S. Webb. Knoxville: University of Tennessee Press.

Wobst, H. M.
1974   Boundary conditions for Paleolithic social systems: A simulation approach. *American Antiquity* 39:147–78.

Work, R. W.
1961   An Archaic site on the Tennessee River. *Journal of Alabama Archaeology* 7:51–75.

Wright, A. J.
1974   An aboriginal quarry in Tallapoosa County. *Journal of the Alabama Academy of Science* 45:17–22.

Yarnell, R. A.
1971   A study of archaeological plant remains. In Archaeology in the Jones Bluff Reservoir of central Alabama, by R. S. Dickens. *Journal of Alabama Archaeology* 17:108–11.

Index

Prehistoric Indians
of the Southeast
Archaeology of Alabama
and the Middle South

John A. Walthall

"I think the study is terrific. . . . Not only because there is a crying need for such studies in the Southeast, especially in such an archaeologically rich state as Alabama, but also because it is very well written. . . . It is a well-balanced study . . . extremely useful to amateur and professional alike."—Charles H. Faulkner, University of Tennessee

---

The geographical area encompassed by the boundaries of present-day Alabama is a rich reservoir of information concerning regional prehistoric cultures. Four decades of archaeological research in the area have revealed a prehistoric culture spanning some 10,000 years and resulted in the investigation of some of the most important archaeological sites in eastern North America. A wealth of artifacts, of compelling interest to archaeologists, anthropologists, and others, has been unearthed.

Research continues, but enough well-established archaeological data are in hand to permit a synthesis of what is known (and what can reasonably be inferred, tentatively)